THE MAGNETIC NORTH

Sara Wheeler is the author of five previous books, including the bestselling *Terra Incognita: Travels in Antarctica*, *Cherry: A Life of Apsley Cherry-Garrard* and *Too Close to the Sun: The Life and Times of Denys Finch Hatton*.

SARA WHEELER

The Magnetic North

Travels in the Arctic

VINTAGE BOOKS
London

Published by Vintage 2010

8 10 9 7

First published in Great Britain in 2009 by
Jonathan Cape

Vintage
Random House, 20 Vauxhall Bridge Road,
London SW1V 2SA

www.vintage-books.co.uk

Addresses for companies within The Random House Group Limited
can be found at: www.randomhouse.co.uk/offices.htm

The Random House Group Limited Reg. No. 954009

A CIP catalogue record for this book
is available from the British Library

ISBN 9780099516880

The Random House Group Limited supports The Forest Stewardship
Council® (FSC®), the leading international forest-certification organisation.
Our books carrying the FSC label are printed on FSC®-certified paper.
FSC is the only forest-certification scheme supported by the leading
environmental organisations, including Greenpeace. Our
paper procurement policy can be found at
www.randomhouse.co.uk/environment

Printed and bound in Great Britain by Clays Ltd, St Ives plc

To mum and dad

Contents

List of Illustrations

Maps

Deep was the silence. Then, in the dawn of history, far away in the south, the awakening spirit of man reared its head on high and gazed over the earth . . . But the limits of the unknown had to recede step by step before the ever-increasing yearning after light and knowledge of the human mind, till they made a stand in the north at the threshold of Nature's great Ice Temple of the polar regions with their endless silence.

Fridtjof Nansen, *Farthest North*

I

Tips about Icebergs

The place of greatest dignitie
John Davis, mariner,
1550?–1605

Herds of reindeer move across ice and snow. Slim-shouldered Lapps squatting on skidoos nose their animals towards an arc of stockades. A man in a corral holds a pair of velvet antlers while another jabs a needle into damp haunch. I make my way towards the outer palisades, where Lapps beyond working age stoke beechwood fires and gulp from bowls of reindeer broth, faces masked in musky steam. The first new snow has fallen, and the Harrå Sámi are herding reindeer down to the winter grazing. A livid sun hangs on the horizon. Sámi, or Lapps, were the last nomadic people in Europe, and until recently castrated reindeer at this place by biting off their balls. In the stockade I take my baby son from his wooden sledge, prowed like a miniature Viking ship, and wrap him closer in his calf pelts.

The Lapps divided the corralled herd, each smaller group husbanded by an association of families (*sijdda*) in pastures close to home. Down at the end of summer, up at the end of winter; the cycle of life above the Arctic Circle. At half past three, the sun vanished. It was the cuspy season between white nights and darkness at noon, the period in which the Arctic turns inside out. The thunderous pounding stopped. Below the corral, people who had come to recover stray reindeer struggled to load them into stumpy horse boxes. In the distance, the lights of Harrå shimmered through a dark haze. The silence of the winter forest settled over the corral, fractured only by the cry of a nightjar. When I came to unwrap Reggie from his pelt, the soft green and orange beams of the Northern Lights swept the sky.

Fifteen years earlier I had spent some time in Antarctica. Its geographical unity and unownedness attracted the younger me, as did the lack of an indigenous human presence and inability to sustain terrestrial life. It was a metaphor for a *terra incognita*; an image of an alternate and better world. I was prejudiced against the complicated, life-infested north. Time passed, and I travelled briefly with the Sámi and their reindeer. I started thinking about the collar of lands round the Arctic Ocean. Fragmentation, disputed ownership, indigenous populations immobilised on the threshold of change – those very things Antarctica lacked appealed to the older me. Especially fragmentation. When I thought about the Arctic, in my mind's eye I glimpsed an elegy for the uncertainties and doubts that are the chaperones of age. Was the Arctic a counterweight to the Antarctic? (The Greeks called it *arktos*, the Great Bear, or Northern Pole Star, and the Antarctic was the *anti- arktos* – the opposite.) Or was it just a frozen mirror image, and I who had changed?

The Arctic is our neighbour; part European; part North American; us. What could be less romantic? And the world seems a wearier place than it did a decade and a half ago. It is the Arctic that captures the spirit of the times. The Arctic is the lead player in the drama of climate change, and polar bears are its poster boys. So I went. On a speck of land in the northern reaches of the Arctic Ocean, the encircling water chaotic with floes, I heard a snow bunting sing. Not a single songbird breeds on the Antarctic continent. The sweet trill of the small black-and-white bird brought the Arctic to life.

Where is the Arctic? An ocean surrounded by continents, and an indistinct geographical zone. The top part – the High Arctic – is a dazzling hinterland where myth and history fuse; a white Mars. The Haughton

4

Crater on Devon Island in the Canadian High Arctic hosts camps of Martian aficionados testing potential housing in preparation for man's arrival on the red planet ('This is as close to Mars as we can get,' one of them told me). The southern limits of the Arctic are moveable feasts. Some consider that the Arctic Circle at 66° 33' constitutes the frontier: people like the farmers in northern Sweden and Finland who wish to claim EU Arctic Farming subsidies. In Canada the definition fails, as swathes of typical Arctic territory (permafrost, permanent ice cover, absence of topsoil and significant vegetation, polar bears, all of these) lie well south of the Arctic Circle. Sixty-six degrees simply marks the point at which the sun fails to set at summer solstice (21 June) or to rise at winter solstice (21 December); climatological and other factors produce divergent conditions at different points on the Circle. The Gulf Stream warms the oceans and the surrounding air to create clement conditions for the subsidy-claiming Scandinavian farmers, and in Finland the viviparous lizard thrives north of the Arctic Circle, whereas parts of the sub-Arctic are colder than anywhere else on earth. The residents of Oymyakon in the Sakha Republic three degrees outside the Arctic Circle once recorded a temperature of -72.11°C (-97.8°F), a level at which trees explode with a sound like gunfire and exhaled breath falls to the ground in a tinkle of crystals. In addition, some cartographers and politicians use the isothermal line to define the Arctic, thus including all the places where the long-term mean temperature of the warmest month is below 10°C. And in the biggest gerrymandered constituency on the planet there are four North Poles.*

I think the southern boundary of the Arctic is most appropriately

* 1. *The North Geographic Pole.* At 90°N, the fixed cap of the earth. 2. *The North Magnetic Pole.* The compass points to this one, and it wanders about. 3. *The North Geomagnetic Pole.* It centres the earth's magnetic field, and also shifts. 4. *The Northern Pole of Inaccessibility.* The point in the Arctic Ocean farthest from land, approximately 680 miles (1,100 kilometres) north of Alaska, at 84° 05' N, 174° 85' W. A fifth pole, *The North Celestial Pole,* is in the sky: the astronomical extension of a line drawn through the earth's axis.

defined by a combination of the treeline and the southern limit of continuous permafrost on land; and by the average extent of winter pack ice at sea.

Since 1900, the mean global temperature has risen by 0.6°C. In the Arctic, the figure is 2–3°. But there is still a lot of ice. In July 2008 I took a Russian ice-breaker across the Arctic Ocean and stood day after day on the bridge with the captain (a saturnine figure who talked too fast, like so many natives of Vladivostok) and we watched the cutaway prow smashing through thousands of tonnes of it. The extent of the ice is not the only critical issue. Unlike the Southern Ocean that swirls around the Antarctic, the Arctic Ocean is more or less enclosed – what marine geographers call a mediterranean sea. Most of the water that leaves flows through a deep channel south-west of the Faroe Islands (it carves through a row of transatlantic sills). In this gap, cold, salty water from the Arctic moves south beneath warm, fresher water from the tropics travelling north. Various 'pump' sites in the Greenland Sea shift these warm and cold currents around the planet. As glaciers melt and water flowing from the Arctic becomes less salty, the pumps could lose power, and a growing body of data indicates that they will turn off altogether. Or will the Siberian permafrost first break down and release tides of carbon dioxide and methane as well as baby mammoths still sporting their ginger hair? Either way, the survival of civilisation as we know it hangs on what happens in the Arctic. Anxiety, panic, concern and scepticism have inflamed the public imagination. As we powered through the ice, I asked the captain what he thought about the big melt. He looked out over the splitting white, took a deep drag on his Troika cigarette, and yelled over the racket of six engines, 'I not know.'

Scientists, for the most part, don't know either. I spent many weeks hunched over holes in the Greenland ice sheet or hauling samples from the slimy bottom of an Alaskan lake. As far as possible I tried to enter the minds of individual researchers to see what made them creative. My own mind was open. History reveals many periods of cooling and warming, and I learned that the science is more dramatic than media headlines indicate, as well as a million times more complicated, nuanced and uncertain. In many respects we do not know how ecosystems will respond to climate change. The Arctic has been the locus for Armageddon two generations in a row now. It was the front line of the Cold War, with both sides pouring money into long-range nuclear bomber installations and lone figures crouching on floes straining to hear enemy subs (or was that a ringed seal scratching its back?). Nuclear holocaust, then apocalyptic climate change: something about the region attracts millennial anxiety. I picked up a scent among the Lappish reindeer and pursued it through the journeys described here. What does the Arctic tell us about our past? What does it reveal of the future?

Besides climate panic, the emergence of the Arctic as an energy frontier has similarly shunted the region into public consciousness. The Arctic already produces about a tenth of the world's oil and a quarter of its gas.* As you read this, geologists and palaeontologists from many nations are chipping indicator fossils from bedrock to locate more. Hydrocarbon extraction is set to remain an economic driver across the polar regions, and issues around the exploitation of natural resources recur throughout these pages: hard-rock mining as well as oil and gas (a hard-rock mine excavates ores from which metals are extracted). Everybody wants what the Arctic has and as a result, shortly after I started working on this book, a simmering international row over ownership boiled over onto the front pages. All five polar nations – Denmark, Norway, Russia, Canada and the United States – set about proving that their continental shelves extend far to the north under the waters of the Arctic Ocean. This, they hope, will secure navigation rights over mineral reserves beneath the seabed. In July 2007 a Russian nuclear submarine sent a diver to drill a titanium flag into the bedrock under the North Pole itself, a gesture that made the

---

* Figures produced in 2007 by AMAP (the Arctic Monitoring and Assessment Programme).

Pole as Russian as gold teeth. The Canadian prime minister went haring up to his bit of the Arctic to express comparable views. In Chukotka, the back end of Siberia and a region the size of Turkey that Russia had forgotten, President Medvedev stepped out of his helicopter onto the tundra to pat a reindeer and listen to some pleasant Chukchi folk songs in a local school. (I was there!) He was the first Russian head of state to bother; no tsar had ever come within a thousand miles of Chukotka. Five days previously, in a speech on Arctic policy to the Security Council in Moscow, Medvedev had flagged the reason for his visit. 'This region', he said, 'accounts for around 20 per cent of Russia's gross domestic product and 22 per cent of our national exports . . . Experts estimate that the Arctic continental shelf could contain around a quarter of the world's hydrocarbon resources.' The main issue, Medvedev insisted, 'is that of reliably protecting our national interests in the region'. Like the diver who planted the flag, Mr President was showing how very Russian it was in the north. That night's television news followed him touring the new supermarket, the first in the region, where he peered into freezers while a supervisor gave a running commentary on cylinders of Arctic Roll made in a factory on the outskirts of Petersburg.

The burst of political concern highlights the transitional state of the inhabited Arctic. In Nuuk I saw a pair of nylon panties pegged on a washing line next to a row of curing seal ribs. Something mysterious and indefinable has outlived cultural collapse. There was the twenty-year-old Inupiat woman with two children; almost everyone in her family was drunk almost all the time, she had never been out hunting, she ate Western junk food and watched *The Simpsons*. 'I sense where I come from', she said, 'when I see the milky ice on the creek split in the spring.' Inuit art has expressed a spiritual connection between man and nature for three thousand years, and in the myths and beliefs of the far north, humanity and the world give each other meaning. *The Magnetic North* describes the semi-inhabited fringes of the Arctic: the transition zone. 'It's not about polar bears,' says Mary Simon, head

of the Tapiriit Kanatami, which represents Canada's 45,000 Inuit. 'It's about people.'

Although the beauties and intractable problems of the contemporary Arctic framed my journeys, I could not ignore generations of explorers. Like the scientists who succeeded them, they went north to unlock secrets. Their adventures frequently descended into a tragic farce of shoe-eating (when they ran out of food) and poetic death, but still; heroic individual struggle is a theme of this book. Who can resist the David squaring up to a Goliath-army of towering bergs? In America, Arctic mania persisted from the Civil War to the First World War – even at a time when Americans were going west, the North Pole and its whaling waters cast a spell, luring Pole-seekers in little wooden ships, in balloons, zeppelins, planes, ice-breakers and submarines. A hundred years ago, in 1909, two Americans on separate expeditions claimed to have stood at the North Pole. Over in the Old World even Pope Pius XI was not immune to worldly longing. As a young priest, Achille Ratti, as he then was, applied to join one of the Duke of Abruzzi's expeditions. Ratti was a keen *alpinista*, but the duke judged that a priest would be bad for morale.

That said, this is not a comprehensive history. I have picked out stories illustrative of themes (the drama of pioneering polar aviation, or the heroism of the Norwegian Resistance); so legendary that it would be perverse to ignore them (Sir John Franklin, shoe-consumer to beat them all); or because I liked them too much to leave them out – though in

IN THE ARCTIC REGIONS.

Expeditions in search of the North Pole are of such absorbing interest that every detail concerning them is the subject of eager curiosity, particularly the Food, which has to be selected with the utmost care. Dr. Kane took with him a supply of about 1,500 lbs. of **Cadbury's** Cocoa Essence and Chocolate in hermetically sealed tins, it being considered the best and most nourishing food, and especially suitable for men requiring all the vitality and strength necessary to the work.

CADBURY'S COCOA stands all tests, because it is absolutely pure (no alkalies being used, as in many of the so-called "pure" Foreign Cocoas). The LANCET refers to it as "representing the standard of highest purity at present attainable." Cocoa, besides being a stimulating and refreshing drink, is a nutritious food, sustaining and invigorating the system probably more than any other beverage. HEALTH writes: "Cadbury's Cocoa has in a remarkable degree those natural elements of sustenance that give endurance and hardihood."

this last category a superfluity of candidates did oblige me to ditch some favourites. I was sorry that Valerian Albanov failed to make the last cut. He was a gifted navigator whose ship froze into the Kara, most dreaded of Arctic seas. Fed by four of the great Siberian rivers, the Kara is frozen for nine months of the year, an annihilating wilderness spread over hundreds of thousands of square kilometres. In 1912 Albanov set off from the Murman coast on a projected 7,000-mile voyage to Vladivostok in search of fresh marine hunting grounds. When the Kara ice closed in, twenty-five men and one woman drifted 2,400 miles in eighteen months, during which time they ran out of fuel and had to chop up the wooden walls of the cabins to keep the samovar going. In April 1914, Albanov and thirteen others set off by sledge for an uninhabited archipelago using a hopeless map and a faulty chronometer. Three men quickly returned to the vessel, but the rest marched on for ninety-two days. They were weak and dreaming of peaches, but Albanov got them there carrying an icon of St Nikolas under his parka. He couldn't keep them alive though. I stood on the headland where nine lie in unmarked graves. A passing Russian boat rescued the other two, Albanov one of them. Those stranded on the ship were never seen again.

When I left the Sámi to their herds back in 2002, my Lappish host presented me with a bracelet made from the base of an antler. More bangle than bracelet, as the two ends didn't quite meet, it was a handsome object that I liked very much – I fancied that it smelled of smoke and beechwood – and it sat on my desk for many months as I mapped out my journeys. One day, as I fingered the bangle, I hit on the idea for a structure. I would make a circular, anticlockwise journey – Siberia to Alaska to Canada to Greenland to Spitsbergen to Lapland and back to Russia, to the White Sea. The ends would not quite meet up. The voyage would be a series of small journeys spread over two years, each planned to shed some dim light on the enigmas of the Arctic. Russia was a natural starting point, as it has more Arctic territory than any other country, 5,000 miles of coastline that unspools from Europe to the Pacific and a wilderness of tundra in which everything has evolved in response to cold. The southern boundary of Russian permafrost coincides with the treeline, the unguarded frontier that loops from the Finnish border, south of Murmansk, across the White Sea and chops off the top of the Urals before proceeding through the Norilsk nitrate fields and dipping into a U-bend on the central Siberian plateau. The coniferous forest below, a wide and monotonous sub-Arctic sash known as taiga, is the salient ecological feature of all northern Russia, a little-known region haunted by mythical spirits and gulag ghosts. Chekhov said that only migratory birds know where the taiga ends.

Twenty-six different ethnic peoples have herded and fished the Russian Arctic for centuries, yet they are invisible in most versions of the national past – unlike the dashing horsemen of the southern steppe or the turbanned anglers of Lake Baikal. Their Arctic land, like the Federation itself, is split by the Urals, the mountain border separating Europe and Asia. The Asian part of Russia, one twelfth of the land-mass of the earth, consists of Siberia and the Russian Far East, and Chukotka, where Medvedev inspected the Arctic Roll, is as far as you can go without running the risk of bumping into Sarah Palin. This was to be my starting point. Nine time zones from Moscow, the region is closed to foreigners, and has, in a quarter of a million square miles, no soil in which anything can grow. (As one traveller said of the mountain basins of north-eastern Siberia, 'twelve months of winter, and the rest is summer'.) Roman Abramovich chose Chukotka as his fiefdom: because of the region's low tax base it suited him to register his companies in Chukotka, and while he was at it he got himself elected governor. Small children run around wearing Chelsea caps. Maybe the reindeer will be next.

Tundra looks the same whatever the longitude, but whereas Chukotka is continental, the true Canadian Arctic has crumbled into a glaciated archipelago. In June 2007 I went there to join a small, publicly funded geology project. The island was bigger than Switzerland, but nobody in Toronto had heard of it. Every day I went off in a helicopter with a pair of geologists and a local man who waved guns at polar bears; every night the scientists met in a tent in the middle of camp and discussed what they had observed in a session they called Rock Talk. Out on the tundra, as bull caribou spooked us and horned larks looped high, Inuit polar bear monitors told me about killing spiral-tusked narwhals in the bay and playing Poker Stars on the Internet.

Across the Davis Strait, on the top of the Greenland ice sheet, a bulbous-topped pole resembling a parking meter plugs the most sacred site of Arctic science – the hole from which, in 1993, a team of researchers pulled two miles of ice cores that awakened the world to the speed of contemporary climate change. I camped nearby, on a dot

of the ice cap, with a team of atmospheric chemists who spend three or four months each summer in temperatures of -30°C, measuring halogens coming off the snowpack in parts of one or two per trillion. The Arctic is jammed with paradox but there in Greenland one struck me forcefully. In the northern hemisphere, the people who live furthest from pollutants are the ones most affected by them. A leading public health expert has said that in the 1990s, many Greenlanders were so toxic they would have qualified as hazardous waste. The marine food chain is among many complex factors in this catastrophe, as it passes some of the deadliest pollutants upwards. The bio-accumulated toxins are stored in fat, and indigenous peoples eat a fat-rich diet. The Arctic Monitoring and Assessment Programme recently logged data revealing that endocrine-disrupting chemicals handed up the food chain have triggered changes in the sex of unborn children in the first three weeks of gestation, resulting in the birth of twice as many girls as boys in some villages in Greenland and among the Inuit nations of eastern Russia. The Svalbard archipelago, which includes Spitsbergen, is further north than Greenland or Russia and the secrets of its toxic status are only beginning to emerge: not in humans, as there are none, but in bears, seals and whales. The bowhead whale has a long story to tell. A small (50-ton) male harvested in May 2007 had a harpoon embedded in its neck blubber. One of the busy whaling yards in New Bedford, Massachusetts manufactured the weapon in 1890, when Benjamin Harrison was president and Herman Melville growing old in obscurity. Slow growth and long life are characteristics of polar organisms: an Arctic poppy takes two years to husband the energy to form a two-millimetre bulbil. This is biological haiku.

Pollution, plunder, the gleeful killings of the Norse sagas – the Arctic is not a white Garden of Eden. All kinds of degradation crop up in the Inuit past: these pages contain a story of the deliberate slow starvation of an orphan. And there is epic cruelty in the north. History is a catalogue of man's inhumanity to man, as one knows all too well, but in a monastery on the White Sea where many thousands of gulag prisoners died, I heard and I believed that in all the terribleness, 'the murderers have not killed the spirit. The spirit lives.' There was something indefinably redemptive folded up in the layers of Arctic mystery. Explorers, scientists, rogue writers – we were all on its tail.

*   *   *

In Ittoqqortoormiit, a municipality the size of Great Britain with a population of 562, a girl in Wrangler jeans and Nike trainers drinks Coca-Cola with her sealskin-clad grandmother. Uncluttered polar landscapes reveal differences lost in the south. Semi-subsistence marine mammal hunters still harpoon walrus in north-west Greenland, and if the solitary Inuit no longer stands motionless over a seal hole for twenty-four hours at a stretch, his father did. (Compare the Comanche taming bison on the plains. He is as remote as Odin.) Above all else, the stripped-down Arctic exposes the way each country has treated its indigenous peoples. Every nation devastates native cultures, even if it doesn't actually kill everyone off. Russians did it with bureaucracy, Americans with money, Canadians (in the end) with kindness. Swedes and Finns did it with chainsaws that chopped down forests. And everyone did it with booze and syphilis. Acculturation is a theme of *The Magnetic North*. It is a grim story, but I was not looking for a pretty picture. I was looking 'to see beneath both beauty and ugliness; to see the boredom, and the horror, and the glory'.

The laboratory effect of the polar regions also amplifies national stereotypes. Norwegian expeditioners share a sleeping bag for nine months before suggesting that they might start addressing one another by their first names, Italian aviators emit cubic tonnes of hot air when their balloon crashes and Americans in thrall to the cult of the individual almost kill themselves in the attempt to be first because being first is all that matters. Elsewhere, fools think being British is enough to beat Johnny Savage; slaves of Soviet ideology make two-hour speeches on the role of the Fifth Party Congress while drifting on a pane of ice 1,000 miles from land; and Danes quietly go native in Greenland, where getting married involves moving to her side of the igloo. Propaganda? Mussolini despatched airships to illustrate the technical brilliance of a rejuvenated Italy; Dickens transmogrified the shoe-eating failure of Franklin into a fine victory in which 127 dead sailors were right and the Inuit, who were still fishing, were wrong; Stalin used aviators to deflect attention from the show trials, and shot his aircraft designers when the planes crashed. Where is post-war American anxiety more solidly visible than the lonely DEW line radar stations strung out across the western polar lands, the raw poetry of the name winning through despite itself?

Bathed in Arctic clarity, the Greenland Vikings enter the realm of parable. Theirs was among the most bizarre colonies ever to have

flourished. Greenland is an inhospitable land offering marginal opportunities for the pastoral farmer, but when a longship glided into peaceful fjord waters in about 980, Erik the Red and his warriors fell in love with a patch of lush meadowland. The 5,000-strong colony thrived for almost half a millennium. Greenland Norse lived like their kin in Fennoscandia: under feudal conditions in a federation of chieftains, taking care over their churches and cathedrals, killing each other in quarrels with zest, sticking rigidly to pastoralism even when hay refused to grow, foreswearing fish even when hungry, burning wood not blubber even though there were no trees, and sending their crusade tithe to the Pope in the form of walrus tusks and polar bear hides. But after

450 years they all died. The mottled grey walls of their church at Hvalsey remain, dwarfed by mountains and the luminous whiteness of the summit snows, glassless windows looking blindly over the silent fjord 600 years after Torstein Olafsson and Sigrid Bjørnsdatter exchanged wedding vows in 1408. That marriage was the last recorded event in Norse Greenlandic history, the church a lonely monument to what man can achieve, and what he can lose. On a June day the ruins solidified a sense of transience – even reproach. Why did the Greenland Norse fail after such feats of physical and cultural survival? The climate did alter, as over the course of the fourteenth century the Medieval Warm Period cooled into the Little Ice Age, but the Inuit in Greenland survived, and anyway the Norse colonists had weathered climatic fluctuations before. As I set out on my own journey I wondered what lessons were buried beneath the lintels of Hvalsey. I had a photograph folded in my passport of baby Reggie in his little wooden palk alongside a herd of grazing reindeer (he could write now, and had captioned the picture 'A Reg on a sledge!'). When I took it out, I thought of the ruined church at Hvalsey, the sudden failure of the Norse who had flourished for so long, and the uncomfortable truth that the unifying theme of collapsed civilisations is collective blindness to the depletion of natural resources. One wonders how historical hindsight will judge our own pursuit of oil at all costs.

The raw beauty of high latitudes has inspired an elite band of artists and writers and some of their stories crept into my own, especially when they informed a contemporary aspect of the Arctic. In Greenland Rockwell Kent painted with his brush sticking out of a hole in his mitten, and in the 1960s the Togolese writer Tété-Michel Kpomassie got off a ship and tried to live like an Inuit. He was twice the height of everyone else and the only black man for a thousand miles, but he integrated all right – within two months he was hospitalised with a suspected case of gonorrhoea. Many saw art as a flight back to nature. Others invested the Arctic with their own imaginative longings. Arctic stories usually embrace an element of myth, even those purporting to be true. Twelfth-century Norsemen told of mermen and mermaids, while Elizabethan navigators sprinkled their maps with bergs and glaciers created by the optical illusions common in refracted light on the Arctic Ocean. The myth of a circumpolar land that included the North Pole inspired travellers for centuries (some packed dinner suits in the event of royal hospitality upon arrival in the illusory land); when they accepted its non-existence, they pursued another myth – that of an open polar sea that was not occluded in ice (now, of course, that is turning out to be true). The Arctic attracts fiction to its facts with remorseless zeal. The two Americans lied about being first to the Pole, the celebrated 100 Eskimo words for snow are a canard, the fourteen-year-old midshipman Horatio Nelson did not fight off a polar bear as my Ladybird book promised. Though I began to sympathise with the Nelsonian position after a close encounter of my own.

Even in a region of myth and fiction, the chapter now opening in the Arctic is notably uncertain. There is no coherent picture of what the region is or has been or will be. I like that: an opacity, like the drawing down of a veil. There are no answers, only stories, and irreducible difficulties. Both polar regions appeal to something visceral in the spirit, especially in an era when we have lost contact with the natural world. But in the Arctic, unlike its southern counterpart, there is a figure at the centre of the picture. The Arctic is an image of the real world in all its degradation and beauty, and it is intimately connected to us – to our future, our crises and our dreams. John Davis, most sympathetic of Elizabethan navigators and a pioneering scientist in an era before science was partitioned off from everyday life, called the Arctic 'the place of greatest dignitie'. As soon as I read that phrase, I identified with Davis. I love the pared-down existence of polar lands and the grace of their peoples under pressure.

II

No Cows

The Arctic in Asian Russia

I even dreamt of buckwheat kasha. I dreamt of it for hours on end.
Chekhov, 'A Journey to the End of the Russian Empire'

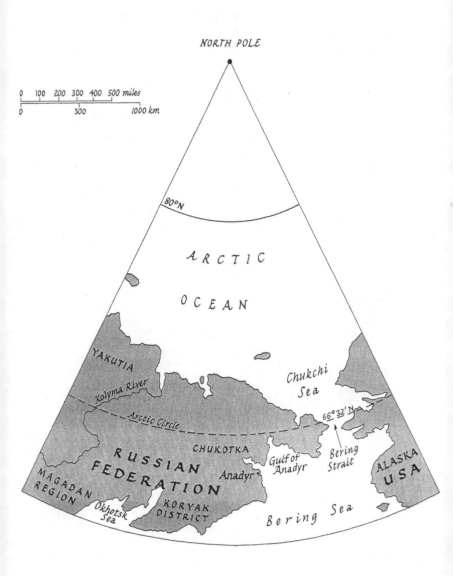

NORTH POLE

0 100 200 300 400 500 miles
0   500   1000 km

80°N

A R C T I C

O C E A N

YAKUTIA

Kolyma River

Arctic Circle

CHUKOTKA

Chukchi
Sea

66° 32' N

Gulf of
Anadyr

Bering
Strait

ALASKA
USA

R U S S I A N
F E D E R A T I O N

Anadyr

MAGADAN
REGION

Okhotsk
Sea

KORYAK
DISTRICT

Bering Sea

In the hallway of a block towards the northern edge of town, a man was tucking a baby into a pram. The handlebar had a circular holder for a baby's bottle or, in this case, paternal beer. The man, short and flat-faced like all ethnic peoples of the Russian Arctic, threw out his chest and swigged hard before sallying into the street. In an office off the hallway, posters advertised Bering Sea Biodiversity, and on a bank of desks miniature Chukotka flags fluttered gaily from jam jars when a breeze sneaked in through the ill-fitting windows. Eduard Dzor was preoccupied with negotiations for an increased whale quota. 'The quota for the whole of Chukotka is five bowhead and 135 grey whales,' he explained as we drank bitter coffee brewed on a portable gas burner. 'Bowheads are difficult to harvest here because they actually swim through Chukchi waters when the surface is frozen, whereas they reach Barrow in Alaska in the spring, so our neighbours there can pick them off from floes. Alaskan Inuit don't hunt greys. But it doesn't mean that those of us west of the Bering Strait might as well switch to grey whales.' As President of the Chukotka Marine Mammal Hunters' Association, Dzor instinctively recognised the role the bowhead played in native Chukchi communities, economically and psychically.

Dzor's people were once known as the bravest polar Russians. As early as the seventeenth century Muscovites considered Chukchi the most savage northerners, natural warriors who regularly raided the Yukagir and Koryak to the south and fought off Cossack bands who galloped as far as the Anadyr River. They ate deer maggots, killed migrating geese by hurling balls at them, and built antler towers as seal-oil lighthouses. They milked their reindeer by sucking the udders and spitting the milk into a bowl made of seal intestine and walrus bone. They lived long, and shored up the world with a cast of evil spirits with pointed heads, while their legends bristled with young girls who shoved their fathers off cliffs and mated with an underwater penis. Young men tattooed their arms with a dot for every enemy killed. In 1769 the defeated Russian authorities abandoned their fort in the Anadyr region, and the Chukchi, alone among northern natives, won a formal truce. An anthropologist who travelled in Chukotka some decades later found women wearing necklaces strung with the handles of broken teacups and pacifying their babies with pipes (they traded both alcohol and tobacco with the whalers). Chukotka was and is uniquely inaccessible by land, and it was this remote location, so far from the expanding empire, that saved the Chukchi from fully-fledged subjugation until well into the last century.

Far from Moscow: but next door to America. Alaskans can see *Chukotskiy Avtonomnyy Okrug* from their kitchen windows, as Sarah Palin memorably reminded the electorate in the doomed 2008 Republican campaign. At one point only five kilometres of pack ice and the Date Line separate the two; yet they share no transport links. Dzor was not the only person I met who had travelled from Chukotka to Anchorage via Moscow and Atlanta. Effectively uncoupled from the rest of the country, Chukotka is so remote it didn't even have a proper gulag. To get to it, the traveller passes through Gorky's land of death and chains. If the sea has solidified he may continue on foot, past Chukotka to Alaska, like the hunters who picked up their harpoons and walked to the uninhabited Americas. Chukotka is not only literally on the edge: it is the edge. Indigenous Chukchi are among the most brutally dispossessed of circumpolar peoples. An ethnic group whose presence predates that of the Russians by thousands of years, Chukchi are, or were, reindeer herders, like most native Arctic Russians, or hunters of sea mammals. In the post-Soviet chaos they are clutching the threads of what they once were and struggling desperately with the consequences

of radical social change. Chukotka is the ideal sub-Arctic environment in which to observe the collision between old and new, as well as enigmatically exotic. As a further incentive to finding my way there, a distinguished regional parliamentarian granted me an interview. Petr Omrynto was a former herder who had risen through the post-Soviet hierarchy to become the sole indigenous representative in the Chukotka *Duma*, or parliamentary assembly.

A place can be too exotic. Like many parts of the Russian Arctic, Chukotka is closed to non-nationals. Forbidden zones were familiar to the point of institutionalisation in the Soviet system, but over forty 'sensitive' cities remain shut off from the rest of the world. In the elation of the mid-1990s, Federal authorities abolished entry restrictions. But they soon changed their minds, as they did about many things, and portcullises crashed down from the Baltic to the Pacific. Aliens without complex sets of official papers are denied access to Chukotka on account of its proximity to America, still in some unspoken sense an enemy. In pursuit of these elusive documents I had spent eighteen months engaged in a process too labyrinthine to warrant transcription here. But I had done it, inserting myself as an artistically inclined scientist onto the books of the Chukotka Science Support Group. I set off at the last possible moment before the Big Freeze, as my papers had not emerged from the catacombs of bureaucratic inertia until the tail end of the Arctic summer. My contact on the ground was Gennady (Gena) Zelinsky, logistics Man Friday for the science consortium. Landing in the capital, Anadyr, was only the first hurdle, he emailed. Getting into town from the airport was the next: one had to cross a bay which in late September might or might not be frozen. Gena sweetly arranged for a colleague to meet me, sending a photograph of a figure resembling a Mongol horseman. I printed out the photograph and folded it inside my passport along with 'A Reg on a Sledge'. In the days before departure I paced around our house, packing and repacking my thermals and following my husband from room to room. A friend said she found it interesting that I was so anxious about this particular trip. Was it the myth of Siberia, the man in chains for ever exiled on the ice fields?

The Transaero 747 to Anadyr took off from a distant runway of Moscow's Domododevo Airport, and, when the doors returned to manual eight hours later and laboured arthritically open, cold air whooshed down the aisles. A squad of armed military personnel stomped on board, planting themselves at the front of each cabin to check documents. When my turn came, a woman sergeant peered at my papers before stretching across the middle row of seats to hand them to her colleague. She was slight, with downy cheeks. But her stiff peaked cap made up for it, and so did her gun. People coughed and stamped their feet in the invading cold. Mobile phones leapt to life. Then the second officer waved me through. At the time, it seemed like a minor Old Testament miracle. In the baggage hall, everyone else's luggage tumbled onto the carousel tightly wrapped in thief-proof blue cling film, so it was easy to recognise mine. Through the glass wall of the arrivals hall, a crowd of Mongol horsemen jostled for position. But my man, his face pressed against the glass, was holding up a sheet of paper inscribed with the Roman letters S – A – R – A. My name had never looked so good.

After warm handshakes and introductions in a language tantalisingly close to English, we boarded a bus of a type familiar from footage of the Korean War. The road followed a conveyor belt trundling wagons of coal across the tundra to a rusting military shipyard. Yuri, my escort, stared out of the window and fiddled with the ripped plastic covering of the seat in front. A sturdy figure with the short, thick legs of all ethnic Chukchi (and of the Inuit they so closely resemble), he had black hair and blue eyes and wore a pair of spectacles with tinted purple lenses. We decanted from the bus, and everyone squinted across the bay at a ferry breasting the water. Platelets of ice turned slowly in the shallows. When the ferry docked, people began pushing to get on. Yuri, moving his head from side to side like a startled tortoise, propelled me into a cabin in which brown frilly curtains heavy with grime hung from windows smeared with salted grease. But the water, an embayment of the Bering Sea, sparkled with cold sunlight, and three beluga fluked between us and the diminutive buildings of Anadyr on the far shore. On the white cliffs to the northeast, the blades of a zigzagging formation of wind turbines lolloped through endless rotations. Yuri's anxieties had vanished, and he chattered for the entire twenty-minute journey, apologising all the time for his 'bad' English while careering forward into exciting hinterlands of syntax. Once the bay freezes (I think he said), passengers travel to town on an ice road. In the short period when the freezing is actually happening, a helicopter shuttles to and fro. But sometimes the machine, leased from another region, fails to arrive. It turned out that the bay was an Arctic Styx: once across, return passage was unlikely. Yuri's sister had waited at the airport for three days, as it was too risky to trek back to Anadyr, in case the plane came and went while one was attempting to re-cross the bay. When I expressed horror at the idea, Yuri shrugged. 'That's nothing,' he said. 'I know person who waited thirty days.'

The main hotel charged $265 a night. So the oligarchs had got this far too. Gena had arranged homestay bed-and-breakfast accommodation through the regional tourist agency, an otherwise mysteriously purposeless organisation. When we docked, Yuri escorted me in a shared taxi van to a block of flats in the centre of town. In a small, two-bedroom apartment on the second floor, I met Marina and her husband Sasha, and we began the first of many 'conversations' in which we battered our heads against a linguistic brick wall. When I hung my parka in their small hall, the wall-mounted coatrack crashed to the linoleum. Neither of my hosts took the slightest notice. The flat was dangerously hot – throughout the Russian Arctic, coal-fired heating is centrally controlled – and Marina and Sasha, both in their sixties, wore shorts and vests, basking in the last rays of the dying star of Soviet munificence. In my room a tin can shaded a bulb that dangled over a Formica table, beaming a tube of light onto the table, and leaving the corners of the room in darkness.

Anadyr, capital of a region well in excess of a quarter of a million square miles, gave one the sense of a being only half evolved – out of the water, but short of the dunes. It had many features of urban development, such as a dozen sets of traffic lights, many of which worked, and a new supermarket stocked with a variety of imported products. All 15,000 residents lived in the five-storey *khrushchevka* apartment blocks indigenous to the Russian far north, but they were, uniquely, freshly painted in primary colours that highlighted the faded greys of the washing strung like bunting from window to window. The town had attracted little metropolitan detritus; one sensed that golden arches were a long way off. Anadyr lacked the hallmark decay of many Russian provincial centres, dumps of stained concrete ringed with semi-rural poverty or industrial decline. There was not yet any advertising, and no wonder, as with an average monthly wage just above $200 there was little disposable income either. Nor were there any kiosks, those functional stalwarts of the landscape elsewhere in the Federation. In the park outside my flat I counted dozens of shuffling *baboushki* muttering to themselves while picking up errant newspaper pages and dropping them into plastic bags. Instead of advertising, the 200-foot walls at the end of the blocks had been painted with attractive images of traditional Chukchi life – a bowhead whale, a fishing boat or a reindeer herd. The murals were even more unusual in the Arctic than the bright, fresh colours on the front walls of the blocks. I wondered what lay behind them.

Gena, the logistics coordinator for the science consortium, had, through sponsoring my official papers, acquired the role of personal minder. He came to pick me up on the first morning on his way to the Hunters' Association office, where the interview with the parliamentary deputy was to take place. The temperature was hovering at 7° above zero, and the park had already blossomed with old-fashioned hooded prams. When I emerged from my block, Gena was leaning against a taxi van. A bluff thirty-five, he was short and stumpy, and almost permanently plugged in to one of his many phones. After shaking hands he presented me with a mobile for the duration of my stay, 'so I know where you are' (was it fitted with a tracking device?). I saw Gena every day when I was in Chukotka. He was kind to me and I appreciated it, especially as he had never really chosen to have me as a ward, and he was always busy. If he put all his phones into his pocket at the same time, one of them would immediately begin to chirrup, and Gena would frown, pull it out, and fire off machine-gun volleys of gruff Russian inflected with the hard vowels of his native Khabarovsk.

Once we were installed in his office, Dzor, the association president, unearthed a pile of photographs and we leafed through images of hunting camps garlanded with rusted oil drums. 'Part of the goal of our organisation,' Dzor explained, 'is to raise living standards. Unemployment runs at seventy per cent in the villages. Food supplies

are even more costly in rural areas than they are in Anadyr as everything has to come in by ship in summer, plane in winter.' Later that
day I paid £8 for five bananas and £5 for three apples. 'There is a lot
of talk in Europe of Russia's emerging middle class,' Gena added. 'I
can tell you there are no middle classes in Chukchi villages.' Sharp-
eyed readers will have noticed the word *avtonomnyy* in the full name of
the Chukotka region. While it is true that Moscow mostly ignores the
furthest outpost of its empire, when it comes to its oil and gas,
Chukotka and its people have no autonomy at all. The issue of how
native peoples should or could benefit from mineral extraction was to
pursue me around the sub-Arctic.

Gena, Eduard Dzor and I sat back in our chairs thinking about
this, returning to the upright to dip our fingers into a bowl of
sunflower seeds. Before anyone spoke, the door opened and a fourth
person came through it, momentarily blocking the light. He was a
tall, square man with teaky skin, black cropped hair, a generous
moustache and exflorescent eyebrows, and his neat, dark suit
displayed an enamel Chukotka Deputy badge on the lapel. Petr
Omrynto, according to Gena, was 'the most famous man in Chukotka'.
He was certainly among the tallest. But there was no mistaking his
Mongoloid features. After a blustery start involving too much ribald
laughter for me to request a translation, Omrynto began to talk. He
liked to talk, especially about reindeer, and Gena struggled to keep
up with a translation. Before entering politics Omrynto had worked
as a herder, ultimately as director of one of the biggest collective
farms. 'Reindeer', he said as he settled into a chair and stretched
his long legs out in front of him, 'are the glue that bind Chukchi
culture and society. Even the word *Chukchi* is the Russian adaptation of the word *chavchu*, meaning reindeer people. During the Soviet
period, we had half a million animals. The Soviets saw us as a
meat factory.'

In the early years state planners had got themselves into a Soviet-
size muddle as they tried to apply Marxist ideology to a society which

had no industry, no agriculture and no formal leaders. First, how were they to prosecute class war in a classless society? 'Chukotka was already communist,' said Omrynto. 'No class, no leaders, no clans.' How then were junior party cadres to find rich, bourgeois 'exploiters' in order to have someone to punish? Unless they identified class enemies among the natives, they risked becoming class enemies themselves. At last someone hit on a solution. The herder with most animals could be the class enemy! This was how de-kulakisation proceeded in the Russian north. It was a caricature of the Arctic capacity to reveal and enlarge systemic social and political expressions. Second, conversion of northern peoples to a sedentary life was an important Soviet goal, yet herders cannot earn a living sitting still: they must follow the migrations. But the Soviets ploughed on. 'One should simply tell the nomads,' read one official document, 'enough of this wandering around; it's time to get settled.' In 1927 a government representative called a meeting in a *yaranga* (the traditional walrus-skin tent held up with whale jawbones) and told a group of Chukchi to elect members for a camp committee. The Chukchi replied that they didn't need a committee because they had always lived without one, and that if they did have one, the number of walrus would not increase. After the Great Transformation of 1928, when Stalin decided to speed up modernisation, officials harangued one another about what to do with the north in interminable plenums, whereupon nothing meaningful happened beyond the expression of rhetoric, the setting of targets and the announcement of five-year plans. By the time news of decisions reached the Arctic north-east, the decision-makers had been shot and their replacements were already formulating new policy – or perhaps by that time it was their replacements' replacements. By 1932 even Stalin realised his pharaonic fantasies were not working in the north. Collectivisation slowed down while high taxation speeded up and low production penalties rocketed; and nothing improved for the Chukchi. Nothing ever improved for the Chukchi. That the herd survived at all was a measure of their tenacity. Their own survival was miraculous. They had not emerged unscathed, or even intact; but Omrynto was living proof that some ineffable integrity had won through.

Through it all, supply lines to Arctic trading centres were so long and so corrupt that little was left by the time goods reached Chukotka except things nobody wanted, such as the fabled 10,000 left-foot gumboots. As everywhere in the circumpolar lands, geography made meaningful centralised state intervention hard, if not impossible. The Soviets went to extraordinary expense in their attempts to homogenise their territory. In the sixties helicopters landed on the tundra to ferry five-year-old Chukchi to boarding schools like herds of reindeer calves. Russian builders put up houses which sank into the permafrost when the top layer softened, attracted snowdrifts, let in the wind, or all three, and sensible Chukchi pitched their *yarangi* outside their new homes: even in the late eighties, of the houses built in the Arctic north for indigenous peoples, only 0.4 per cent had running water. As for the reindeer, they simply refused to cooperate, migrating every year as if nothing had happened.

Omrynto remembered disintegration on all fronts. He was a mesmerising speaker, his deep voice filling the scrappy room and his hands, big as root vegetables, conjuring the shapes of the herd flowing across the tundra. He even exuded the rich, smoky smell of reindeer. 'Between the sixties and eighties,' he said, 'when I was herding, average life expectancy dropped twenty years, to forty-five for men and fifty-five for women.' Omrynto winced, as if in pain. 'Every single good social indicator fell and all the bad ones leapt, suicide and murder rates among them. Whenever it looked like it could never get worse, it did.' De-Sovietisation turned out to be as disastrous as Sovietisation had been. 'In the nineties people starved. I remember going to one village and all that was in the store was vinegar and rice. Don't forget that we had no radio and no roads. Imports just stopped.' The indifference of a market economy filled the vacuum left by the collapse of the communist state. 'They had forced us to become *kolkhozniki* – workers on collective farms. We tried to divvy up the herds, so that every reindeer belonged to someone again, but thieves took the equipment, and it was too late to go back to the old ways, when herders made everything they needed.' The collapse of reindeer herding in Chukotka was the most catastrophic in the Federation – by 2000 there were only 100,000 animals left, and that was the critical number: if the population dipped further, the herd would no longer be sustainable. Chukchi migrated to Anadyr to look for work while Russians left in their thousands when their jobs disappeared along with the old regime. In Anadyr, one resident stuck a fly-poster on a telegraph pole advertising his flat in exchange for a one-way air ticket to Moscow.

Over the past decade, reindeer numbers have climbed back to 200,000. 'We have even started to sell meat,' said Omrynto, 'though the long supply chains kill us.' Gena and Dzor groaned. Not only were there no rail links to the outside world, there were no roads either. The old Russia had gone, but the new one had yet to arrive to replace it. I asked Omrynto what he considered the most challenging problem facing his constituents. 'Alcoholism, without a doubt,' he shot back, suddenly grave. 'Eighty per cent of villagers I represent are drunk on any given day.' Dzor, sitting behind his desk, chipped in, 'Every time Petr comes back from the villages he is in shock.' Everyone looked gloomy. 'You need to add to that other health issues,' Omrynto continued, wincing again. 'Syphilis is still rife in the villages', and here he told a long tale about patients nullifying the effect of expensive antibiotics with drunken binges. 'I see a lot of TB. In the worst post-collapse years of the nineties there was scurvy.' It was the first place I had ever been where scurvy was still close. Cut off from modern food supplies, Chukchi had forgotten which berries or whale organs to eat to fulfil their vitamin C requirements. They were stranded in no-man's-land between the past and the future. What with a sky-high suicide rate and rampant levels of fatal drink-related accidents, it seemed that death was always close in Chukotka. Death, and reindeer.

'But look, I'm optimistic,' said Omrynto, waving the root vegetables. 'Almost everything has changed for the better since 2000. The population is rebuilding. We are the richest in the Russian Far East when it comes to oil and minerals,' and he pointed to a map on the wall marked with coloured triangles indicating potential deposits of this and that, including uranium. Canadian-based Kinross had just wrested the first gold and silver from its Kupol mines above the Arctic Circle. Triangles notwithstanding, the striking feature of the map was its emptiness. The low tundra contours, veined with rivers, were barely settled at all. But the mention of minerals sounded a knell. Oil represented hope to Omrynto. But it had destroyed Siberian polar communities after pollutants and effluents poisoned grazing land in the seventies and eighties. When I stood up to leave, Omrynto leapt to his feet, a bear of a man. He fished a business card out of a deep pocket. It was printed in both Roman and Cyrillic, and before handing it over, he autographed it.

In 1890 Chekhov travelled thousands of miles across Siberia, tramping through mud like jelly, swooning over 'the smoky, dreamy mountains' and 'lithe' rivers and dreaming of turbot, asparagus and buckwheat *kasha*. He crossed the taiga on a sodden grass and dirt track that remained the sole connecting artery between European Russia and its Pacific hinterland.* In the towns ('everything hellishly expensive') the playwright sampled the whores, finding 'Asiatic' bordellos to his taste ('no washbasins or objects made out of rubber or portraits of generals'), and on the whole he loved Siberia, though wind and rain lashed his face 'to fish scales', and he had trouble with his haemorrhoids. When he reached the Pacific island of Sakhalin, among the most feared places of exile, he interviewed 'thousands' of convicts and many smallpox-ravaged Gilyak families. Chekhov had a humane attitude to both groups

---

* The completion of the Trans-Siberian railway in 1903 linked the headquarters of empire with the Far East. It was a fantastically ambitious engineering project conceived as a way of consolidating Moscow's influence and power in Asia.

('Our primary concern should not be our own needs, but theirs,' he wrote of attempts to 'Russify' the Gilyak). He was preparing a travel book, but found it hard to make the leap from fiction to fact in a place where the two were intertwined; he told his brother that when he sat down with his pen and travel notebook he felt he was wearing

the wrong trousers. The main impression that emerges both from his letters and his account, *The Island: A Journey to Sakhalin*, is how foreign he found the landscape. He wrote that he felt like a European there on the edges of the Russian empire. 'It seems to me', he said, 'that Pushkin and Gogol are not understood here.'

News of my arrival had spread, and Radio Chukotka rang one of Gena's phones requesting an interview. I had nothing against the proposal; and refusing anything semi-official in this semi-police state seemed unwise. But when Gena and I arrived in the lobby of the radio station, the receptionist panicked. After long minutes in which she and her colleagues bumped into one another as they rushed to and fro, a man in a suit appeared with a device in his ear. 'Problem,' said Gena after the two had spoken. In the background, people were hurrying around carrying coils of cable. Generalised anxiety about President Medvedev's arrival in three days had resulted in station bosses banning any foreigner who had got through the regional no-alien rule. Specifically, this meant they were banning me, as there were no other foreigners in Anadyr. But Russians meet their difficulties with lateral guile. We arranged to meet the interviewer that night in Gena's flat, and do the recording there.

This reporter, Alyona Vakarit, arrived with a spindly male sidekick and a bag of beer bottles. She was tall and handsome, about my age, with a mane of red hair which from time to time she tossed theatrically. We did the interview at the kitchen table. When the tape recorder was switched off, conversation turned to Chukotka. 'What is the West's opinion of Chukotka?' asked Vakarit. It was difficult to tell her that it doesn't have one. But it turns out that the rest of Russia doesn't have one either. 'National radio announces what time it is in all the zones,' Vakarit complained, 'and ends at Kamchatka, as if that were the end of Russia. But Chukotka is beyond that!' (Kamchatka, the peninsula south-west of Chukotka, long ago entered the language as a metaphor for remoteness; in 1840 Gogol wrote in a letter, 'I would not have hesitated to travel as far as Kamchatka,' meaning, to the ends of the earth, and today the seats at the back of football stadiums are 'out in Kamchatka'.)* 'If they do think of us at all in Moscow,'

---

* Marina Tsvetaeva, among the greatest poets of Russia's bitter years, refers in her 1934 poem 'Homesickness' to her withdrawal into 'my separate internal / World', comparing exile to that of 'a Kamchatka bear without ice'.

continued Vakarit, throwing her hair back in indignation, 'they think of flying dogs, as it is so windy here in winter. And of course the jokes.' The region's most significant role in the Federation is as the butt of a thousand jokes. *A Chukchi comes into a shop and asks: 'Do you have colour TVs?' 'Yes, we do.' 'Give me a green one.'** In the old days travellers returned to the capital with tales of a people who had mouths on the top of their heads and ate by placing food under their hats and moving their shoulders up and down. 'They think we have to stay connected to our houses with ropes in snowstorms,' moaned the thin sidekick, 'and that we still all earn big salaries.' In the Soviet era, civil servants received 'the long rouble' to compensate for the hardships of polar posts. Those inflated wages had perished with perestroika, along with a raft of other state subsidies.

My landlords Sasha and Marina were hunched over the kitchen table when I got back, each using a teaspoon to tease individual salmon eggs from a roe. Once they had amassed a batch of the gelatinous orange spheres, they sealed them in jars. The rest of the salmon poked out of a bucket in the sink. The next morning they were still at it, though a badminton racket had been pressed into service. Sasha was gently rubbing a fresh block of roe over the strings so the eggs fell onto a plate. It was less labour-intensive than the teaspoon method. Where had the badminton racket come from? Possibly a landfill site, as it had already reached a scientifically interesting stage of decomposition. The eggs were delicious.

On Saturday the sun was gone, and white horses played on the bay. In the shortening days, you felt winter shouldering in: cold air tickled high in the nostrils, and distant vistas shivered in advance of their

---

* Ethnic Chukchi naturally fight back. *A Chukchi and a Russian go hunting polar bears. They track one down at last. Seeing the bear, the Chukchi shouts, 'Run!', and starts running away. The Russian raises his gun and shoots the bear. 'Russian hunter bad hunter,' says the Chukchi. 'Now you haul this bear ten miles to the* yaranga *yourself.'*

swaddling snow. The bunting-washing hung stiff as salt cod. The interview with Omrynto over, I had planned to explore the area. But I had not reckoned on an absence of roads. Anadyr was a prison and I was an inmate, along with the rest of the population. To take our minds off incarceration, a brass band played stirring tunes on the steps of the House of Culture, a central-casting Soviet monster with a swooping metal roof and a facade that said, 'Don't come in here.' On the gritty shore behind, a group of men lit a barbecue with a blowtorch. Everywhere else, the town was out for its constitutional. The Mongol horseman impression at the airport had been misleading. I was expecting to find a city of Tartars, but in physiognomy I found Moscow-on-the-tundra. The horsemen who rode up from the shores of the Black Sea in the thirteenth century proceeded no further than the wealthy principalities of Rus. Their blood had diluted the southern populations, hence the frequently expressed assertion that in the north, one finds 'the true Russia'. Indigenous groups represent a small minority throughout the far north, and there are more ethnic peoples in Moscow than in Anadyr. Still, the juxtaposition is striking: a Mongol minority in the Arctic and a Mongol majority in the south, the two separated by a thousand miles of long-nosed Russians.

If the town had a centre, it was the new supermarket. All roads led to its swing doors: if anyone wanted to meet, they did so on its forecourt. It was the first supermarket ever to exist in Chukotka and nobody could stay away, preferring to go in three times a day to purchase three separate items rather than get everything at once. In this respect and others Anadyr was different from any other town I had ever been in. Cars tended towards the large and flashy, mostly land cruisers with names such as Toyota Tundrabird T4, and the majority had the steering wheel on the right side, which is the wrong side. Gena explained that the Russian Far East imports fleets of knackered or sub-standard Nissans and Toyotas from Japan. Doesn't it seem odd to spend an unfeasibly huge sum of money on a car which has the steering wheel in the wrong place?* Also, in a town known to be almost crime-free, why were both the supermarket and the Coffee Studio crawling with security guards? 'They're a status symbol,' Gena revealed. The shadow economy, so vigorous in the Russian Federation, was barely stirring in Chukotka, and the protection racketeers who had taken over many of the roles of state in the first years of democracy elsewhere in the Far East, notably Vladivostok, were non-existent. Connections, however, were everything, and you could get anything that was in short supply if you knew the right people. And that was like breathing to a Russian.

I sensed an unfathomable paradox at the heart of the city. Apartment blocks were externally pristine and uniquely bright, but their stairwells still stank of urine, and someone had invariably stolen the light bulbs. The split-level Coffee Studio above the supermarket offered a world-class range of cocktails, but each lurid glass cost almost half the average weekly wage. Gas-guzzlers lumbered through the streets like tanks, but on the stable dunes east of the docks a pair of old Chukchi hunters were smoking fish for the winter outside a *yaranga*. Stranded on the margins of the Federation and the continent, Anadyr was struggling to plug in to the global economy and the free world. One was unable to shake off the image of a police state. I had to register with the authorities within three business days of arrival, or incur a heavy fine. When one day I bought *pirozhki* (meat turnovers) and sat on the steps of the telephone exchange eating them before going in to look at emails at one of the public terminals, a policeman approached me and began barking. When I stammered that I didn't speak Russian, he shouted, 'No eat!' and waved me off angrily with a thumb. Young people over-compensated in the rush to catch up with the world they watched on television. The collective female wardrobe was a horror show of synthetic

---

* I may have underestimated the practical issues. How easy would it be, I asked a mechanically-minded friend when I got back, to move a steering wheel from one side to the other? 'Well,' he said, after some reflection, 'it would be easier to turn the car over and put the wheels on the roof.'

frilly shirts, cheap jeans and high-heeled plastic boots with studs, buckles and anything else the Chinese manufacturer could glue on. Young couples flocked to the Coffee Studio simply because it had an English name, whereas that fashion had long run its course in Moscow. The Studio had its good points. In it I found the only decent espresso machine in Anadyr. But it also had banks of plasma screens belting out Muscovite music videos day and night. Inside the tinted windows of the Studio, Moscow was a faraway paradise of the Chekhovian variety ('Oh to go to Moscow!' the eponymous Three Sisters wail as they fend off provincial stupor.) But Irina and her family were an arm's length from the capital. This lot were four thousand miles away.

Anadyr was a microcosm of the whole of Arctic Russia, a place where sequinned trousers co-exist with persistent, elemental toughness. The post-Soviet transition had been disorientating for everyone, but one couldn't help feeling that it had hit hardest up in this forgotten corner.

It was already owl light when I hurried up the wooden steps of the cathedral for the five o'clock Saturday service, and the taffeta sheen of the golden domes had flattened. The whole building, appropriately scaled up from the modest local churches, was made of weathered aspen boards: a magnificent chalet of a cathedral. Inside, candlelight flickered over painted faces, the tidal drone of a male choir rose and fell and ponytailed young monks strode around noiselessly, following the muttered instructions of the priest, a tall, broad figure whose stomach swelled tight against the black fabric of his robe. Puffs of incense smoke trailed woozily among the dozen worshippers, and they shifted from foot to foot, touching their headscarves. Here were the obedient servants of the eastern Church quietly commemorating their martyrs, their lilting low prayers echoing back to a time before oligarchs and collectives, though not before reindeer. Here too was the abiding spiritual calm that the Soviets failed to obliterate, coming down on us few like a benediction.

Or was it? The peace of the cloisters was not, regrettably, the one that passed all understanding. Father Agafangel, the officiating priest, was embroiled in a fight with his bishop that had just made the national press amid a hailstorm of denunciations. The bishop, a known nationalist renegade and arch-conservative, had himself publicly denounced the Patriarch for his support of democracy and cellphones. (A week after my return, the Patriarch dismissed the bishop.) Chukotka attracted misfits and outsiders. It was a tough place to live, but if I heard a refrain, it insisted that life in Chukotka was better than it used to be. And if there was a name in the refrain, it was that of Roman Abramovich, maverick outsider extraordinaire.

In 1995, in one of the most profitable privatisations of that chaotic decade, Abramovich and Boris Berezovsky had bought national oil conglomerate Sibneft for $200 million. Abramovich knew nothing of Chukotka, but he registered his companies in Anadyr to benefit from its low tax base. Municipal budgets rocketed, and in 2000 the electorate returned Abramovich as governor with a robust 99 per cent of the vote. In addition to his tax millions, Abramovich invested heavily. He paid for the illumination of Anadyr's streets, and for buses to run through them. (There were two bus routes, and both were free. It took sixteen minutes to get from one end of the main route to the other.) In the first four years of his tenure as governor, capital investment in Chukotka increased twelvefold. The wind turbines flapping on the clifftops were among his many schemes, and it was he who had paid for the 200-foot murals of whales and reindeer, having hired a modish Moscow design consultancy. Abramovich didn't like the fact that he couldn't eat well on his monthly visits to the rim of Russia. He was fond of the folksy German restaurants he had patronised on business trips to Munich, so he built one and flew in a Bavarian chef. I had dinner at this place, which Abramovich had called *Baklan* (Cormorant). It was near the cathedral, and featured home-brewed beer and a live oompah-band. I ordered sauerkraut with a Russian twist, the twist being an absence of cabbage. A visitor returning to Anadyr after a ten-year absence would find it transformed by the Abramovich millions. Besides the supermarket and the Coffee Studio with its Harvey Wallbangers, both urban and rural living conditions had improved from the nadir of the nineties, as had healthcare (rural scurvy notwithstanding). Abramovich was more popular in Chukotka than anywhere else in the world, including Stamford Bridge, home of Chelsea FC, and Omsk, where he had bought and invigorated the Avangard ice hockey team. Meanwhile, Sibneft began to drill in Anadyr Bay, and the poor remained as disenfranchised as they always had been. But Abramovich couldn't do anything about that. Or could he, if he wanted? I did hear dissenting voices. Yelena, an articulate gallery owner in her fifties, told me she wished the authorities would spend less on paint and more on pensions. 'These walls have to be repainted every year,' she said, gesturing out of the window of her craft gallery near the *Duma* at the flats on the other side of Otke Street. 'Food is expensive, and there is still malnourishment among the poorest. There is too much attention paid to appearances and not enough to the substance of people's lives.'

Yelena had approached me in her gallery as I pored over captions beneath the artefacts with a pocket Russian–English dictionary. Introducing herself as an English-speaker, she peered with me into glass cases filled with walrus-bone whales and men. 'Look at this polar bear,' said Yelena, fishing out a hoe handle featuring a recumbent beast. 'If you tip it this way, the bear's body looks like a human face. Masses of early Chukchi carvings depict anthropomorphic animals and zoomorphic humans. It represents a belief in the inter-relationship of all living beings.' Many pieces were exceptionally beautiful. 'The interesting thing is,' Yelena explained, 'animal–human interchangeability was a feature of Stone Age art – from, say, 20,000 years ago. It vanished everywhere else, but the fact that it was still going strong here in Chukotka between about 100 BC and AD 100 is a reflection of our isolation.' That again. 'And of human tenacity.'

Abrupt climate change froze the carvers out at the end of the first century AD, and archaeologists have found few artefacts from the next 1,500 years. 'When Russians began arriving in the 1600s,' Yelena continued, picking up a sealskin scraper, 'they traded new tools and materials. Here's a copper helmet – see the verdigris?' Fine garments hung on the walls of the third room. 'The artists went on absorbing the influences of whoever was around,' said Yelena, pointing at a beaded coat. On the north-east Chukchi coast, a community of 1,500 Inuit speak Yupik, like west Alaskan Inuit. Until the 1950s, the two groups regularly camped together on the sea ice off one of the islands straddling the US–USSR border. In the end Soviet authorities banned the visits on the grounds that it was unfair to show American Inuit how well their Soviet kin lived. 'In the thirties,' said Yelena, 'Eskimo at Naukan on the Bering Strait started making sealskin carpets in which traditional geometric motifs appeared alongside Soviet symbols. Sculptors don't go in for symbolism any more; it's mostly representational figures.' She showed me a trio of doe-eyed seal pups playing on a floe. It was the kind of thing one might buy at Boots. These carvers too had absorbed the spirit of the age. Unfortunately, it was ours.

In September 2005, in Russia's largest corporate takeover, Gazprom acquired 72 per cent of Sibneft for US$13.01 billion. Not a single one of the many investigations into tax evasion within Sibneft had stuck. Since the sale, municipal income in Chukotka had plunged. Abramovich

stood for a second term as governor, even though he didn't want to; pundits said that his friend Putin pressurised him into it. He resigned in July 2008, five months after Putin had done the same, without completing his second term. But he was still there, and not just in the sulphurous glow of his streetlights and the ditties blaring out of his German restaurant. He was gazing into the tundra from the windows of every building, as he was standing again in the forthcoming parliamentary elections, and his team had not taken any chances when it came to the distribution of posters. I was loitering outside the *Duma* one day, waiting with Gena's friend Anatoli for another friend who was supposed to be delivering a box of computer cables. Anatoli was an Anadyr-born engineer who had trained in Virginia; his father, a mining consultant, had taken a secondment in the US, and the family had been able to accompany him abroad. Although Anatoli had returned to Anadyr to work for a mining firm, he was keen to get out again, and to go to Moscow. The *Duma* was an unassuming neoclassical building hard by the main street, facing its own small car park. As we waited, Anatoli explained that Abramovich was not just standing to be a deputy. 'He wants to be chairman as well,' he said, scanning the traffic. 'Why aren't there any posters of the opposition?' I asked. Anatoli turned to me with a look so withering that I blushed. 'Effectively there is no opposition,' he said, his tone of voice indicating that he was addressing a person with a small brain. 'Except some insane far right party which nobody takes seriously. You must know that we don't really choose whom we vote for.' Anatoli tugged on his nineteenth cigarette of the afternoon. 'Since 2004, even the governor is appointed by the president unilaterally – I mean, technically the *Duma* has to ratify the appointment, but it's a rubber-stamping procedure. It's all part of Putin's system of Vertical Rule.' Had that been a good thing? 'In some respects it was needed, as tinpot governors were treating their territory like a personal fiefdom. They were like Cossack-trader warriors. But it has gone too far.'

An aircraft-sized Nissan squealed into the car park, and once it had stopped alongside us, a figure emerged carrying a cardboard box. Greetings were exchanged, the box handed over, and the aircraft-jeep wheeled away down Otke. Anatoli tucked the box under one arm, pulled up his collar with the other hand, and we set off back to Gena's flat. 'In the middle nineties,' Anatoli finished up, 'we had more democracy in Chukotka and less money. Now we have less democracy and more money.' From which we can conclude, I said, that democracy is a bad thing? But at that he just laughed bitterly, and lit another cigarette.*

A dairy stood halfway down Gena's street. Workers bottled milk products in the back and sold them in the front. I had been inside and bought yoghurt. Later that day, drinking tea in Gena's kitchen, I asked where the cows grazed. 'No cows,' Gena said. 'Powdered milk, imported from Voronezh.' Improvisation was the key. It always had been. Elena Russell grew up in the fifties and sixties in a barracks in the Bilibino goldfields, where her father was a geologist. After Elena was born the midwife stitched her mother up with the portal vein of a reindeer. The family ate powdered vegetables, powdered egg, powdered everything, except reindeer. When she was a teenager, Russell wrote in her autobiography, 'Moscow came up with the idea of building the world's first atomic power station within the Arctic Circle,' but it was hard to find a site in Bilibino, as 'wherever the bulldozers crashed through the earth, there was gold flashing back at them'. Surveyors took many weeks to get to Chukotka from Moscow, their planes delayed in Omsk for so long, according to Russell, that they had time to get divorced, have their teeth crowned and grow a long beard. But despite the challenges, engineers built the reactor.

When Russians eventually rode east out of their European enclaves and crossed the Urals, they came like conquistadors. They wanted sable, a commodity in such demand that at one stage it accounted for

* Two weeks after I returned from Chukotka, Abramovich was returned as a deputy and as parliamentary chairman, polling, according to the Central Election Commission, 97 per cent of the vote.

a third of imperial revenues. Yet the Russians were in the dark as to what lay behind the Urals. The odd wanderer brought back stories of tribesmen who froze to the ground in winter (besides having their mouths on top of their heads). But the rewards were fabulous: a single hunt could make a man's fortune. In the sixteenth century, freebooting Cossacks rode east in bands of fighter-explorers, trading tin, flour and beads for fur. It was the beginning of the great territorial expansion of the tsarist state, and imperial foot soldiers followed the sables across the wide Siberian rivers that surge from the Mongolian steppe to the Arctic coast: first the Ob, then the 3,400-mile Yenesei ('cramped by its banks', according to Chekhov), then the Lena. In 1639, the first Russian saw the Pacific. He and his colleagues traded with Chukchi herders who had tattooed faces and fragments of walrus ivory pierced through their upper lip. By the end of the eighteenth century the entire Arctic coast of Asia belonged to the empire in addition to the many thousands of square miles to the south. Moscow had conquered Siberia through a mix of individual fortune-seeking and government policy, the latter a reflection of a profound Russian longing, expressed since Peter the Great, certainly since Catherine the Great, to populate the spaces to the east. Tolstoy referred to it as a 'mission'. The indigenous peoples, lumped together as Tartars (originally Tatars), simply got in the way of this quasi-mystical vision of a continent-wide Russian state. They rose up from time to time, but the allure of the Russian's goods, and the superiority of his arms, always triumphed. According to one tale, a Tungus herder once accepted a chunk of bread as a gift from the first Russian he had ever met. After chewing it for a while, the herder said to his friend, in their own language, 'Good.' Then he took a cracker from the Russian, ate it, and said, 'Delicious.' After that the Russian offered a spoon of sugar. 'Don't even think about killing these good men,' the Tungus told his friend after consuming the sugar. So they threw away their bows and arrows and tucked into more bread, crackers and sugar.

The most attractive item among the goods was vodka, and the

Russians exploited the native fondness for their spirits. One traveller reported that among the Ostiak (Khanty) people on the Ob the usual procedure was 'to give each Ostiak a cup of good vodka, free of charge; then sell the first bottle for one rouble; two more bottles – mixed half and half with water – for one and a half roubles; and then three bottles of pure water for three roubles each'.

After the fur traders, poor farmers straggled through the passes of the Urals into the unfeudalised lands of Siberia, followed by religious dissenters fleeing the control of the Orthodox Church. But the immigrants who made an indelible mark on history were exiles and prisoners; in English and every other European language, 'Siberia' is synonymous with penal servitude – a Russian heart of darkness. The Arctic in particular was ideal for prison camps: so far away that everyone in Moscow forgot about the prisoners' existence; too remote for viable escape; and a really horrible workplace. By 1753, when the tsar abolished the death penalty, the range of offences punishable with Siberian exile included fortune-telling, taking snuff and driving a cart without using reins. The nineteenth century alone saw a million convicts march into oblivion, the journey itself a two-year via dolorosa which killed thousands. Many stayed in Siberia after their release. In *House of the Dead*, the fictionalised account of his own incarceration and his first great novel, Dostoevsky conjures a kind of Asian Australia peopled with former prisoners.* (Sentenced to death for his involvement in a group that printed anti-establishment literature, Dostoevsky was standing in front of a firing squad when he learned that his punishment had been commuted to four years hard labour.)

In this great continent-empire on which the sun never set, nobody

---

* Who can forget Dostoevsky's prison bath-house? Two hundred men in a room twelve paces square, the floor inches thick in slime, the convicts, their leg chains clanking, piled on benches pouring dirty water onto the shaven heads of the men crouched below – a phantasmagoria of crimson steaming bodies ridged with the scars of the lash. 'It was not heat: it was hell.'

had the slightest interest in the Chukchi, or any other Arctic peoples. A distinguished nineteenth-century observer referred to them as 'half-thawed humanity', going on to call the Chukchi 'descendants of fish'. (Aren't we all?) In *Anna Karenina*, the heroine's husband, government minister Alexei Alexandrovich Karenin, embodies the theoretical attitude of Moscow to its distant northern tribes. The important thing was to commission plenty of commissions. Karenin determined, 'if it were to turn out that the position of the national minorities was really what it appeared to be according to the official data in the hands of the committee, that still another scientific commission be appointed to investigate the reasons . . .' Unfortunately nobody could make out, from the information submitted to the commission, whether the minorities were starving to death or perfectly all right, a state of affairs necessitating a further commission. As usual, fiction could not compete with fact. In 1827 two commissions had actually spent eight years à la Karenin counting natives.

That said, Russian efforts to colonise and modernise rarely got beyond 60°N, and the Arctic regions remained largely unmolested outside the prison camps. Peasants had never settled on the tundra: how could they? There was no wood for the *izbi* (huts) and no black earth which steamed after spring rains to nourish rye, buckwheat, flax, hemp or turnips. The authorities mostly ignored their Arctic responsibilities, concentrating their energies on the fratricidal theatricality of Russia's volatile southern frontiers, or poking around in the Balkans. After all, the northern border could not fray.

Besides the Chukchi who once hunted seal from coracles with obsidian-tipped spears, Khanty men fished the Ob from leaf-shaped dugout canoes, bands of Evenk built bark-covered tepees in the forest and Dolgan clans migrated with the reindeer, pulling huts mounted on ski-runners, called *balok*, between the Arctic coast and the Yenesei hinterland. The many languages spoken across the Russian Arctic and sub-Arctic include Turkic, Uralic, Tungus-Manchu and Ket, the latter unrelated to any other tongue. Most of the peoples were and remain reindeer-based, and no group was originally fully settled. The nature of herding and hunting requires periodic movement: you have to move with the reindeer and marine mammals, even if the authorities make you live in a house. A minority everywhere, and lacking political and economic muscle, the northern peoples have never had Transcaucasian-style elites to act as spokesmen.

Piers Vitebsky's affecting book *Reindeer People*, published in 2005, distils nearly twenty years fieldwork in Sebyan, a community of a few hundred Tungus-speaking Eveny in the vast east Siberian Republic of Yakutia, also called Sakha.* Well over 2,000 kilometres west of Anadyr, Sebyan is still very far indeed from Moscow. Eveny have herded reindeer among the Verkhoyansk Mountains for many generations, following the spring and autumn migrations and surviving winter temperatures which cause human teeth to shatter. Their technical vocabulary is one of the largest in the history of speech, featuring, across all dialects and regions, 1,500 words for parts, shapes, diseases, diet and moods of reindeer. Eveny have a wide range of nicknames for their beasts, and are not as isolated from the rest of the world as one might imagine: in the 1990s a male reindeer who never tired sexually was called Bill Clinton. Men, women and children wear, almost exclusively, garments made from reindeer, with the result, according to Vitebsky, that ethnic Eveny look and smell like reindeer. Each hollow hair has such fabulous insulating properties that the blood and organs of a dead deer do not freeze under uncut skin: they ferment.

Vitebsky's portrait is deeply sympathetic. He camped with Eveny herders for many months, living with them a life that was an interplay between ice and fire; he learned that cold is the basic state in the universe, while heat is a limited resource. His book is infused with the perfume of larch and resin, and with the meaty smell of a reindeer-camp fire.

* Eveny (formally known as Lamut) are not the same people as the more numerous Evenk (Tungus) living to the west.

An entire ecosystem has evolved round the deer. One particular female fly hovers around a reindeer's nostrils and shoots in a jet of eggs when the animal inhales. Ten months later, a baby fly cannons out fully formed when the reindeer sneezes. But as the nineties progressed, Vitebsky writes of Sebyan, alcohol tightened its grip. 'The village came to resemble a horror movie in which people succumbed one by one

to a zombie plague ... each time I returned, I found that someone I thought would hold on for ever had gone under.' That might be the saddest line I ever read about the Arctic. The advent of aviation had reduced mobility rather than increased it, as young people no longer learned the skills of long-distance travel – skills that are gone for good once they vanish. *My vymyrayuschiy narod*, an Eveny elder told the author over the campfire and the vodka bottle; we are a dying people, a people on the verge of extinction. There are about 17,000 Eveny left. They accept what is happening to them (according to Vitebsky), sensing that they, like all peoples, are clinging to the face of the earth for a fleeting moment. Noting how much they have been through since the

Russians invaded their land, Vitebsky concludes that their 'inner spiritual life and reserves of irony allow them to survive, even while they see their world for what it is. The emotional journey of the reindeer peoples of Russia has been hard, and the feeling of loss that I sense in so many does not come from naïve nostalgia, whether theirs or mine. The Soviet ideal of progress was based on a rejection of the past: graves were to be forgotten, children were to be separated from their primitive, deported or murdered parents, dead shamans were not to be reborn. This catalogue of sacrifices is now seen to have been in vain.'

The expansion of the gulag system facilitated the fanatical industrialisation at the heart of Stalin's vision for Russia and almost completed the spiritual annihilation of the small peoples. The gulag existed at least in part to address the imperial failure to harvest the natural resources of remoter regions. After Stalin unveiled the second Five-Year Plan in 1932, geological expeditions set out over the tundra in search of fresh sources of coal, gas, oil, gold, nickel, graphite – anything the government could extract with enforced labour and use or export. Traditional hunting grounds and reindeer pastures emerged as major repositories of resources from phosphates to mica and tungsten, and armies of *zeki* (prisoner-workers) built mines, refineries, ports, power stations and factories, all connected to service cities by networks of railways and roads.

One hesitates to nominate the 'worst' Arctic gulag. The worst was the one you were in. But three of the harshest were Vorkuta in the west, Norilsk in the middle, and Kolyma in the east, all not only isolated but virtually inaccessible. In the summer, prisoners endured the martydom of mosquitoes, and in winter they froze to their bunks. In Vorkuta, the temperature only struggles above zero Celsius for four months a year. If a person fell into the snow on the march to the mine, his body lay unnoticed until spring. In the multiple camps of the Kolyma region abutting Chukotka, prisoners could down pickaxes in the goldfields when the temperature fell to -50°C. But in the winter of 1928–9, the rule changed to -60°C. Only the camp commander had a thermometer, the regulation did not apply to woodcutting teams, and the wind chill was not part of the equation. By 1940, Kolyma was producing one third of the world's gold, and every kilogram cost a human life. Slave workers travelled to Vladivostok by rail, crammed into Stolypin compartments in which robbers took their food and clothes, then north on one of Andrei Sakharov's 'death ships of the Okhotsk Sea', disembarking at Nagayevo, the port serving Magadan, gateway to the Kolyma River valley. Out of every hundred men who built the road connecting Magadan with the web of gold camps, one survived. The pits themselves filled up twice a day with blasted ammonal, and the miners coughed up bits of their lungs. Virtually nobody made a successful escape. According to Solzhenitsyn, when prisoners tried to run away from a Kolyma camp, the authorities baited local ethnic Yakut people with rewards for turning them in such as dried herring, flour and tea. Children shouted, 'There's a herring coming' when they spotted a stranger. (Yakut had little cause to think fondly of Russians, prisoners or not.) Between two and three million died working the mines and camps of the north-eastern gulag. Teacher and journalist Eugenia Ginzburg survived for eighteen years – just – and after reading her autobiographical account of the children's camps at Kolyma, I felt as if I would never read another book again.

By 1952, the Kolyma complex covered an area three times the size of Texas. Soviet historians call this period 'the opening up of the far north'; just as the Cold War unsealed the Canadian Arctic, the gulag brought infrastructure and people to the Russian north. When Khrushchev closed most of the gulag camps, incentives attracted a fresh immigrant population to sustain the new industrial base. One might have assumed that the north with its permafrost would at least have been immune from the ravages of Khrushchev's crazed agricultural policies. But minerals under Khibiny (later Khibinogorsk, subsequently Kirovsk) in Russian Lapland provided the Soviet Union with its entire requirement of apatite for phosphate fertiliser. Thus in a twist of geography the unfertile landscapes of the sub-Arctic enabled the meadows of Transcaucasia to bear fruit. In the sixties, geologists found massive reserves of oil and gas directly under reindeer pasture in the West Siberian and Timan-Pechora basins. Pipelines were poorly maintained, if they were maintained at all, and leaks resulted in chronic contamination which badly affected herders. In 1994 a 52-kilometre section of pipeline in the Komi Republic ruptured in twenty-three places. A dam thrown up to contain the spill made the situation worse when in excess of 100,000 tonnes of oil poured over the land and into the Kolva and Usa riverways. Fourteen years earlier, in 1980, the oil and gas condensate well Kumzha-9 in the Pechora delta suffered a blowout. Engineers detonated an underground nuclear explosion in an attempt to arrest the flow. This failed, in part because workers drilled the well for the nuclear device in the wrong direction. It took the Soviets six-and-a-half years to repair the blowout. Every day of that period, two million cubic metres of gas and hundreds of tonnes of condensate spewed out of the well.

Communist mismanagement reduced the country to economic ruin and left a legacy of rotting industrial plant – rotting literally, and metaphorically. Most Arctic factories cost the exchequer more than they put into it, so, naturally, after the regime fell, the new leaders in Moscow had to close them down if they were to have any hope of rebuilding an economy. As a result, many of the industrial towns that spearheaded the Soviet 'mastery of the North' are dead or dying. Gena referred to the port of Providenya in Chukotka as 'Death City'. Shipping had dropped off along with everything else and Providenya, which once had a meat processing plant, a tannery, a dairy, a factory and even a film studio, was little but a wilderness of broken windows, its population of almost 15,000 shrunk to 2,000 or fewer. Down at Petropavlosk, the abandoned Kamchatka fleet rusted in the harbour. The Arctic Ocean ports of Chersky and Tiksi had fallen to precipitate decline, as had Magadan, the mining town on the Okhotsk Sea that once funnelled hundreds of thousands of prisoners to the camps of the north-east. The Russians who stayed are practically destitute.

Whilst failing production centres have shut down, the few successful enterprises have acquired a life of their own. It was a paradigm of what was happening across the sub-Arctic belt. Industrial pollution, vigorous as a virus, delivers some fresh ecological catastrophe to the tundra as every month passes. As mentioned at the start of this book, the Arctic produces about a tenth of the world's oil and a quarter of its gas.* Most of that comes out of the Russian Arctic: 80 per cent of the oil, and as much as 99 per cent of the gas, according to figures produced in 2007 by AMAP (the Arctic Monitoring and Assessment Programme). In an optimistic gesture towards integration, the resource-rich Yamal-Nenets region depicts on its crest a pair of polar bears, a reindeer and an oil derrick. But flares burning off gas in Gazprom's Yamsavey gasfields near Nadym in Yamal are among many releasing pollutants onto a vulnerable ecosystem in which cold and dramatic seasonal variations inhibit recovery. In the pan-polar pollutant stakes, however, the nickel city of Norilsk on the Taimyr Peninsula emerges a clear winner. Twenty-four hours a day, seven days a week, three metal smelting plants pump out waste which even company directors admit is mostly sulphur dioxide. Situated just east of the Yenesei, on which it depends for transport, Norilsk is the largest city in the world above the Arctic Circle. In 2007 Norilsk Nickel published metals sales totalling 15,909 million US dollars. Its board of directors includes Oleg Deripaska, one of the young oligarchs who made quick billions from the resources of the far north. In addition to its role as the world's leading producer of nickel (295,000 tonnes a year) and of palladium, the key component in catalytic converters, the group, via global subsidiaries,

---

* As long ago as 2000, the United States Geological Survey judged that 'the Arctic contains 25 per cent of the world's undiscovered hydrocarbon reserves'. This much-quoted statement, a shibboleth in the context of Arctic politics, is one which the USGS no longer officially endorses, some say because its experts now consider the figure to be higher.

produces cobalt, rhodium, silver, gold, iridium, ruthenium, selenium, tellurium and sulphur, as well as ranking among the largest producers of platinum and copper (423,000 tonnes a year). Its critics say it is also the world's largest producer of acid rain. According to company figures, the total amount of sulphur dioxide produced by the three Norilsk plants is almost two million tonnes a year – a figure which has only decreased by about 16 per cent since the last days of the Soviet Union. Once in the atmosphere, this gas turns into acid rain. Men in Norilsk have the highest lung cancer rate in the world, and one local doctor, Svetlana Golubkova, recently told a BBC reporter who managed to get in (like Chukotka, Norilsk is closed to foreigners) that 'very, very few healthy children are being born here'. Greenpeace Russia cites evidence that acid rain has spread across an area equivalent in size to Germany. The deputy general director of Norilsk Nickel, Tav Morgan, told the BBC that the company was taking action to cut pollution. 'For the period up to 2015–2020,' Morgan said, 'we expect to reduce sulphur dioxide emissions by approximately two-thirds.' But he later admitted it was hard to guarantee those figures because company men were still developing the technology to facilitate reduction at any pace.

I was no longer the only westerner in Anadyr. Gena had acquired a house guest, a Fairbanks-based German anthropologist who had procured an entry permit to conduct field research. He had been working in the settlements to the north for three months. He was also a cook, and on Sunday prepared a meal of Teutonic heft for me and Gena. Tobias Holzlehner was a sharp-eyed university lecturer with woolly ash-blond hair, and his *Spätzle* dumplings were delicious. A fluent Russian and English speaker, he was collecting data for the multi-authored project *Moved by the State: Perspectives on Relocation and Resettlement in the Circumpolar North*. From 1957 to the mid-eighties, the practice of *ukrupneniye* had 'centralised' semi-nomadic Chukchi reindeer herders and walrus hunters, rounding them up into purpose-built factory towns. The goal – to boost production – was never achieved;

the consequence, as Petr Omrynto had indicated, was social and cultural disaster. Over the following days, as I learned about his work, Tobias introduced me to Restaurant Anadyr, up the pedestrian avenue from the radio station. I was always hungry by lunchtime: the underemployed tourist bureau advertised their accommodation as B & B, but one B would have been enough, as no breakfast ever made an appearance. To arrive at the Anadyr one entered a large, anonymous building and mounted a flight of swerving wooden stairs, entering the restaurant, on the first floor, though a pair of saloon swing doors inlaid with frosted glass. The cavernous room featured improbably high ceilings, strip lighting, net curtains and, at the far end, a low stage equipped with a drum kit and two standing mikes. A pair of mini-skirted elderly waitresses with dyed hair ferried carafes of vodka to lone diners. A tower of white bread teetered on every linen cloth, and alongside the prices the menus displayed the weight in grammes of each portion – a relic of the Communist years. On successive days Tobias and I worked our way through the fare, devouring cabbage soup, pickled herring, liver stroganoff with puree, pork dumplings and doughy *pelmeni* packets stuffed with beef. After the purgatorial flash and blare of the Coffee Studio, the Anadyr was old-fashioned heaven. The teaspoons had holes punched in them. 'So they can't be stolen,' said Tobias. Was it stigma that made them unstealable, or their unsuitability for certain teaspoon-orientated tasks such as . . . but I couldn't think of a single one, except melting rocks of crack cocaine.

The 'disaster' Tobias had witnessed in the villages was not the result of Soviet collectivisation, but of the years following 1991. He returned to the subject again and again, using the phrase 'post-apocalypse' to mean 'after the collapse of the Soviet Union' – for example he spoke of the abandoned villages he had visited as 'post-apocalyptic ghost towns'. He told me he was interested in how people relate to their empty villages when they return. 'Why do they go back?' I asked. 'To hunt,' he said, 'and to escape the shattered utopia of Soviet modernisation.' In the words of Yuri Slevkine, author of the best book on what Russian academics call 'the small peoples of the north' (*malye narody Severa*), 'No matter how fast the circumpolar peoples adapted to their changing economic circumstances, for most of them it was not fast enough.' Like every regime that had preceded it, the new Russia that emerged after the collapse failed to embrace its indigenous peoples, particularly when Putin's 'vertical power' strategy removed the little autonomy enjoyed by the regions. This was particularly evident in Chukotka. The Russian nationalism that seeped into the space left vacant by Communism further alienated peoples not considered quite Russian enough. When powerful voices of the right express a longing for a traditional Russia, they do not mean reindeer and walrus.

After many years working with indigenous peoples in the Arctic, Tobias had an informed idea about the reality of their lives. But he was able to find redemption in the spirit he encountered among the hunters who had not succumbed to despair and booze. More than once, as we were talking over a diminishing tower of bread, he cited Hemingway to express what he discovered in Chukotkan villages: *The world breaks everyone and afterward many are strong at the broken places.* 'They have a certain resilience,' Tobias continued. 'They have carved out a place in a hostile world.'

The following morning I went to Abramovich's *Fitness Centre* (three-foot Cyrillic letters spelled out the English words over the entrance). It was as if a spaceship had landed. Abramovich and his people had foisted the aspirations of Chelsea footballers' wives onto the permafrost, and their gym dazzled the eye with its array of Swedish equipment. I set to, working my way from machine to machine as hip-hop rasped from the Finnish speakers and sunlight poured through the windows, lacquering the leather seats of the exercise bikes. Besides me, only one customer disturbed the columns of fine dust suspended in the sunshine. He was an impressive specimen, biceps and pectorals bulging as he cracked his gloved knuckles before swinging a few hundred kilograms over his head. He too looked as though he had landed from Outer Space. Had Abramovich imported him with the treadmills? Eventually he spoke to me, apparently asking if I minded a window being opened. 'I'm sorry,' I said. 'I don't speak Russian.' Wreathed suddenly in smiles, he advanced towards me, gloved hand extended in greeting. '*Americanka!*' he wrongly concluded. His well developed eyes widened in awe. 'My hero is very much Arnold Schwarzenegger. He is your friend?' I floundered as he pumped my hand, crushing a few unimportant bones.

Later, after borscht and dumplings at the Anadyr, Tobias showed me round the museum, another product of Abramovich munificence. The modern rooms were a showcase for what Chukotka had once been, and was now. The top floor consisted of a themed display of Chukchi life, traditional and modern: *yaranga* to GPS, bone togglehead harpoon to steel togglehead harpoon, seal oil lamp to locally-generated nuclear electricity. When we arrived at the top of the stairs, an elderly attendant put down her crossword book and shuffled heavily across the polished wood in her slippers to switch on the lights. 'Governor Abramovich's special project,' she said, gesturing towards an array of interactive displays. She watched us closely as Tobias translated the Russian panels below the models, and, when we turned back to the stairs, she rushed over, slippers whooshing. We had missed a display in the corridor, a glass case devoted to the Chukchi writer Yuri Rytkheu, the most famous figure to emerge from the region in the twentieth century, or ever. When his first book came out in English, Hemingway sent him a telegram which read, 'Way to go.'

Rytkheu was born in 1930 on the easternmost tip of Chukotka; his father was a hunter, his grandfather a shaman. One of the first of the post-war generation of Soviet-educated native intellectuals, like his contemporary, Kirgiz writer Chingiz Aitmatov, he spent much time away from his homeland and made it in Moscow as a party man, which of course was the only way you could make it. (Both Aitmatov and Rytkheu died in 2008, revered as cultural heroes.) In his lifetime Rytkheu sold hundreds of thousands of copies of his novels, magical dramas set among his own people. Critics perceive him as a Soviet stooge, and it is true that in his fiction he praises, for example, the relocation of Chukotka Eskimos and the blond-haired Russian heroes who made Chukchi dreams come true. In his 1981 autobiography, Rytkheu lathered Soviet housing with praise (much better than those crummy old *yarangi*). But like Aitmatov, he could be critical below the surface, especially after Krushchev's thaw. One had to read between the lines. Whatever the truth, Rytkheu points up the difficulties faced by intellectuals in regimes that wield an excess of power. When the choices were silence, compromise or death, it was braver to compromise than to keep silent, and dying wasn't going to help anyone, as even Hemingway acknowledged. Osip Mandelstam tried to steer a middle course, writing public odes to Stalin while reciting lampoons in private. He died in a transit camp in Vladivostok at the end of some bitter December.

Rytkheu and his indigenous contemporaries were caught up, whether they liked it or not (they didn't), in the Soviet notion of The Long Journey. This was the process by which the unenlightened Chukchi or Kirgiz herder 'attained consciousness', which meant catching up with everyone else and becoming a paid-up *Homo sovieticus*. Ideologists perceived the Soviet role as one that brought light to polar darkness, and Rytkheu enshrined the metaphorical progress towards truth in his fiction. To ensure the success of The Long Journey, folklore too had to be Sovietised. One anthropologist recorded a song the progress-obsessed regime had introduced among the reindeer herders of the Arctic north:

> *The northern lights are flashing cheerfully!*
> *My heart is filled with joy!*
> *When I get back, I'll start listening to the radio.*

Stalin's non-Russian peoples had no place in a technologically advanced brotherhood. They were an embarrassment. And it wasn't just their 'primitive' ways. Nationhood itself was a capitalist snare, according to Lenin, and the aim of socialism was to merge nations.

When it came to forming policy, Soviet social scientists squared circles with unfailing regularity until the next kink in the great socialist path revealed fresh puzzles. Committees grappled to create theories into which they could shoehorn the northern peoples, much as Karenin had done before them. Why should ethnology not alter to suit the changing demands of ideology, as the Soviet version of history did? But the fact was that indigenous cultures were among the many things Stalin determined to destroy, in the south as well as the Arctic. He liquidated the Buryat lamaseries along the Russian–Mongolian border with their medieval libraries and statuary, and murdered thousands of lamas. His henchmen burnt the tenth-century Alan churches in Karachai-Cherkessia. During the Great Patriotic War he deported two million Chechens, Karachai, Balkars, Ingush and others from their ancient homelands. Further north, shamans were obvious examples of the anti-scientific backwardness he had vowed to root out. Party stooges took shamans from many tribes up in planes and said, 'You say you can fly, here is your chance.' Then they pushed them out.

As for Rytkheu, he wrote in Russian. He had to, at least at first: Chukchi was not a written tongue. The many Arctic languages posed a problem for the Soviets in their commitment to *likbez* (the liquidation of illiteracy), but they were confident that it was one a committee could solve.* In 1930 members appointed to that committee, sitting in session in Moscow, decided to codify the northern languages in Roman script. Factories duly printed primers and distributed them throughout the land, though no teacher could use them, as Russians could not read Roman writing, and anyway the corrupt and interminable supply chain meant that primers in the wrong language frequently arrived above the Arctic Circle. Concepts were even harder than linguistics. The Chukchi primer bizarrely translated 'the First of May', the great Soviet holiday, as the English word 'Christmas'. In 1938 Cyrillic replaced the newly created northern writing system and the linguists who had devised the latter

---

* By the late 1920s, Union-wide, ethnologists had identified 192 languages.

were arrested on the grounds that the Roman script was 'a bourgeois alphabet'. So that solved that problem.

My benevolent landlord was bent on solving a linguistic problem of his own. Sasha had acquired a Soviet-era Russian–English primer, and took to lying in wait for me with specifically prepared phrases. 'How does it strike you here?' was one. We fought through many sessions, undaunted by the evidence that no matter how hard we tried, the primer refused to supply an answer to any of its own questions.

After a gruelling bout with the primer on Saturday morning, when Sasha did not have to go off to his job as a delivery driver, I set off on a hike across the tundra. Sunlight bounced off the mosses of the plain, lingering on the water pooled in swampy hollows. Only the faintest breath of wind moved the blades of sedge, and silence hung heavily, except for the *whee-hee* of Aleutian terns. The oceanic surface of the earth puckered with low growths of cottongrass, stands of alders, or a bilberry bush. When I turned away from its bitter grandeur, the castellations of Anadyr rose, self-contained as a medieval citadel. That day the smoke from the central heating plant went up straight, like a plumb line. Then my phone rang. It was Gena. He asked me where I was, and when I told him, he exploded. 'What are you doing? You are not allowed to leave the town. This is a border zone! You will be picked up by the police and I would be held responsible,' he thundered, 'because I am your official sponsor. You have let me down.' 'I'm sorry,' I whined, felled by this well-judged combo of hurt and aggression. He ordered me to return immediately ('I'll meet you outside the supermarket'), and, in case I hadn't got the message, lobbed a Parthian shot. 'Be careful where you tread. There are land mines.'

The following morning, in preparation for the one-day presidential visit, gangs of workers filed into the park outside my window soon after sunrise, picking up stray bits of rubbish and stuffing them into hemp sacks. The regional authorities were taking no chances: they had even repainted the zebra crossings. Medvedev arrived at ten, and Anadyr was tense all day, unfamiliar figures in dark glasses patrolling its streets and Federal choppers buzzing across the sky. By 6 p.m., several hundred Russians were swarming around the entrance of the Chukotka Hotel hoping for a final glimpse of the big man. People tugged at their collars and stamped their feet as the chill of a leafless polar autumn gusted in from the bay. I wedged myself alongside a group of women on the platform at the top of the supermarket steps, looking down at the crowd, and at the police line holding it back. A security van blocked both ends of the road. Despite the menace of the vans, and of the tall, stocky men who stood smoking by the hotel entrance, the night had a fairground ambience. A pair of schoolboys wrestled one another to the pavement, parents rocked prams, and mobile phones, held aloft, captured pictures of a Black Maria backed up tight to the double doors of the hotel.

At 8.20 p.m., three men in suits hurried out of the hotel lobby. A murmur rippled through the crowd. Two more men appeared, carrying silver metal cases. Then it was him. A thrill swelled among the people, they clapped, and whistled, and their cameras flashed. It was really him! We had assumed Medvedev would bundle straight into the back of the Black Maria, avoiding the crowd and the sniper's bullet. But he didn't. He strolled to the side of the vehicle, acknowledging the cheers by raising both arms and smiling. He was wearing a thigh-length leather jacket, and, like most famous people, he was short. Then he got into the van through the sliding side door, a small fleet of limousines appeared, and the cortège drew away. The flushed crowd dispersed in a thrum of chatter. I returned to my billet on Otke Street, keen to report a presidential sighting to Sasha and Marina, who were playing bingo in the kitchen with neighbours. They had been watching events unfold on television, and had even unearthed a large Federation flag with which they had draped the top of the fridge. The television station was replaying Medvedev's speech to the Security Council earlier in the week; the one in which he said, 'Our biggest task is to turn the Arctic into Russia's resource base for the twenty-first century.'* In a single generation the Arctic had shifted, in the minds of herders, pensioners and presidents, from backwater to repository of hope and wealth. To support its claims to the Arctic seabed, Russia had already funded two expeditions, to the Mendeleyev underwater mountain chain in 2005 and to the 1,200-mile Lomonosov Ridge in 2007. Promises had been made of scientific evidence demonstrating that Russian boundaries extended, on the continental shelf, well beyond the 322-kilometre (200-mile) economic zone granted to the Arctic nations under international law. So the northern frontier, no longer a fixed line, had become as fluid as its southern counterpart. And Russians, like their neighbours, were pouring in resources. A few days after Medvedev's visit, on the plane leaving Anadyr, I sat next to a young man who had just finished an expedition. I recognised the unkempt hair, wind-scoured face and unshaven chin. An engineer for the Federal government, he revealed, over packets of stale sunflower seeds and tins of out-of-date orange juice, that he designed submarine robots which could explore the seabed. That summer he had been working with a team of twenty scientists on the ice-strengthened *Akademik M. A. Lavrentyev* in the Bering Strait.

Gena was leaving on the same day as me, flying down to Khabarovsk to join his wife and son. Tobias had evidently hosed him down, and there was no further mention of my poor behaviour. He even gave me a parting gift. It was a walrus baculum (penis bone), two feet long with a face carved on the tip. The walrus has the largest baculum, absolute and relative, of any mammal. After this pleasant episode Gena and I went to the airport together, planning to cross the bay in a Second World War barge, one of a fleet operating as shuttles on flight days (where the barges

---

* This was a case of déjà vu several times over. In 1986 Gorbachev emphasised the crucial economic role of the region in a speech delivered in Murmansk in which he promised to open up the Soviet Arctic. Fifty years before him, an older generation of Soviet apologists called the Russian Arctic, 'Tomorrow's America'.

had been when I arrived, there was no clue). Taxis had converged to wait on the bank, drivers and passengers smoking furiously in the weak late afternoon sun. Beluga were fluking in the bay again. In the shallows, ivory shards of porcelain ice washed in and out with the ragged edges of the waves from the barges. As the horn of our own barge lowed, I looked back for the last time at the central heating plant puffing out its dark grey steeples, Abramovich's five-storey paintings of reindeer glowing in the last of the sun like postage stamps, and dogs scavenging on the docks. All around the town, the sky reached down to the tundra. All quiet on the Eastern Front. Like a lot of far-flung and neglected places, Anadyr had grown on me. It had its own charm. But God, it seemed far, and remote, and nothing to do with anywhere else. Not only is Chukotka not Siberian – it's not really part of the Russian Far East either. Petr Omrynto had said as much. 'Separate and on our own!' he had cried out more than once as his root vegetable hands excavated sunflower seeds in the Hunting Association office. If Russia's lawless edge lingered anywhere, it was in Arctic Chukotka. No wonder the inhabitants referred to the rest of Russia as 'the mainland'.

It was the period in which airlines were going bankrupt all over the world – in July oil had reached a new record of $147 a barrel – and financial disaster had engulfed the developed world. Only two airlines flew to Anadyr from Moscow: Domododevo and Transaero (even Aeroflot didn't bother). Domododevo had that week ceased operations, though the government was negotiating a bailout, and when I got to the airport, the incoming Domododevo flight from Moscow was listed on the board as 'awaited', even though it had been due for three days. Whey-faced passengers were sleeping on the bucket seats in Abramovich's new terminal. Gena's airline had in fact also collapsed, but the government had stepped in, this time more decisively, as the airline sold the only route south from Chukotka to the Russian Far East. We sat in the coffee bar and waited. People around us were engaged in obsessive wrapping of luggage in tape and blue cling film as an anti-theft measure. 'Are cases often robbed here then?' I asked Gena, nervously eyeing my own bag. 'No, never,' he said.

III

500 Alaskan Whores

The American Arctic

America's really only a kind of Russia.

Anthony Burgess,
Honey for the Bears

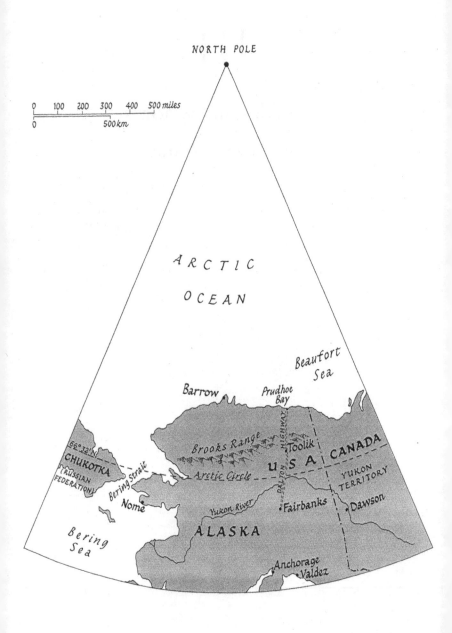

Thirteen thousand years ago – possibly earlier – the first Americans pursued herds of mammoth and bison eastwards over the Bering Strait land bridge. Some kept going east to the edge of the ice sheet, others dropped south. Many stayed in what became Alaska. They paddled their seal-skin *umiaks* to the fairs of Kotzebue Sound to trade with ancient rivals, thousands of slender craft looping the floes towards camping grounds infused with the stench of reindeer and blubber.

Metaphorically as well as physically outside the rest of the USA, the 49th state still beckons the free spirit, the dreamer, the pioneer. Yet there is much of America in Arctic Alaska and its history. Just as Chukotka cannot conceal its Russian context, Alaska reveals the unbridled force of the entrepreneurial spirit and the open conflicts of a democratic country. Here are the environmentalists and the oil executives; the dispossessed, the vulnerable and the truth-seekers; indigenous hunters and refugees from the Lower 48. Chukotka has no roads because successive governments couldn't afford any. Alaska has one of the greatest roads on the planet – the fabled Dalton Highway, the only land route to the Arctic Ocean, the all-time über-road that met every engineering challenge in the sacred service of oil. Could this 414-mile technological triumph hold the key to the American Arctic experience? I went to Alaska to take a road trip on the Dalton Highway – and to follow the Trans-Alaska pipeline that sashays alongside.

Before the pipelines, Alaska had another road to riches. The story of non-renewables in the Arctic is not over, but no matter how long it continues, the Klondike will always set the standard for thrills. The Klondike goldfields were in Canada, but the shortest routes to them went via Alaska. The rush began in the 1860s, when a Hudson's Bay Company clerk at Fort Yukon, on the great bend of the Yukon River where it touches the Arctic Circle, reported that a missionary had seen so much gold in a local river 'that he could have gathered it with a spoon' (one wonders why he didn't). Prospectors began arriving in the upper Yukon valley in the early 1870s, finding mainly placer gold until, in 1896, an American sieved up a nugget on Rabbit Creek, a tributary of the Klondike hastily renamed Bonanza Creek and staked out from end to end. In July 1897, a prospector disembarked from his steamer at Seattle with 90 kilograms of gold in his suitcase. It was Klondike now, or bust. Over the next twelve months, in excess of 100,000 men and women stampeded to the goldfields, many crossing into Canada over the treacherous Chilkoot Pass from Skagway – the symbolic precursor of the Dalton Highway. In the last half of 1897 alone three thousand horses started up the single-file White Pass adjacent to the Chilkoot. Barely one survived. When a horse fell on the trail, men coming behind trampled over it, so that by the end of the day nothing remained but a head on one side and a tail on the other. Even when they were over the mountains, prospectors had to build boats to float down the Yukon rapids and on 800 miles to Dawson City, the gold town hard by the border; either that or mush in over the ice. Besides spreading TB through the indigenous communities, killing hundreds, many newcomers left the hostile Klondike half-dead, or indeed dead. Meanwhile, Dawson City flourished. The currency in the saloons was gold dust, weighed in scales on the bar at $16 an ounce. Prostitutes had their own scales, though the best among them charmed prospectors out of their entire poke. Girls singing on the stage of the Savoy or the Monte Carlo were pelted with nuggets (in a friendly way, and they got to keep the nuggets if they weren't brained). Meanwhile shortages in the overcrowded town meant that salt was the same price as gold. Typhoid broke out in 1898, and undertakers worked round the clock to embalm bodies in preparation for shipment to loved ones in the Lower 48. In an attempt to avoid starvation, Canadian authorities imposed a one-ton supply minimum on each prospector. It took forty climbs to haul the ton up the one-in-three gradient of the Chilkoot Pass, even after entrepreneurs had set up chains of buckets. Those that survived kept coming back. It was the finding that counted, as Robert Service, the poet of the Yukon diggings, well knew:

> *There's gold, and it's haunting and haunting;*
> *It's luring me on as of old;*
> *But it isn't the gold that I'm wanting*
> *So much as just finding the gold.*

Claims were bought, sold, bought back and restaked. When, in 1898, a greenhorn found placer gold at Cape Nome on the south coast of the Seward Peninsula in west Alaska, thousands raced out of Dawson and tore across to found the settlement of Nome. By the summer of 1900, 12,500 men and women were camped on the beach. Three years later they stampeded again, out of Nome to Fairbanks. That was the last of the big rushes.

At about that time, Hudson Stuck, archdeacon of the Yukon, travelled 14,000 miles across Arctic Alaska by dog sled. 'What is the Alaskan legacy,' he wondered of the lust for gold that had brought southerners to the northlands, 'of all those thousands of men and hundreds of thousands of dollars they brought? Those creeks, stripped, gutted, and deserted; this town, waiting for a kindly fire with a favouring breeze to wipe out its useless emptiness; a few half-breed children at mission schools; a hardy native tribe, sophisticated, diseased, demoralised, and largely dead – that seems the net result.' He well knew, he said, the 'low-down white' of Service's ballad, and he endorsed the asperity of the poet's judgement. 'It is unquestionable', Stuck wrote, 'that the best natives in the country are those that have had the least intimacy with the white man.'

Stuck's aim was to bring succour of the Episcopal variety to the far-flung Inupiat, an Inuit people who shared a similar ethnic heritage with the Chukchi; but he also loved the Arctic. He respected both 'Eskimo and Indian', knowing each well, and expressed contempt for government workers who taught Inupiat to call themselves Mr and Mrs (he made the acquaintance of a Mrs Shortanddirty), nonetheless relishing the spectacle of 'a native woman in a Merry Widow hat and a blood-stained parka gutting salmon on the river bank'. Imitation of the white man, he warned without irony, was a perilous strategy. On a fork of the Chandalar River he conducted funerals of babies who had died of diphtheria. (The valley of the Upper Kuskokwim had almost been depopulated by the disease.) In 1912, people there prayed daily to Our Sovereign Lady Queen Victoria and Albert Edward Prince of Wales, both long in the ground, like the babies. Stuck knew all the ice – crumble ice, shell ice, rotting ice, thin sheets of overflow ice (the latter the most treacherous on a river, and the most frequent cause of tenderfeet losing their feet, and sometimes the lives went along with the feet). At seventy below it was impossible to break trail, and at those times, when Stuck was stuck, he and his native boy had to snuggle in the tent and wait it out. When occasionally he came across a group of Inupiat who had not been saved he ripped through the Incarnation, Crucifixion, Resurrection, Ascension and what he called the cardinal rules of morality. So much for not imitating the white man. It was a Five-Year Plan by any other name; but Stuck was saving souls.

Out for twenty hours at a stretch ('my moose-hide breeches froze solid'), carrying a translation of the Bible and the Book of Common Prayer, Stuck wore caribou socks, and claimed one day that his Adam's apple froze. He went from creek to creek, giving divine mass to native and prospector alike in a roadhouse or a store or a tent with a cloudy seal-gut window, the flock with frosted parka hoods and white breath, snowshoes under their arms. The service was adjourned when a dogfight broke out, cold air shooting in like a steam jet while someone went outside to separate the offenders. When two different local groups were present, two interpreters were required, with the result that a

twenty-minute sermon went on for an hour. Stuck's book records the soft-tissue of Arctic history: the perishable bits. He writes of buying fish with packets of gold dust, and of burying lone prospectors who had frozen to death. Nothing dented his enthusiasm. He wrote of 'the bounding of the spirit' induced by an Arctic sunset, concluding that 'surely for its pageantry of burning, living colour, for purity and depth and intensity of tint, the Far North with its setting of snow surpasses all other regions of the earth'.

Besides diphtheria, Stuck identified TB and whiskey as the chief dangers threatening the well-being of Arctic Alaskans (some would also add Bible-bashing Christianity), and of these two, whiskey was the worst. In the archdeacon's view, all laws controlling it amounted to 'a dead letter' in so large a country. Alcohol abuse was as old a story as contact itself in Russia and America alike: it was among the experiences shared on both sides of the Bering Strait. A traveller in the 1880s already talks of the 'whiskey howl' of the Indians, and of a tribe 'whiskied nearly out of existence'. But Inupiat, masters of land-fast ice, had lived unmolested for centuries throughout the Alaskan Arctic before the arrival of missionaries and traders. A yearning for the white man's goods only set in when Inupiat began to convert the spoils of the hunt into dollars during the 1870s. Whalebone corsets and buttons brought the cash in first, followed by fox furs. When nobody wanted either whale or fox, Inupiat were obliged to take salaried employment, as they could not now return to their old ways: they were dependent on the store and its booty, as were their Siberian kin. The story resonates round the Arctic. Less than a century after the first fur was exchanged for a glistening silver dollar, the main Inupiat settlement, at Barrow, famously the most northerly town in the Americas, functioned purely as a cash economy, and people hunted only on their day off.

Before heading up the Dalton Highway and following the oil pipeline to the Arctic Ocean, I heard a lot about 'the freedoms' of Alaska. There is a great deal of it in which to be free. By far the largest state in the union, at 572,000 mi^2 Alaska is a fifth the size of the entire Lower 48 and six times the size of Great Britain. It has 100,000 glaciers and, with only a twentieth of 1 per cent of the land developed, 1.06 people per square mile. State licence plates bear the slogan, 'The Last Frontier'. Arctic Alaska lies at an even further remove – isolated wilderness by the standards of a region that considers itself reasonably isolated and wild as it is. Covering a third of the state, with a tiny fraction of the population, Arctic Alaska is the last frontier of the last frontier. Yet the white man has repudiated the romance, first making the Arctic a Cold War battleground. Between 1955 and 1957 the US and Canada set up a chain of fifty-eight Distant Early Warning radar stations – the DEW line – along the 69th parallel, linking Alaska with Canada, Greenland and other Arctic islands. Then, when the notion of two superpowers and their titanic struggle had expired with the twentieth century, a fresh set of white men turned the Arctic into an energy frontier. In a rapine quest for natural resources, the outsider came to Alaska to take oil, just as he had done in Siberia. Hudson Stuck had identified TB and hard liquor as precursors of destruction. Oil was next on the list. Like a talisman for the circumpolar Arctic in its pitiful entirety, the Alaskan paradise yielded up the serpent.

Inupiat hunters have known where oil seeps for generations. By 1919, men from Outside knew where it might flow faster still: the US government had just published a report revealing an unusual 220-million-year-old sandstone and gravel formation under Prudhoe Bay. Subsequent earth heaves had locked in deep porous rocks capable of capturing migrating oil. But the Arctic was hostile territory, the season was short, and nobody knew how to extract the oil. The US navy, however, had already converted its warships from coal to oil, and just in case supplies ran short, in 1923 President Harding designated 37,000 mi² (95,000 km²) of the North Slope Naval Petroleum Reserve Number 4. Investors included Laurel and Hardy and a constellation of other stars who, in 1936, poured movie dollars into a Hollywood oil consortium. Geological teams and wildcatters began arriving in Fairbanks before heading north with armies of seismic crews, between them drilling over 150 wells between 1901 and 1951 without a single discovery of commercial viability. With Eisenhower in the White House, the Federal government released previously closed lands cheaply for private oil exploitation, spurred by Iran's decision to nationalise its petroleum business. In 1957 the *Anchorage Times* announced the first proper strike in 3-inch headlines. It happened on the Swanson River in southern Alaska. Two years later, statehood became a reality, Alaska beating Hawaii to full membership of the union by eight months. Half a century later, state legislators are still feuding about oil.

The next fortune was surely to be made on the North Slope and, with the relaxation of Federal controls in the sixties, explorations shifted to the top tier of Alaska. BP was among the first to buy leases. Significant Arctic oil began to gush in 1968 when Atlantic Richfield struck below Prudhoe Bay. The residents of Fairbanks literally danced in the streets. BP struck a year later, and other companies followed. As strikes proliferated, Wall Street too caught oil fever. But the companies still had to transport the crude to market. Tankers could only get in to Prudhoe Bay for two months each year. In mid-1969 the three major players – Atlantic Richfield, Humble Oil (now part of Exxon) and BP – announced there was to be a pipeline whatever the engineering challenges. Environmental groups put up a fight, but they faced a losing battle after OPEC countries restricted production in 1973. Nixon signed the Trans-Alaska Pipeline into law the following year.

The 800-mile pipe was to decant at the northernmost harbour that doesn't freeze in the big white of an Alaskan winter, and that was Valdez on Prince William Sound. Halfway down the pipeline corridor, Fairbanks boomed again. The oil companies set up a consortium to design, construct and maintain the pipe, but before leaping the technical hurdles, it had to clear the political ones. Any pipeline had to cross land occupied, but not owned, by indigenous peoples, and the spirit of the times meant that public bodies and private companies alike were unwilling to trample literally over their rights (as both groups had done for two centuries). Native organisations sprang forth to the rallying cry of Federal tyranny, and it quickly became clear that there would be no pipeline without appeasement. So it was that in 1971 the Alaska Native Claims Settlement Act passed into law. In exchange for surrendering their ancestral lands, the settlement gave approximately 75,000 Inupiat and other groups $962 million in cash, and 44 million acres (about a tenth of the state's land, but in return for surrendering any claim to the other 90 per cent). Religion and diphtheria in 1900, money and land in 1971. Life was looking up for Alaskan Inuit. Reservations were out of vogue and there were to be none in Alaska.

Instead, twelve new regional corporations managed the wealth, investing half the money and disbursing the other half. The Act was designed to bring indigenous peoples into a business economy like all good Americans. ('Into the mainstream of American life', legislators called it. Passing the buck might be a more appropriate expression for what they did.) It was also designed to clear the way for large-scale non-native mineral extraction. Which it did.

Much has been written about the way in which the 1971 Settlement Act transformed native Alaskans into capitalists. The terms of a much earlier act allowed each individual to claim 160 acres. But there were few takers, as private ownership was not a familiar concept. But when the new Act craftily set a claims deadline, many felt they had better get in while they could, and they did register claims, despite the fact that this was in violation of their customary principles. Bad feeling inevitably followed. 'The sense of private property that has been jacketed upon them [native Alaskans] is uncomfortable, and incompatible with subsistence harvesting and its changeful cycles,' wrote one commentator. 'Eskimos should make laws for those people outside,' an Inupiat told an anthropologist. It was not all bad: in 1972 the North Slope Borough, an Inupiat initiative headquartered in Barrow, became the first native government set up by an Arctic people. It taxed the Prudhoe Bay oilfields, and Barrow itself became the richest settlement in the USA. Americans had hit on a capitalist solution. But it destroyed a culture as effectively as collectivisation.

As for the money: piranhas swam into view, offering advice, stock, trucks, lunch. Anthropologists called what they saw 'rapid acculturation'. Unwise investments proliferated, as did whiskey. Scenting a story, the *New Yorker* despatched John McPhee to Arctic Alaska and the upper Yukon in 1976. The fine book that came out of the assignment, the bestselling *Coming into the Country*, returns obsessively to the Native Claims Settlement Act. A strong objector to the net effects of the Act, McPhee noted that all the Hungwitchin people had to do to get their share of the money was 'turn white'. He camped and travelled among the Kobuk River peoples, and among both white settlers and Hungwitchin of the Eagle region. A future Pulitzer winner, McPhee conveys the tension between preservation and development, especially acute in the seventies, and besides revealing deep sympathy for the indigenous peoples of Alaska, he also lovingly records a series of unsentimental portraits of white settlers who had stuck it out.

On 20 June 1977, oil flowed. Would it turn out to be the most significant day in Arctic history? Soon 1.2 million barrels a day were speeding to Valdez to meet 25 per cent of US oil needs, and as the state received about 12 per cent in taxes on every barrel, dollars erupted over Alaska like lava from a volcano. The legislature in Juneau established a Permanent Savings Fund. That was a good thing. Corruption, fraud, racketeering, Teamsters Union scandals, organised crime, aborted impeachment proceedings, carpetbagging and lucrative oil industry contributions to political campaigns – they were bad things. To a certain extent the pipeline became a paradigm of 1980s greed, just as Russian oil became a paradigm of oligarchical enrichment a decade later. The industry got the tax and accounting breaks it wanted – it had the right people in the legislature to defend its interests – and effectively emasculated state mechanisms to protect people and the environment. Then came 24 March 1989. The 987-foot supertanker *Exxon Valdez* ran aground on Bligh Reef with 1,263,000 barrels of crude on board. The captain, almost certainly drunk, had been trying to avoid icebergs that had calved off the Columbia Glacier. Almost eleven million gallons of crude ran into Prince William Sound. Remember the television pictures of oil-stricken sea otters and tar-strangulated gulls? But the Exxon PR machine was ready. The Russian solution to accidents was to nuke the evidence. The American way was to spin the message. But the net result was the same: environmental disaster. Exxon beamed images round the world of flotillas of omnisweepers and maxi-barges sucking up spilled oil, and of 15,000 workers scrubbing rocks. (After the first few days PR gurus decided the scrubbers weren't cleaning, they were *treating*.) One could imagine oilmen Laurel and Hardy joining in, Hardy scrubbing industriously and Laurel subverting his efforts. Exxon released footage of 250 sea otters being flown to rehabilitation centres where they dined on crab; to the joy of the world, all 250 survived. It cost Exxon $90,000 per animal. The rest of the otters died. If the PR men were smirking, the joke was on us. At least 67 per cent of the spilled oil was never recovered. Private contractors working on the clean-up became known as spillionaires.* Still, to this day many Alaskans back the oil companies when they make claims for more development, among them representatives of the Inupiat-owned Arctic Slope Regional Corporation. The dawning awareness that the fanatical combustion of fossil fuels might have a deleterious effect on the network of earth systems is little in evidence in Alaska.†

Beginning 70 miles above Fairbanks, the 414-mile Dalton Highway crosses both the Yukon River and the Arctic Circle, finally running out of ground on a coast nearer Chukotka than anywhere else. The only land route to the Arctic Ocean, and built exclusively to service oil transportation, the Dalton ravages one of the last true wildernesses on the planet, an Arctic Serengeti teeming with wildlife. The truckers, who think of it tenderly as their own, call it the Haul Road.

The Dalton begins just outside Fairbanks, Alaska's second city. The Arctic Science Division of the University of Alaska Fairbanks had extended an invitation to its research facility at 68°N, and even offered a seat in a truck on a delivery run from Fairbanks. As the vagaries of weather called for a flexible departure date, I got to Fairbanks and waited for a telephone message. With a population nudging 31,000, the place is flat and boring, featuring a proliferation of strip malls and

---

* Repercussions of the spill affected salmon fisheries around Prince William Sound and Cook Inlet for many years. Yet in June 2008 the US Supreme Court slashed the damages awarded against Exxon. Commercial fishermen continue to find oil on the shoreline of Prince William Sound.

† On average it takes 25 calories of fossil fuel energy to produce one calorie of protein.

clapboard houses and a generalised tang of neglect. Urbanisation, you
get the feeling, is skin deep: a moose, six feet to the collarbone, was
rooting on the side of the freeway at the end of the slip road to the
Northern Nugget, the motel where I was beached until I could ride
the Haul Road. On one really bright day I could see the outline of
Denali on the skyline, the tallest peak in the Americas, but mostly a
dank and oystery cloud front sat on the horizon until the reprieve of
darkness. Alaska was still a lonely place. On my way to the shop at
the end of the slip road, I found myself nodding a greeting to the
moose. His was the only familiar face in Fairbanks. Quietly desperate
for company, I spent one afternoon on the steps of the Northern
Nugget with a group of sourdoughs just in from the back country.
They were sucking on a quart of Jack Daniels which they passed round
between them, a farting terrier at their feet. A 'sourdough' signifies a
true Alaskan, after the frontiersmen who took sourdough starter on
the trail.* It was the most ancient method of bread making: keep a
piece of raw dough back before baking a loaf, and use it to start the
next loaf. And so on, for years. This lot had been panning without
success around the creeks of the Koyukuk River, a major tributary of
the Yukon in the region of the Arctic Divide. It was a horrible day,
the grey sky gelatinous as frogspawn. An undercurrent of truculence
occasionally broke the surface within the group, like a whale's fin.
Costive conversation listed, for my benefit, towards the definition of
the contemporary sourdough. Bread was no longer involved. According
to a ham-faced lummox in a plaid jacket, 'Y'ave to have piddled in the
Yukon River.' This met with general agreement, and the Jack Daniels
went round again. 'You,' chipped in a man with a hat resembling a

* The practice of carrying a lump of dough from home to start the first camp loaf
took off during the California gold rush (and Sourdough Sam remains the mascot of
the San Francisco 49ers), and prospectors followed suit when they headed for the
Klondike. Sourdough was more reliable than yeast, which tended not to survive the
journey – though it had to be kept warm, and the prospectors took it to bed with them.

doughnut, pointing at me, 'you're a *Cheechako*.' Fortunately I knew this word as Alaskan vernacular for a tenderfoot or greenhorn – someone from Outside who was new to Alaska. So I wasn't tempted to punch doughnut-head. *Cheechako* originated from Chinook jargon, a pidgin trade language of the Pacific Northwest. (I later learned that the word is often used to signify homosexual, but that wasn't what the man meant.) Someone else droned on about the quantities of gold he had panned on a previous visit; all hat and no cattle, as they say in Texas. 'Why dint'you take us back to the same creek?' asked another, reasonably enough. The oracle was Delphic on this point. The man in the plaid jacket dropped the bottle (ham-fisted too). It smashed on the bottom step. Nobody said anything, because they had already drained the whiskey. The failed prospectors were departing for Anchorage, 358 miles to the south, early the next morning, leaving the moose and me to battle it out. Doughnut-head stood up, swaying gently. His face was smooth, without any of those small wrinkles produced by thought. 'Want to come to my room?' he asked me with a winsome squint.

Two days later, I left. I was riding the Haul Road. It was the only route through Arctic Alaska, and therefore the only land passage to the splendours of the North Slope. It was also the ultimate cipher for what Americans had achieved in the Arctic. I was in the passenger seat, and next to me, behind the wheel of a truck marked with the logo of the University of Alaska Fairbanks, sat Jeannie. She was an Idaho-born outdoorswoman, once an oil worker on the rigs, now an employee of the university maintenance crew. Travelling in a pickup of a size never seen in Europe, Jeannie was heading all the way to Deadhorse, where she would collect a consignment of hauling equipment, then travel back down the Dalton Highway to my destination, the university science camp at Toolik Lake. Toolik was a long way from anywhere and Jeannie, whom the university had posted at the camp for the summer, worked two weeks on, two weeks off. Meaty as a wrestler, with cropped hair the colour of hay, she was an old hand on the Haul Road, and a steadying presence when eighteen-wheelers hurtled past, catapulting rocks at our windscreen.

We had pulled out of Fairbanks in the morning, jouncing through boreal birch forest, already gilt-edged, stands of aspen, evergreen spruce, and alder. And hundreds and thousands of willow bushes. The shallow valley floors were golden with cottonwood and flecked white with tassels of sedge, and on the low ridges, against a background of glowing green, the rich cream of reindeer moss reflected the rays of the sun. We stopped at a prospector's cabin on the Chatanika River, its angular, chipped logs knocked up with axe and augur by some amateur panner moiling for gold. The capital that followed the old-timers brought derricks and suction dredges that ingested and spat out the earth, heaping the land with pyramids of tailings. Two 55-gallon steel fuel drums lay on their sides under the cabin's single window. 'Alaskan state flower,' said Jeannie. Initially nervy and reticent, she had thawed as the population dropped away, and besides chattering about the wonders of the Alaskan wilderness, she sometimes turned towards me just to flash a wide smile. I was pleased to be heading into the Arctic Divide with such an amenable companion.

The Sitka spruce, elsewhere so mighty, shrank as the latitude – monitored on the GPS on the dash – crept towards 66. A keen and proficient cabin-builder, Jeannie always looked out for short or leaning trees if she was considering buying a piece of land. 'Lean's a sign of permafrost,' she said authoritatively, 'and you can't build on that type of land. Take a shovel to it, feels like you've hit concrete. If you drill through, whatever you build will droop as the frost softens.' Permafrost underlies a quarter of the earth's surface.* Prudhoe Bay oil workers once drilled a shaft through 2,000 feet of it, and in Siberia, in Yakutia near the Upper Markha, salt miners have tunnelled through four-fifths of a mile of permafrost. Most of it is very old. In Alaska and the

---

* By definition, any material that has remained frozen for two or more summers constitutes permafrost.

Yukon, it might be in excess of two million years. (Unlike most of the Canadian High Arctic, during the last glaciation Alaska had no ice sheet lid to keep out cold air.) Who knows what is locked in those cubic miles of earth? When a cliff collapses in Siberia, a woolly mammoth regularly emerges, a beast not seen alive for ten thousand years.

'Howdy buddy,' a male voice crackled over the CB radio, waking me from a pleasant reverie. 'I'm right behind you, and I'm not gonna be able to stop as I slide down the hill over the ridge ahead.' I looked up from the passenger seat to see the rear-view mirror filled to its frame with a monster fender powering towards us in a cloud of coffee-coloured dust. 'I'd be grateful', continued the voice, 'if you could pull over to let me pass.' That would be a yes, then. The Dalton Highway was a macho stereotype: the biggest got priority, just for being big. If you disagreed, you got flattened.

The road was built with private money in the 1970s to carry goods to the oil rigs at Prudhoe Bay and the adjacent service town of Deadhorse. In winter, members of the Alaska transport department flood the entire highway with water mixed with gravel to create a smooth, hard surface with good traction; when water freezes in the culverts that run under the road, they squirt steam down special chimneys sticking up at one end. In summer, they pack the surface with calcium. But it's tough, lonely going, whatever the season. CB radio, according to Jeannie, is 'a matter of life or death', as are at least two spare tyres, and the permanent illumination of headlights.

A glint of the Yukon flashed through the birch trunks and my spirits soared. A vital link in the history of the American far north, the 2,000-mile Yukon still lives up to its legend, at least at the Dalton crossing. An Everest of a river, it surges through a 3,000-foot-wide gorge in an opaque riverine highway of its own. Once it was the focus of life in the Alaskan interior, and gave access to the Shangri-La of the Klondike. But to indigenous peoples, it signified much more: a lifeline to fresh hunting grounds when the weather changed or the caribou altered their route. In the 1970s the plan to ford the Yukon presented civil engineers with one of their most taxing challenges. To start with, air temperature ranging between 32° above Celsius and 50° below required a differential of two feet to allow a bridge to contract and expand. The steel box-girder construction that now links both sides of the Dalton Highway has the pipeline strapped to its side. As you approach, you can see the slope. Since 9/11, the combined presence of bridge, pipeline and riparian Pump Station Number Six have necessitated a heavy security programme – imagine the value, to a terrorist, of cutting off both the oil supply and vehicular access to Prudhoe Bay. Security personnel keep a twenty-four-hour vigil close by the north shore stanchion; when we passed, a guard from the day shift was eating a sub sandwich in his van. So far, spillages have been either the result of drunken pranks, or accidental. An Athabascan teenager had recently shot at the pipe with a high-powered weapon, continuing to fire until he made a hole. He went to prison, and 200,000 gallons of crude went into the tundra.

We had set out from Fairbanks in warmish autumn conditions, but around the Yukon the temperature dropped, an Arctic zing supplanting currents of mild heat. Something in me unclenched. Heading at last north of the Yukon, the pipeline, saviour of Alaska, led the way in a majestic zigzag. We stopped to wait for a young grizzly to get up from the middle of the road. He was licking his front paws. The Dalton cuts through good hunting land, but if you want to use firearms rather than a bow, the law dictates that you walk off the highway for at least five miles and hunt the backcountry. Then you have to walk out again, shouldering your caribou . . . it was a joke at the white man's expense in Chukotka, but a reality in Arctic Alaska.

The pipe had been part of Jeannie's life for a long time. 'Greatest engineering feat of the twentieth century,' she said, 'and the largest private construction job in history.' Superlatives all round. 'See the zigzag?' She pointed at the silver Zs on the hillside ahead. 'Protects against earthquake damage. Had a 7.9 Richter scale quake here in '02, and neither the pipe nor the big Yukon Bridge so much as bent an inch. I was here! And see that pump station? One of a dozen built on refrigerated foundations. Each has a Rolls Royce jet engine inside.' I felt obliged to take an interest in the complexities of pipage. What, I enquired, was the function of the foot-long white bars sticking up from the sides of the pipe? 'Conduct away heat created by the friction from waxy crude,' Jeannie explained. 'Operators can alter the flow via a series of 151 valves remotely controlled in Valdez. The big fear with turning valves off, though, is oil stopping, as it congeals then. Big disaster!' I could see the Yukon Flats in the distance, hedged to the east by dim grey hills.

Construction began in November 1973, with 21,000 workers camped on the job. As a concession to environmentalists, engineers had incorporated more than 500 animal stations into the route. The solution to permafrost was to elevate the pipe on stilts for 420 out of the total 800 miles. The stilts were fine – noble even – but the hillsides covering the buried portions resembled artificially cut ski slopes, revegetated in lurid green. The pipe itself had a certain sleek, technical beauty. Overall, it wasn't ugly. It was unobtrusive.

'Two miles to the Arctic Circle!' announced Jeannie, quietly triumphant at having made it to 66 degrees of latitude without even a flat tyre. I too felt more than a pang of excitement: the invisible frontier ahead was the gateway to a mysteriously silent America. Ice now skimmed the hillsides, and beaver lodges damned the creeks. At the Circle itself, marked with a sign, we stopped to eat the Alaskan picnic Jeannie had taken some trouble to prepare for my benefit: sockeye salmon jerky smoked in her back yard (she called it 'squaw candy'), home-baked bread, wild cranberry muffins and a flask of dark coffee. Jeannie could kill, skin, gut and quarter a caribou without assistance, and often did. Solitude and the backcountry had proved more reliable than human company, and she played a man's game on the Haul Road. She had even made herself look like a man. But she didn't really care about beating the other guy. She didn't long to drive a bigger truck. It was just a way of surviving. As we finished the meal, a formless silver unity of drifting fog moved across the mountains ahead of us, and for a few minutes we let a creek do the talking. Then, evidently moved by some mysterious working of memory, some deep-sea fish stirring in the murky depths of her unconscious, Jeannie began telling the story of the death of her Labrador Susie.

'Eleven years we went everywhere together, before she had a stroke. She was lying on the bed next to me and she lost control of her bladder. She was embarrassed. A month later she died in my arms wrapped in a bedspread on the edge of the vet's parking lot. I kept her body in the freezer for four years. When the power died in an electrical storm and the freezer went off, she got doused in salmon juice, and I had to bury Susie then.' She stood briskly to clear the debris of the picnic, bowing her head to concentrate on the empty Ziploc bags. Was it the polar emptiness that had prompted her to unfold her emotional landscape and lay it on her gingham picnic cloth? While I fussed around pretending to help, a man's tread brought the Arctic Circle back, and a thin, raggedy figure in his twenties appeared wearing oily Carhartt dungarees and a baseball cap stitched with the logo of a flying saucer.

'Wonder if you ladies could help me?' the figure asked in softly modulated tones. 'I'm set to do a little gold-dredging up north, and my vehicle's broken-down half a mile up the road. Would you ladies be kind enough to take me on to Coldfoot, where I can telephone my nephew in Fairbanks and have him come up with a spare part?' It was against university regulations to take hitchhikers, and I could see that Jeannie was uneasy. Years of employment on the lower rungs of the oil industry ladder had taught her the importance of obeying rules. The wilderness was all well and good, but a pay cheque was better.

'We'll talk to you when we're done,' she told the supplicant, who nodded and stole away. I was deeply anxious. It would be tantamount to murder to leave a man on his own without supplies in temperatures that at night fell well below freezing. The rules had not been made for the Arctic.

'He might write the university a thank-you letter,' Jeannie said as we stuffed the remnants of the picnic into a pack. This seemed unlikely.

'Couldn't you', I ventured, though it seemed as if I were stating the bleeding obvious, 'ask him never to mention the ride to anyone?' I could see she knew she had to take him, but she didn't like it.

The fellow, 'Alaskan native and native Alaskan', had staked a claim. He had learned the trade, he informed us from the back seat, during a stint working as a driller for a large commercial company. After an industrial lifting accident in which he had injured his back, he had been officially designated Disabled, and was presently operating as an independent prospector, camping out at the diggings like an old-timer. He had already found small quantities of gold, which he had sold to the Fairbanks refinery. 'Just gone up to $700 dollars an ounce,' he said confidently, 'and there's much more out there. There's gonna be gold in every creek in this state with gravel in it.' He claimed to have equipment worth in excess of $50,000, but I rather doubted it. His car, which we passed, wouldn't have fetched twenty (dollars, not thousands). His manners remained impeccable, even when Jeannie was less than forthcoming. You got the impression that he was inured to unfriendliness, pressing on regardless.

'What are you ladies up to so far north?' he asked politely.

'Oh, just out taking some photographs,' said Jeannie breezily. This seemed about as plausible as the flying saucer buzzing away from the man's cap and out of the truck window into space. I shrank into my seat, saying nothing.

'Look at that,' I said, as we hurtled forward into the Arctic.

'What?' said Jeannie at the wheel.

'There was a sign,' I said, 'to a place called Gobbler's Knob.'

'So what?' she said. Fortunately the conversation was brought to a premature close by flooding over a portion of road, requiring Jeannie to slow to a crawl and stop talking. By the time that hazard was behind us, we were almost at Coldfoot, a destination touted as the major settlement on the entire Haul Road. Located on Slate Creek, the camp was named after prospectors who got cold feet and turned back. During the mini-boom of 1902 Coldfoot Camp had seven saloons with wind-up phonographs, a post office, a jail and ten whores, the latter referred to as 'sporting girls'. That's how it was with the rushes. Each one pulled in a campload of hangers-on. One sourdough said, 'If Stefansson [a controversial early twentieth-century Arctic adventurer] could get to the North Pole and discover gold, there'd be 500 Alaskan whores there inside three months.' We drove into a car park surrounded by six low buildings made from abandoned construction containers. This turned out to be Coldfoot. The hiker went off to telephone his nephew from a booth at the back of the truckers' cafe. We followed him inside. Particles of cooking grease filmed every surface of the steamy interior. A plaque on the wall recorded a temperature of 97°F (36°C) in 1988, and below it a sign noted that the following year Coldfoot had experienced -60°F (-50°C) for seventeen days in a row. Jeannie and I both ordered the Special, pork-belly soup, which was excellent. A third sign indicated that we were at the last gas station for 239 miles. So after paying for our soup, we filled up. The gas pump was faulty, and kept cutting out, so Jeannie had to put in a cupful at a time. A passing trucker recognised her Idaho Vandals cap (she was a fanatical supporter) and conversation about the team's woeful recent performance took us up to a full tank. I slipped back inside to mouth goodbye to our hitchhiker, who was yelling into the receiver, evidently not finding his nephew receptive to the 250-mile round-trip rescue plan. He seemed somehow helpless – which was how I felt, as I so wanted him to find a chunky nugget. When I returned down the Dalton to Fairbanks a week later, his broken-down car was still marooned on the Arctic Circle. I expect it is still there today, embraced by permafrost and mammoth carcasses.

Before we settled back into the Dalton's mesmeric rhythm, the metropolis of Wiseman (population twenty-one) loomed out of the tundra. A layer of porridge ice rustled on a river abutted by vegetable gardens and cabins sprouting solar panels. But the mountainous silhouette in the background brought back the pages of Bob Marshall. One of the few frontiersmen who left a record, Marshall settled in Wiseman and wrote about the Arctic Divide in prose that will last until the glaciers return to the North Slope.

Born in 1901 in New York City, Marshall spent childhood summers roaming the Adirondacks before going on to train as a plant physiologist and forester, rising to the position of Chief of Recreation and Lands in the US Forest Service. He made four trips to Arctic Alaska in the thirties, studying tree growth at the northern timber line. Deeply engaged with the conflict between wilderness subjugation and wilderness preservation, Marshall wrote of 'the emotional values of the frontier' and urged conservation, not development. Some places should remain unknown: as Will Ladislaw had already declared in *Middlemarch*, they must be 'preserved as hunting grounds for the poetic imagination'. The 1930s is more foreign than the Arctic now but Marshall's plea to conserve polar wilderness resonates as clearly as it did when he was crawling over spring ice to wrap a tape measure round a spruce trunk.

Marshall's bestselling *Arctic Village* told of fifteen months based in a cabin in Wiseman. It took two weeks then to get from New York to Fairbanks, and from there Marshall flew the last leg. When he returned to Wiseman for a second visit, the hundred residents, a mix of whites, Inupiat and Athabascans, held a dance at the roadhouse in his honour. In Wiseman Marshall found beauty, tolerance and freedom that compensated for the many things lacking at the roadhouse store. He was attracted, he said, by 'the glamorous mystery of unknown worlds'. Marshall writes of hooking grayling 20 inches long, of siwashing (bivouacking without a tent), of dining on grizzly steaks and moose tongue, knocking off first ascents, unpacking his dendrograph after wading through 9 feet of last winter's snow in August, naming mountains and gulches and marvelling at his luck in finding paradise. He describes diving head first into his sleeping bag to change a film in the dark, cooking biscuits in the midnight twilight, hauling his raft across Squaw Rapids, then hiking back to Wiseman to read about the

Depression in a four-month-old copy of *Time*. When it rained, he lay in his tent reading Meredith's *Diana of the Crossways*, enough to send a normal man into a coma on Fifth Avenue, let alone at the headwaters of the Koyukuk. In the winter he went mushing, starting out from Wiseman in the starlight, cooking cornmeal for the dogs, trampling soft snow down with snowshoes to make camp, cutting spruce boughs on which to set his stove. The maps he made, some published by the USGS, are works of art. There weren't any roads to draw, but a delicate network of streams and rivers that resemble, on the page, the microscopic vessels in a pair of lungs in an anatomy book. When Marshall first arrived, Wiseman was dominated by gold-diggers from '98 who had stayed on. Some were snipers, men who reworked old mining ground. It was always the failures who stayed.

A modest man immeasurably moved by what he called 'the humility of grandeur', Marshall died of a heart attack on a train from Washington to New York when he was thirty-nine. 'Exploration', he had written, 'is perhaps the greatest aesthetic experience a human being can know.' The Arctic had attracted so much shoe-eating that one could lose sight of the spiritual exhilaration of exploration. Of the heavyweights, only Fridtjof Nansen communicated a sense of the true subjugation of the ego that discovery can bring. 'If we perish,' he wrote, 'what will it matter in the endless cycle of eternity?' Nansen is the presiding spirit of my Arctic story. A long-faced Norseman with a touch of the Sphinx, he was born near Christiania (the former name of Oslo) in 1861, and in the course of a tumultuous life became an outstanding scientist, diplomat and humanitarian as well as a record-breaking explorer who led the first crossing of Greenland. A Nobel Peace Prize was among many laurels bestowed for his work as a League of Nations High Commissioner, in the course of which he had originated the Nansen Passport for refugees. Following independence in 1905, he became his country's first ambassador to the Court of St James's, and at one point almost rose to the position of Norwegian prime minister. Perhaps that is why he was a better explorer (and

writer) than the rest: he did other things, a man for all seasons. Nansen sensed at a profound level the 'yearning after light and knowledge', and, almost uniquely, was able to marry that understanding to physical capability and snowcraft.

Shortly after Wiseman, the valleys deepened and the forest capitulated to semi-iced North Slope tundra. Northern harriers and rough-legged hawks circled above a flock of wild Dall sheep on the steepest hillside. Linked now to a stranger by the intimacy of Susie's death, Jeannie gunned the truck into the foothills of the Brooks Range, the 700-mile limestone uplift which arcs across Alaska, the end of a spine that starts with the Andes and surges north as the Mexican cordilleras and the Rockies. Here its mountains mark the border between the Arctic North Slope and the Yukon River Drainage – what some call the Arctic Divide. It was Marshall's country, the land he had skewered so lyrically in words. And I saw what he had seen. Behind the first row of low hills, blunt 8,000-footers rose in waves, deeply incised by broad, U-shaped glacial valleys. White birch skirted the lower slopes, while patches of snow remained in sheltered spots just above. As we crested the first pass, the Koyukuk curling ahead, a Japanese cyclist whizzed by, head down and upturned eyes murderous with misery. You have to admire a man who has pedalled through the Brooks Range. But I wished he had looked as if he were enjoying himself.

The Brooks' limestone needles shot into cirrus cloud, proportion subordinated to the height imperative, as in an El Greco painting. Jeannie had become more voluble as we approached journey's end. She had started to shout out the name on each sign. The road builders were keen on signage, and the forks of the rivers were capable of infinite subdivision, facilitating a maximum number of marker posts. 'The West Fork of the North Fork of the Chandalar River!' Jeannie yelled. As an act of preparation for the descent waiting on the other side of the highest pass, she got out to lock our hubcaps. For the first time, full slopes of ice foreshadowed the Big Freeze. The highway dropped away steeply on either side. Jeannie climbed back into the cab. The sun was setting, and the sky painted rosy pink. When the valley was in shadow, level sunbeams continued to pour onto the white higher slopes in an effect of ravishing beauty, and the ice reflected and refracted purple light like cut crystal. Then all except the tips became dead white, and we experienced the transfiguration of alpenglow. When the shadows crept higher and submerged both slopes and ridges, alpenglow still lingered on the highest peaks, until eventually these too were quenched, glowing points going out like stars. We had crossed the Arctic Divide.

Half an hour later we trundled into polar flatlands. Jeannie bantered about road conditions over the radio with a passing trucker. She suggested that wheel chains would be required in a few days. 'Yep,' agreed her interlocutor. 'Reckon it's the last time we'll go barefoot this year.' Then we passed no one for fifty miles, and we both fell silent, woozy with the heady emptiness of the Dalton and the fug of the cab. Jeannie's loyalty to the concept of progress enshrined in the Haul Road was touching. She was as certain as the missionary Hudson Stuck that the American way was best. Perhaps a conviction of rectitude characterises all significant endeavour. The Stalinist collectivisers had been sure they were right to nail down nomads who had roamed the Russian Arctic for many centuries.

We spent the night in a Deadhorse blockhouse. Disintegrating volumes of soft porn stood in chronological order on a shelf in my room, a bathetic end to the greatest road trip on earth. In the morning, I took a walk before breakfast. Deadhorse was a ratty ex-mining settlement of the central casting variety just fifteen miles from the holy springs of Prudhoe Bay, Pump Station Number One and the high security 'Pad' housing 1,400 BP workers. You could faintly see industrial smoke trails in the sky over the horizon, emanating, according to Jeannie, from stacks burning off not oil but gas. For three decades people had been talking about plans for an ambitious but as yet non-existent gas pipeline all the way down to Chicago. As for Deadhorse, it was a dead loss. 'Best thing about it,' Jeannie had told me in advance, 'is the cat at the general store.' At the store, where the cat was not in evidence, we drank weak coffee to fortify us for another stint on the Dalton. An odour of frankfurters leaked from behind the clapperboard partition separating the public part of the store from its private recesses. The natural light beyond the windowpanes was bright, but the gloomy room required the illumination of a weak and shadeless overhead bulb that dangled at eye level, threatening to clout the careless customer. A notice pinned on a board alerted the Inupiat workforce to a forthcoming general meeting in Barrow 200 miles away to discuss proposals to raise hunting quotas. Barrow Inupiat eat bowhead – picking them off from floes, as I had learnt from envious Chukchi – and the ritual hunt remains an important social and cultural landmark. 'We as Inupiat have been the guardians of the Arctic for thousands of years,' subsistence bowhead hunter Charlie Hopson from Barrow recently told an environmental journalist. His daughter had joined him on his whaling boat, but his son was working as a mechanical engineer at Prudhoe Bay.

'What keeps you here?' I asked Jeannie as we drained our coffee and prepared to leave. 'It's not what's here,' she said. 'It's what's not here.'

Back on the road, we headed south to Toolik Field Station in the foothills of the Brooks. You could see the camp from way off, crouched a mile from the Dalton on the south-east shore of Lake Toolik. A half-arc of prefabricated trailers jacked three feet off the tundra; a berm of cargo crates; a couple of Caterpillar forklifts with their buckets in the air. At noon Jeannie swung into a gravel yard and pulled up outside one of the prefabs. We got out. A thermometer on the outside wall revealed that it was -5°C. Jeannie opened the fridge-style door and we went through a lobby heaped with boots and parkas, entering a galley in which a bearded man was doing a jigsaw at one of a dozen tables and simultaneously eyeing an open laptop next to the scattered pieces. This was Ford, the Toolik maintenance manager. It turned out that he was constructing an image of the Sahara and monitoring the health of his generators, which were linked to the laptop.

Now owned and managed by the Institute of Arctic Biology at the University of Alaska Fairbanks, Toolik Field Station was founded in 1970 as a camp for the labourers hacking the Dalton Highway out of the permafrost. As it was the end of September, the scientists had left, installed once more in the laboratories of their home institutions. In order to absorb the landscape of the Arctic Divide, I had arranged with the university to spend a week with eight Toolik support staff while the station was quiet. On the gravel tracks outside the galley, the occasional golf cart trundled equipment and stores between modular labs and science Jamesways, but otherwise little was going on beyond a general battening down for winter. That suited me fine. Behind the galley, miles of boardwalk criss-crossed the tundra. Most of it facilitated a twenty-year ecology study looking at the breakdown of soil carbon. For many years the station has been operating as a monitoring and testing ground for investigations into the Arctic's role in global climate change: researchers measure – for example – fluxes in the levels of greenhouse gases released as the active layer above the permafrost softens in spring sunshine.

Ford showed me to a guest dorm with eight rooms. As I was the only guest, I got to choose. It was hard, as they were all the same. Ford went through the ropes. Grey water, including sewage, got trucked out to Prudhoe Bay at a cost of 75 cents a litre. So we were limited to two two-minute showers a week during which we were required to turn the water off while lathering. This explained the cardboard plates and bowls in the galley. It was more environmentally friendly to burn cardboard than to truck out dirty washing-up water.

I padded the labs. Technicians maintained one of the freezers at -80°. In the Antarctic I had once looked after a gas-powered freezer used to prevent things getting too cold. Sometimes at Toolik I kept the others company. One afternoon I motored out to the middle of the lake with Sherri, a science technician from California with *Baywatch* looks to complement a Masters in marine biology. She had to haul in a floating meteorological station before freeze-up. After sucking the season's data from the device onto a laptop, we pulled up the anchors, which were plastic crates full of rocks. Mostly, I hiked the hills and valleys, watching the highway snake north in a rolling cumulonimbus of brown cloud. A series of smaller satellite lakes clustered round Lake Toolik, itself not yet frozen, though the streams decanting from it were filmed with ice, and the banks crackled under my boots. Alluvial rock filled the valley floor between camp and Jade Mountain, and outcrop merged into block-fields of glacial till, a vegetation known as *barrens*. Going up Jade, the low bushes thinned out, and I found myself walking over disintegrated schist and volcanic tuff before following a ridge to the summit. The high mosslands to the east dropped off in 1,000-foot gorges, and on the other side a permanent icefield bunged the head of a basin, its greenish lower slopes tinted with blueberry leaves. The sun came out, and I lay down in the deep silence, conscious of what Marshall called 'the unreality of a freshness beyond experience'. I pondered the open vastness of an Alaskan landscape far from the choked marine freeways of the Inside Passage, the cloud forests of the Alexander Archipelago, the alpine bowls of the Mat-Su Valley, or the gothic rainforests of the south dense with western hemlock and Sitka spruce 8 feet in diameter. The Arctic existed in a different dimension to the rest of Alaska: simultaneously stunted and soaring. I had come to glean something of the American polar experience, but here I had found something universal. I suddenly understood Marshall's 'humility of grandeur': that overwhelming yet deeply comforting sense of one's smallness and unimportance in the thunderous hugeness of the Arctic Divide. I must have fallen asleep while I was thinking, and when I opened my eyes a wild sheep was looking at me. I could feel the warmth of its breath on my cheek.

Meanwhile the pipeline glinting into the distance continued pumping its millions of barrels to the hungry multitudes. There was something inevitable about its presence even here, in one of the last true wildernesses. Oil, on one reckoning, has been the single most important factor in shaping environmental history over the past fifty years, not just in Alaska, but everywhere. Cheap energy became a distinguishing feature of the twentieth century, and the harnessing of fossil fuels, along with population growth and technical innovation, constituted its determining characteristics. I lay lazily in the cool sunshine and wondered what John Muir would have made of it. A vigorous environmentalist who founded the Sierra Club, and widely regarded as the father of US National Parks, Muir said Alaska was among his great loves. His 1915 classic *Travels in Alaska* is a work of uplifting enthusiasm: like Marshall, he proselytised the values of conservation and, like Nansen, he recognised the enlightenment discovery can engender – and he shared Nansen's poetic touch. 'The setting sun fired the clouds,' Muir wrote. 'All the world seemed new born. Every thing, even the commonest, was seen in a new light and was looked at with new interest as if never seen before. The plant people seemed glad, as if rejoicing with me, the little ones as well as the trees, while every feature of the peak and its travelled boulders seemed to know what I had been about and the depth of my joy, as if they could read faces.'

Muir emigrated to America from Scotland when he was eleven, but never lost his Dunbar accent. A sinewy Celt with dark curly hair, he enjoyed preternatural stamina, and thought nothing of walking for twenty-four hours at a stretch. He was a self-taught glaciologist, and one of the very few white men in nineteenth-century Alaska not hell-bent on gold. He wrote a lot, but words came, he said, 'slow as a glacier', and anyway he thought that 'one day's exposure to mountains is better than a cartload of books'. Like many writers who have celebrated the transfiguring power of landscape, Muir sought in his travels a medium with which to engage with wilderness. He found it in Alaska. He spent a lot of time on the trail zoned out with joy. 'I was too happy to sleep,' he writes more than once. Muir's grateful nature is especially moving when one learns he had been deployed as a slave by his father, a tyrannical religious zealot and characteristically dour Lowland Scot. Clearing a homestead in the Wisconsin backwoods, Muir senior worked the child John for sixteen or seventeen hours a day. When John was sent to chisel a well through eighty feet of sandstone, he was poisoned by carbon dioxide and pulled out unconscious. But the old man sent him down again the next day. Muir grew into living proof of the fortitude of the human spirit; of the cup perceived half full; of the importance of killing self-pity. One chink in the armour lies in his often repeated observation that the indigenous groups with whom he stayed 'are fond and indulgent parents . . . In all my travels I never heard a cross, fault-finding word, or anything like scolding inflicted on an Indian child, or ever witnessed a single case of spanking, so common in civilised communities.' And his father had not knocked the faith out of him: Muir turned the old man's harsh Protestantism into benign pantheism, though he still saw God's hand everywhere in the Alaskan glaciers. Green rhetoric is debased currency now but at the time civilised Americans hailed Muir as a seer. A shaggy-bearded writer-activist promoting a distinctive mix of science and spirituality,

Muir considered himself a conservation lobbyist who encouraged people to value a world in which human beings were not dominant. His brand of what he referred to as enlightened utilitarianism would have a place today.

We had a light cycle, just as I had experienced in Chukotka. September was the true Arctic cusp, the brief period in which days are light and nights are dark. But there was something else at Toolik: auroras. Even before the sky darkened, faint flickers smeared the sky. At eleven or twelve, an unseen hand switched on the Northern Lights – or rather, drew them, as they were like a rippling and fluorescent curtain that swished to and fro until dawn. Night after night I stood outside my dorm watching an evanescence of strands emerge from the drapes to curve inwards and outwards. One time the curtains vanished and the end of a primrose bow twisted in on itself before bellying rapidly from east to west. I waited. Globules of bright light materialised in another part of the sky, pulsed, then stretched into ribbon streamers and thrashed in quick, jerking movements, like whips cracking. The end of the ribbons frayed when they curved, a prismatic fringe altering from fat baby fingers to lace filaments, elastic threads of light shifting from greens to yellows and purples. At other times bars of light marched in close-packed succession, transforming themselves at a set point into solid white lances. Then suddenly the shimmering decayed, leaving only the powdery course of the Milky Way.* As Gertrude Stein said, 'Paradise – if you can stand it.'

In the evening, at ten or eleven, Ford lit a fire in an old metal drum and stood close, nursing a bottle of beer. The points of the flames

* The Northern Lights (aurora borealis) are caused when electrically charged particles stream from the sun and strike atoms and molecules of oxygen, nitrogen and other gases in the upper atmosphere. Subatomic particles break off and collide, liberating energy in the form of light. Oxygen atoms produce some colours, nitrogen atoms others, and the forces involved are immense. In 1989 an aurora knocked out the lights in the north-east of the USA and Eastern Canada for six hours.

flared white as they leapt in the Arctic air, and the unmediated heat burned the cold off exposed skin. Ford chose to live not in a dorm but in a windowless shipping container with a fridge door. He had made it cosy over the course of several seasons by building a wooden bunk and a set of shelves crowded with bookmarked books, unfinished volumes that lay around like partly eaten sandwiches. Like everyone else he worked a fortnight on, a fortnight off; and when he was at Toolik he revelled in as much solitude as he could find. Ford enjoyed a busy family life in Fairbanks, and the Arctic represented the Other. It was easy to see it like that: a pristine oasis far from the rain-splattered streets of home. After a few more beers, Ford grew very lyrical on the subject. But I was beginning to see that the Arctic is more than just a sanctuary. It is not a symbol. It is a living reality, with all the problems and horrors and joys reality brings.

The landscape inched towards freeze-up. A flock of ptarmigan nesting in willow bushes on the eastern flank of the lake grew whiter, shedding tortoiseshell summer feathers as they hopped towards a tasty morsel. Each day, the far reaches of the lake had frozen further inwards, the slushy, granular snow-ice on top – what Thoreau said looked like frozen yeast – collecting in ridges that traced contours on the white rind. There was everywhere a sense of hardening, of battening down. The earth seemed to be hurrying forward into the next phase of its cycle. Each day another of the tarns had frozen to an opaque whiteness. One sensed them snapping shut in the night. Ground squirrels were maniacally caching before the big sleep, and over to the west, three or four caribou hoofed around, temporarily separated from their herd as it migrated south.* A pair of yellow-billed loons that nested

---

* The *siksik*, as Inuit call the ground squirrel, is the only Arctic mammal which hibernates deeply. A polar bear merely becomes dormant; a *siksik* gets close to suspended animation, its body temperature dropping below freezing. Inuit consider the *siksik* attractive, and its skin is used to clean newborn girls so that they will be pretty too. They clean a male baby with the forehead skin of the bull caribou –

on the lake were preparing for their own long winter journey. *Toolik* is the Inuktituk word for the common or yellow-billed loon, a bird with many uses among the Inuit. The parents of an infant son may touch the baby's lips with a loon beak, to give the boy a strong, clear voice for the drum dance. The Toolik *toolik* had produced two chicks. One died almost immediately, and the survivor was unfledged. The loons were together on a different part of the lake every day. I hoped to see them go before I myself headed south.

'If it's succour with nature you want, everyone thinks Alaska's it,' Paul said.

We were all huddled in Winter Quarters, a dorm next to mine where the staff staying through till March were preparing to hunker down for the long, dark haul. People were nibbling on freshly plucked cranberries and glugging from the array of end-of-season bottles. It was already late, and we had come inside after viewing a spectacular aurora. Paul was a technician who had notched up seven Alaskan winters. As he came from Minnesota, he didn't find anywhere cold. Like his colleagues, he had a science degree, and like them he had chosen to come north and work as a technically competent dogsbody in order to experience the Alaskan Arctic. It was another kind of American dream: not the pursuit of riches, but of freedom and communion with nature. (Paul's Russian peers would have liked the option.) 'Alaska's come to occupy this weird place as ultimate wilderness in the collective American psyche,' he continued. 'Yet so many of the assholes who come up here haven't a clue how to survive in the wilderness. I mean, look at Chris McCandless.' McCandless was

---

pangniq. Both skins must be present at the confinement, in case. The caribou close to Toolik are Grant's caribou, from the Western Arctic herd. The word caribou comes from Mi'kmaq (one of the Algonquin languages of Eastern Canada), and literally means 'snow shoveller', referring to the way the beast scratches at the snow with its hooves to find food.

a cause célèbre in the Lower 48, and a lost cause in Alaska. John Krakauer immortalised his enigmatic story in a book called *Into the Wild*, and Sean Penn had made it into a decent Hollywood film. The protagonist was an intellectually gifted elite athlete from an affluent east coast family, and in 1992 he had selected sub-Arctic Alaska as the setting in which to live out a wilderness fantasy. McCandless was the enlightenment seeker, the man who walks to a different drumbeat, the idealist in flight from the trappings of urban America. Having changed his name to Alexander Supertramp, he packed a rucksack with a small gun, salt and a book on berries, and strode out. Four months later, a party of moose hunters found his corpse in the shell of an abandoned bus. He had starved. When the news broke, sourdoughs queued up to criticise, pointing out that the many essential items 'Supertramp' failed to take with him included a large-calibre weapon, an axe, a map and a compass. Yet as the story acquired the patina of legend, to thousands of others McCandless came to represent the archetypal Romantic hero, the loner who repudiated the sterility and hypocrisy of conventional society and pursued noble American ideals of freedom to the end. Like everyone else, he was convinced his route was the right one. Sherri was among his many supporters. She was the Californian technician who had taken me out in the boat.

'I think what he did', she said, 'took more courage than getting some crummy banking job and a house in the suburbs.'

'He was a narcissistic fool living out an ill-considered fantasy,' retaliated Paul, rising to Sherri's bait. 'For food, McCandless took a 10lb bag of long-grain rice! Reckoned he was going to eat berries and shoot game with some crummy little gun!'

Whatever the criticism of McCandless and others like him, the fact remained that having looted Alaska of salmon, logs, gold and oil, Outsiders had now found it another role. It had become a stage for introspection; the place where the brave and the true escaped civilisation and divested themselves of the worthless trappings of society.

Either that, or a stage for the machismo of the Iron Man variety, exemplified in the 1,150-mile Anchorage-to-Nome Iditarod, a dog-mushing contest touted as 'the last great race on earth'. This was Jack London territory; it was he, more than any other writer, who had fostered the image of Alaska. London went to the Klondike from his native California when he was twenty-one. He found not gold but a fecund source of literary inspiration. As he said later, even though he never made a cent from gold, 'I have been managing to pan out a living ever since on the strength of the [Klondike] trip.' That's the spirit. *The Call of the Wild* was a bestselling sensation in 1903, and London rocketed to celebrity status. Restless, hardworking and addictive, he was so famous that his first divorce made the front pages all over America. McCandless had long been obsessed with London. In his last weeks he had carved 'Jack London is King' into a piece of wood.

At the same time as London was finding what he needed in the Arctic, two other Americans were using it to seek fame in another way. One of them, Robert Peary, is still the best known American explorer of all time, if you don't count Neil Armstrong. Peary was the antithesis of Alaska's John Muir and Bob Marshall: he perceived the Arctic as a place to be conquered, rather than a peak on Darien with a view that lifted the soul. It was once a widely held position in the USA, for by the start of the twentieth century, Americans had overtaken Britons in pioneering Arctic exploration, as they had done in so many fields. It was therefore not surprising, in 1909, that the two men who announced that they had, independently of each other, reached the goal of centuries and stood at the North Pole hailed from the United States. Peary and his rival Frederick Cook were a strange pair, yoked by history but with little in common. Peary, born in 1856 to a family of New England merchants, was a tall, tireless showman addicted to fame. One polar historian judges him 'probably the most unpleasant man in the annals of polar exploration', a hotly contested field. The neurotic and megalomaniacal Peary had staying power, at least: on expedition after expedition he smashed his way through Smith Sound to the top of Greenland, marching on even after eight of his toes snapped off. On 6 April 1909, he and his black manservant Matthew Henson stood on the ice at 90°N – or so Peary claimed. It was, he wrote in his journal, 'the finish, the cap and climax, of nearly 400 years of effort, loss of life, and expenditure of fortunes by the civilised nations of the world, and it has been accomplished in a way that is thoroughly American'. Both Peary and Henson left offspring in the Arctic, taking away instead three 37-ton iron meteorites sacred to the Greenlanders, as well as six live Inuit specimens, four of whom quickly picked up alien germs and died in Washington. The meteorites are in the Smithsonian. One of the surviving Inuit, the boy Minik, found out that his father's bones were on display at the Natural History Museum.*

In any event, Peary learned, before reaching home, that Cook claimed to have forestalled him at the Pole. A Manhattan doctor nine years Peary's junior with extraordinary piercing eyes, Cook was as affable and charming as Peary was tense and humourless. Like his rival, he was a man of solid polar experience, and in 1898 had acquitted

---

* Peary brought the six Greenlandic Inuit back from his fourth polar expedition in 1897 and put them on show at Brooklyn's Excursion Wharf. The group included seven-year-old Minik and his father Qisuk. 'It was like a land', the boy said later of his first weeks in the USA, 'that we thought must be heaven.' Minik went to school in the Bronx, played football and learned to say his prayers. His father died four months after their arrival, but Minik only learned in 1907 that staff at the Natural History Museum had faked his burial and that Qisuk's bones were on display in a glass case. After twelve years Minik sailed back to north-west Greenland, but he couldn't speak Inuktituk, or skin a seal. He said he felt like 'the loneliest person in the world'. In 1916 he returned to New York with another expedition, and appeared briefly in vaudeville theatres as a fur-swathed Eskimo before taking US citizenship and working as a lumberjack. The bones of his father and the other three Inuit who had quickly perished remained in boxes in the museum basement for years. In 1918, Minik died in New Hampshire. In 1993 his father's bones were returned to Greenland for a proper burial.

himself well in the Antarctic with Amundsen. When the sensational story of his arrival at the Pole broke, mobs swarmed round him wherever he walked and 'Dr Cook hats' sold in their thousands. (Two feet tall, brown and furry, one newspaper said the hat looked as if you could boil it up for soup in an Arctic emergency.) The battle for paramountcy between Peary and Cook received unprecedented coverage, initiating one of the most bitter newspaper wars of all time, the *New York Times* backing Peary and its rival the *Herald* batting for Cook. The steady but deadly accumulation of evidence that unmasked Cook began with the revelation that he had faked his photographs of the Pole by cropping a set he had taken in Greenland six years previously. Peary was triumphant – until it emerged that his speeds were dubious and his lack of observations suspicious, and that his records also failed to withstand scrutiny. Informed sources agree that neither man reached the Pole. But the Arctic attracts fiction to its facts until the two are indistinguishable, and the Peary legend lives on, just as he planned.

When we woke the next day, a hard frost had transformed the landscape. In the middle of the morning, snow even fell briefly. The tundra was stippled white, with sand-coloured swirls around the ground willow. On the hills rime crusted the brown slopes where not even willow could get a purchase. The lake itself had lightened to a bright silver. It too was stippled when a north-westerly soughed in from the ocean. I hiked east to a smaller lake that was already frozen, its ice thick-ribbed, thinning and smoothing at the centre like supple glass. The knife ridges of the Brooks were of a piece with the rest of the landscape. This was after all the end of September: the whiteing of Alaska. I sat down at the far end of the lake, wishing I could draw. Close up, powdery crystals piled half an inch deep on the fragile, bending stalks of foliage. Around the roots, clusters of black, globular droppings nestled among leaves, twigs, smooth pebbles and rocks textured with lichen. Clumps of moss grew tiny lawn-green trumpets. It was almost windless by three o'clock, and half the sky was a cold, fresh blue – a toothpaste blue – but a layer of cloud had moved over the sun's half, opaque and grey in the middle, and translucent and white round the edge. Beyond the cloud, a wall of wide rays, faintly golden, fell among the Brooks. Cold began to bite.

A pair of shaggy Russian permafrost scientists arrived in camp, and in the morning I sat on the galley deck talking to them over toast, their consumption of which was unstinting. It was a fine Alaskan morning, mild and mellow, and a raven landed on the deck. A yellowish haze had spread over the east, and the tintinnabulation of a swift-flowing brook animated the landscape in the foreground. The Russians, based at the University of Alaska Fairbanks, had spent the week poking temperature probes deep into permafrost, a task they had repeated all over the western hemisphere. 'Permafrost', explained the shaggier of the two as mouthfuls of toast and jelly vanished into the wilderness of his beard, 'represents a unique record of long-term temperature cycles. It's a better record than the atmosphere, because we see trends more easily.' Permafrost offered up an accurate record of the past; the Russians were collecting data with which to predict the future. Like a peat bog or a coal deposit, permafrost acts as a storage unit for accumulated carbon. If it melts, organic material frozen for millennia will begin to break down and give off CO_2 or methane. Was that going to happen, that was the thing. 'As a general trend,' said the less shaggy one, 'we have seen temperatures rising. Here at Toolik we know that between 1979 and 1994, the average surface temperature in summer rose by nearly 3°F. As warmer air aerated the upper soil levels, the tundra did begin to release carbon dioxide. But we are not sure the Siberian permafrost will ever release all its hundreds of thousands of tonnes of methane.' I found it reassuring when a scientist said he wasn't sure. 'It depends,' continued less shaggy, 'if there were natural causes for the warming. If there were, the cycle will, eventually and presumably, be reversed. If the temperature rose as a result of anthropogenic activity, on the other hand, yes, methane will pump out, along with tonnes of organic carbons – from dead animals, for example.' So is the cause of temperature rise anthropogenic? 'Some of it is. The question is, how much?' That did indeed seem to be the question. But by then they had eaten all the bread, and they got up and left.

On the day before my last one I drove 50 miles north with Sherri to retrieve a data logger left in the field by a departed science group. The treeless expanse of the North Slope had reddened to an un-Arctic russet. To get to the logger, we left the Dalton on a track heading a short distance into the Arctic National Wildlife Refuge. When we arrived, I went off to take photographs while Sherri disconnected the wires. The 19.2-million-acre Refuge constitutes a single protected area encompassing an unbroken continuum of Arctic and sub-Arctic ecosystems, from the boreal forest of the Porcupine River plateau to the barrier islands of the Beaufort Sea. About the size of South Carolina, or Scotland, it remains the only area on the North Slope on which Congress specifically prohibits petroleum development. Whether the ban will remain in place is a contested issue. Somehow, one knows who the winners will be. It's just a question of when. Sherri came to find me, and we headed home, the sky infused with the valedictory amethyst of sunset. Night had fallen by the time we rolled into camp. Condensation like smoke was floating off the lake in billows. Sherri and I hurried into the galley, and fell upon our dinner. The next morning, I left, back down the Dalton with Jeannie. Before climbing into the truck, I took a last walk around the lake to find the three loons. But they were gone.

IV

Rock Talk

The Canadian Arctic

A geologist who saw it on my desk told me that they now reckon that type of stone to be something like a thousand million years old. What has it been, before there were any men to throw it, and where will it be when you and I are not even a pinch of dust? Don't cling to it as if you owned it. I did that ... None of us counts for much in the long, voiceless, inert history of the stone ...

Robertson Davies, *The Manticore*

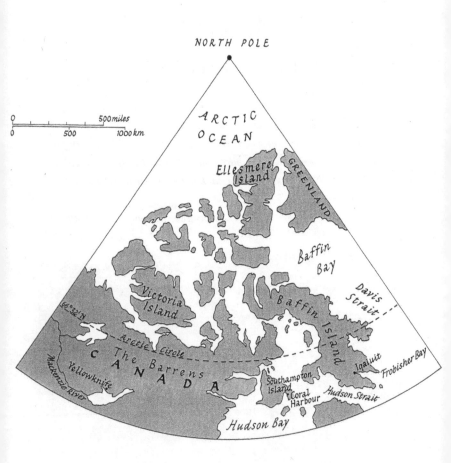

NORTH POLE

ARCTIC
OCEAN

500 miles
500   1000 km

Ellesmere
Island

GREENLAND

Baffin
Bay

Davis
Strait

Victoria
Island

Baffin Island

66°32'N

Arctic Circle

The Barrens

CANADA

Iqaluit

Frobisher Bay

Mackenzie River

Yellowknife

Southampton
Island

Coral
Harbour

Hudson Strait

Hudson Bay

A full 1,300 miles from Ottawa, Iqaluit squats at the bottom of the fifth biggest island in the world.* Now the capital of the largest Canadian Territory, the site was just another white ice plain until 1941 when the US government, shocked into action by U-boat attacks on its aircraft carriers, activated a plan to establish a chain of airfields in Arctic Canada to ferry planes to Britain under the terms of the Lend-Lease Act. Machines could not yet fly non-stop but, starting out from three points in the USA, they could hop across the North Atlantic. A staging airfield was required in Upper Frobisher Bay, and Inuit guides selected a site on Koojesse inlet where the Everett mountains rise from the coast. Construction of the airfield that grew into Iqaluit was one of countless logistical challenges war brought to the polar regions, especially as a barrier of islands dotted and dashed across the deep water channels leading to the head of Frobisher Bay. Once the installation was up, it turned out that maintaining gravel runways built on permafrost was a Sisyphaen task reliant on brute force and patience. But by 1943, US Advance Air Base and Weather Station Crystal Two

* 1. Greenland. 2. New Guinea 3. Borneo 4. Madagascar. 5. Baffin Island. Neither Australia nor Antarctica qualify, on account of being continental landmasses.

was operational on the Iqaluit site, and a permanent Inuit settlement had grown up with it, its members obliged to wear dog tags because military personnel could not tell them apart.

By that time the staging route was already obsolete. Allied anti-submarine warships had neutralised U-boat activity, aided by airborne radar units and protective air cover. In addition, flights over the Greenland ice cap had a dubious record. The death blow came when, as a result of advances in aeronautical engineering, planes with extra fuel tanks were able to leap from Goose Bay in Labrador to Great Britain. But military interest did not end with hostilities. The US incorporated the airfield into its Pinetree Line of long-range radar bases, and in 1955 the embryonic Iqaluit became the construction centre of the Cold War DEW line operation that reached halfway across the circumpolar lands. After that it transmogrified into a Ballistic Missile Early Warning Site and a station for a squadron of KC-97 mid-air refuelling tankers that supported nuclear bombers. The military finally moved out in 1963, B-52s having made the Arctic obsolete once again, from the point of view of a bomber pilot.

Freed from military control, the community settled into a quiet civilian existence. In 1987 administrators named it Iqaluit. It was there that I had my first experience of Arctic Canada. I was in transit en route to a geology camp on Southampton Island in the north of Hudson Bay, and while waiting in town to hitch a ride on a resupply flight, I squatted in the flat of a friend who was in the field, and had the place to myself. The sky lay on Frobisher Bay tight as Tupperware, and chained dogs howled all night, lupine whines that carried far out over the water.

For the first few days the temperature hovered at a midsummery 5° above, and in the mornings the sky was striated, like bacon. Two wide paved roads forked through sections of Iqaluit's small, semi-urban sprawl, while sand roads careered around the place, or gave up in roadblocks of mud and ice. The jostling pack ice of the bay dominated the scene – that, and the beach in the heart of town, damp sand crowded with rowing boats, motorised dinghies, locked wooden storage huts, ambulant dogs and leaking mounds of rubbish, signature of the inhabited Arctic. Unequal rows of stilted low-rise apartment blocks radiated from the beach like spokes. Public buildings included a gleaming hospital, a tax office and a new francophone school for the tiny French-speaking community at 65°N. Signs appeared in three languages to reinforce the Canadian-ness of the nation's newest territory: French, English and Inuktituk in both the Roman alphabet and in syllabics, a script invented by missionaries. As a result, all the signs were huge. I went into the North Mart supermarket, where a notice in the baking section indicated that vanilla essence was available, but that due to its 'special status' it could only be produced following consultation with the management. I enquired about the incarceration of the harmless vanilla essence. But it turned out not to be harmless at all. It ensnared the innocent. 'Do they swig it or sniff it?' I asked a shelf-stacker. 'Drink it,' he revealed with a grin, acting out the gesture of raising a vessel to his lips, 'if it's all they can get their hands on.' Failing to find anything tempting in the supermarket, I tried the restaurants. There were a dozen, none good, though you could get a passable lunch at the Discovery Inn, if you could stomach the ambience and decor – tiny, high windows, sulphurous lighting and a smell of something that might once have been alive. A few hundred yards from the school and the swanky hospital, the backyards on the muddy streets outside the Discovery disgorged broken-down white goods and soiled cardboard boxes. Stooped old Inuit sat around doing nothing, children skidded on home-made skateboards and podgy teenage girls plugged into iPods drifted around in *amautiit* duffels, a flat-faced and soot-headed baby peeping from every hood. When I spoke a word of greeting, a person invariably replied cheerily. One child enquired after the provenance of my freckles, and older women looked on with gummy smiles. Shreds of the internal robust endurance of Inuithood had outlasted the troubles, for now.

They should have called it Fattytown, not Iqaluit. Obesity was a sad symbol of cultural collision. It represented exile, metaphorically speaking; exile from the traditional Inuit environment and its complexities of meaning. Cut off from a country diet, people had ballooned into grotesque parodies of the white man. Canadians had tried hard to put things right. But they couldn't turn the clock back. In his book *Arctic Dreams*, after describing the annihilation of bowhead

whales in Arctic waters, Barry Lopez turns to the present. 'This time around, however, the element in the ecosystem at greatest risk is not the bowhead but the coherent vision of an indigenous people. We have no alternative, long-lived narrative to theirs, no story of human relationships with that landscape independent of Western science and any desire to control or possess.' These are issues that go to the heart of being human; their resolution controls our ability to be fully ourselves. The Inuit might appear drunk, fat and stoned, but they just about still know something we have forgotten.

When a countrywide survey quizzed the public on what it means to be Canadian, the majority of respondents cited 'not being American' as the primary characteristic of nationhood. As a secondary badge of identity, Canadians pointed to the existence of 'our north'. 'We are a northern country,' its citizens repeatedly asserted in the poll. 'We have our Arctic.' It is true that the Arctic occupies a higher percentage of the Canadian landmass than it does in any other country. Yet, despite the central position of the Arctic in the national identity myth, only 100,000 out of 33 million Canadians reside north of sixty degrees of latitude, the political boundary of the polar provinces (and roughly the treeline).* Most are Inuit. My geologist-campers seemed to understand both sides of this paradox instinctively. 'Hardly anyone I know', said one, 'has ever set foot north of sixty.' Many countries are burdened with too much history, but as Prime Minister Mackenzie King once said, Canada has 'too much geography'.

'Inuit can't rely on Canadian staples like forestry,' explained the publicly-funded chief of the geology project as we cuddled up to a stove in a soggy mess tent. 'Nothing is ever going to grow up here. Toyota will never fly in a factory to build the new Prius. It's too far from anywhere else for much tourism. Our main aim at this camp', he continued, 'is to see what the land can produce in the way of natural resources which will stimulate an economy.' An acrid smell rose from the socks drying over the stove rail. Inuit had exploited their environment in collusion with the Arctic for many centuries, curing seal hides with spittle; catching bowhead with bone harpoons; conjuring gods and spirits from the ice to invest the universe with meaning. Southern interlopers came for whale oil, then blue-fox fur, then hydrocarbons, and then (now) diamonds and gold. Encounters between the two groups were never harmonious, but once the land was consolidated into a single nation, proper trouble started – the kind of trouble, it turns out, that never goes away, taking on a life of its own and playing out unenvisaged dramas that resonate throughout the circumpolar north.

The nomads who fished the inlets of the Foxe Channel during a period of Arctic cooling between about 600 BC and AD 1000 carry,

* The treeline in North America in fact dips up and down quite a bit. In Alaska and the north-western parts of Canada it lies a long way above the Arctic Circle; in Hudson Bay it falls as far as 53°. The southern limit of continuous permafrost, similarly, dips a long way south in the Hudson Bay area. This is because the pack ice on the shallow waters of the bay lingers until midsummer, leaving no time for the water to warm up. Summer temperatures on land near Hudson Bay are as a result cooler than those near larger bodies of water such as the Arctic Ocean and Beaufort Sea.

posthumously, the 'Dorset' name, after a cache of artefacts that surfaced at Cape Dorset on Baffin Island. Using chipped stone tools, a Dorset man or woman once carved a male swan half the size of my little finger out of walrus ivory, an exquisite bird with its neck arched, its feet extended and its beak open as it clamoured to a female out on the tundra; another craftsman made a perfect stylised gull's head from driftwood weighing less than a sixtieth of an ounce. While waiting to leave Iqaluit, I had made friends with a collector who had allowed me to handle the gull's head. It was less detailed than my Siberian penis bone, but more evolved. Many Dorset carvings depict anguished human faces locked in a grotesque scream, calling to Munch and us, across the centuries.

The Dorset people, their successors and their descendants respected the land to a religious degree. It was all they had, and they cherished it with attitudes and behaviour that encapsulate the essence of Inuithood. Generation after generation, people sang of creation myths and a land once peopled with superhuman hunters who invested every glacier with a past. The stories tied them to the land. And the land provided. Puffballs of *pualunnguat* cottongrass healed a baby's umbilical, formed a portable *qulliq* lamp wick and did a hundred other things; the purple flowers, black berries and matted shrubbery of *paurngait*, or crowberry, made mattresses and medicine and, later, cleaned gun barrels; creeping willows relieved toothache and, mixed with rancid blubber, made a tasty chewing gum. Inuit honed their survival skills to a degree of perfection almost unknown among the milk-drinkers of warm latitudes. In lean times, a seal hunter sat next to his sea-ice hole resting his bare feet on an empty caribou-skin bag (*tutiriaq*, in the western dialects), as he knew the lightest scrape of footwear, amplified below the ice, chased away the seals. The women not only cured hides with spittle, they also chewed their menfolk's boots every morning to unfreeze the leather. In 1929 a white ornithologist asked two Aivilik hunters from Southampton Island, where the geology camp was situated, to draw a map of the whole island coastline – longer than that of Vancouver Island – from memory. When set down next to a modern map, the resulting sketches are accurate to a quarter of a mile.

Inuit perceived the environment as a revered partner: interlopers like Peary and the other Pole-seekers saw it as an enemy to be beaten into submission. As they had few skills with which to take it on, many expeditions culminated in farce, disaster, or, at the very least, a bout of shoe-eating. In the last of his voyages to Baffin Island, in 1578, Elizabethan buccaneer Sir Martin Frobisher shipped up 300 Cornish miners in a fifteen-strong fleet. The men duly mined 1,100 tons of

ore. When Frobisher got it home, he found that what glittered in the rock was not gold but pyrite. Nobody knew what to do with it, so it was used to repair Kentish roads. Until the Dalton Highway, they were the most expensive roads ever laid. Others had more luck: merchant-adventurers made fortunes from whales, and chartered companies did the same from furs. The Hudson's Bay Company, founded in 1670, effectively handled the exploitation of all the land draining into Hudson Bay for the British crown. According to their royal charter, company men were 'true and absolute Lordes and Proprietors' of a landmass comprising nearly 40 per cent of modern Canada. In the early years, hunters brought so many beaver pelts to the trading posts that Company men acquired the money and confidence to send mapping expeditions north, to find out if there might be a Klondike of furs there. In 1771 Samuel Hearne, a young Company-sponsored seaman, became the first white man to see the north shores of the North American continent, and his book recounting the expedition remains a classic of the genre. Hearne was that most compelling example of the species, the reflective man of action. Fluent in Athabascan, over a period of three years he travelled more than 3,500 miles across the western sub-Arctic with a party of up to 200 Dene men, women and children, living with them their eternal cycle of feast and famine and smearing his face with goose fat to ward off insects.* *A Journey from Prince of Wales's Fort in Hudson's Bay to the Northern Ocean* offers an unflinching portrait of people Hearne greatly admired (this despite the fact that his first guides robbed him, leaving him to eat not his shoes but his buckskin jacket on the march back to Prince of Wales Fort). He praises, for example, the stoicism of the Chipewyan, a subgroup of the Dene. At one point his party stopped for a woman to give birth, resuming again, after her fifty-two-hour labour, as soon as the infant appeared. The nursing mother then had her sledge hauled for her – for one day. But it wasn't all good. The twenty-five-year-old Hearne had to watch his companions hack a party of Coppermine River Inuit to death for no reason at all. 'First, we war,' chief guide Matonabbee informed an alarmed Hearne in advance of the massacre. 'Later, we survey.' When he returned to England, Hearne met Coleridge, who later cited the older man's anecdotes as an influence on his unfinished ballad 'The Three Graves'. Coleridge said he wanted to show that the 'witchcraft' of the Dene – the workings of their imagination, in other words – was 'not peculiar to savage or barbarous tribes', and in the ballad he changed Hearne's Dene people to English ones. Some critics think Hearne was

---

* The Dene are a group of peoples, including the Chipewyan and Sahtu, living across a wide region of northern Canada. Dene were the first to settle what are now the Northwest Territories.

a model for the Ancient Mariner. He said that as a young man he had been inspired by the story of the fictional Robinson Crusoe. Alexander Selkirk (the real-life Crusoe) inspired Defoe; Defoe inspired Hearne; Hearne inspired Coleridge – and so it goes.

The Hudson's Bay Company lost its monopoly, traders pushed north, Britain began to cede control of Canada. Through it all, in the collective imagination of lower latitudes the image of the Eskimo remained that of a primitive and uncorrupted nature-dweller who played little part in the national narrative.* There was not yet any meaningful contact between the two groups. Instead, one of the first documentary films – perhaps the best ever made – played up the white man's idea of an Eskimo. The film was *Nanook of the North*, the director a dogged Irish-American called Robert Flaherty who pitched up, in 1920, among a group of Inuit in Port Harrison (now Inukjuak) on the east coast of Hudson Bay in northern Quebec. I saw Flaherty's film for the first time in the final year of primary school (I was eleven), and it opened my eyes to the idea that man and the wilderness were not enemies. It might have been that film that set me on a path of polar investigation. Like Coleridge, Flaherty found his subject in the Arctic, that 'fabulous land where Indians were still Indians', by which he meant compared with semi-assimilated aboriginals further south, who no longer conformed to any idealised white model. He had been trying to make a polar film for years, and had travelled with dogs in northern Ontario and the Hudson Bay region as a kind of geographer-explorer, mostly in the pay of an iron prospector, working closely with Inuit

* White men adopted the Algonquian word 'Eskimo' as a blanket term for all indigenous peoples of the north. The word means *eaters of raw meat*, and it was coined as a term of abuse, as Algonquin and indigenous northerners were enemies. 'Eskimo' refer to themselves as *Inuk*, plural *Inuit*, which signifies, 'true man'. In Inuit legend, all other races are the product of the coupling of a woman and a dog. The Inuktituk word for white man, *qallunaaq*, plural *qallunaat*, literally means 'big eyebrows'. It could have been worse.

and other groups. On the 1920 expedition he used Akeley cameras fitted with gyroscopic tripod heads and lubricated with graphite rather than oil, which froze. For a year, living in an abandoned fur-trader's cabin near Inukjuak, Flaherty filmed the daily life of his neighbours. Difficulties queued up for attention: insufficient daylight, dry snow in the lenses, film that shattered in the cold (that was only the start of it), but Flaherty sailed home to New York with 75,000 feet of film. It turned out that he had a gift for drama and the instincts of an ethnographer. The edited version of his film was and remains a triumph. Who can forget the footage of the hunter Nanook steadying his *umiak* while, from the impossibly tiny hole at the stern, one wife emerges, then another wife, then a series of children of ever-decreasing size, and, finally, the dog?

Nanook's story captured the imagination of the world. At the Capitol Theater in New York the movie grossed $43,000 in its first week. Cinemagoers wallowed in images far from the brittle landscape of Scott Fitzgerald's Charleston-twisting metropolis, and the film's reputation spread to lands where moviegoers had to be told what snow was. *Nanook* catered to the eternal fascination with the noble savage who led his life in a natural paradise untainted by the horrors of civilisation. It also revealed something timeless about the human spirit. A still of the plucky little hunter was used to sell ice cream; the thirty-eight-year-old Flaherty became a household name; in Malay, *nanuk* entered the language as a word for a strong man. The Canadian Eskimo was an international star, leaving the Eveny, the Chukchi and all the other Russian herders out in the cold, unknown in the outside world, as they remain. Of course, the depiction of Inuit life the world swallowed was a romanticisation. Thirty years after *Nanook* first enchanted me, I read new material about Flaherty and his filming. This was another Arctic myth, another case of semi-fictionalisation. In 1923, life expectancy in Arctic Canada was twenty-eight. Two years after the film opened, Allakariallak, the man who played Nanook, died of what was probably TB. (Flaherty, in thrall to his vision and with an eye on

commercial potential, put it about that Allakariallak perished of starvation while hunting caribou.) But nobody below the treeline was interested in that. Much later it emerged that there had been romance all
round. Flaherty had had an affair with Alice 'Maggie' Nujarluktuk, the
woman who played Nyla, one of Nanook's wives, and when he left
the Arctic – never to return – she was pregnant with their son.

As the population of Canada climbed, Arctic interlopers, increasingly,
were settlers from lower latitudes rather than plunderers on a brief
visit to make film or take fur. When Federal authorities brought the
Arctic Islands into the new Canadian Dominion in 1880, they institutionalised the antagonistic relationship between Inuit and everyone
else. Nowhere was this more apparent than in the desperate story of
government-sponsored relocations – desperate in several unforeseen
ways. Josephie Flaherty, the film-maker's son, was among the victims.
He had never met his father.

Three decades after *Nanook*, the Canadian government moved twelve
Inukjuamiut families up to the uninhabited Ellesmere Island 1,500
miles from their home along with an unrelated group of five families
from Pond Inlet (Mitimatalik) on Baffin Island. I changed planes in
Pond Inlet once (from a twelve-seater to a three-seater). It was bleak,
but the second pilot said you didn't know what bleak was until you'd
been to Ellesmere. In 1953 and 1955, the eastern Arctic Inuit started
new lives at Craig Harbour (later Grise Fjord, now also Nusuittuq,
and still Canada's northernmost settlement), and Resolute Bay
(Quasuittuq) on the adjacent Cornwallis Island. The Department of
Northern Affairs and National Resources (as it then was) and the Royal
Canadian Mounted Police (the Mounties of *Boy's Own* legend), citing
a paternalistic motive, had concluded that as some Inuit were starving
due to lack of game, it would be irresponsible not to try to find at
least some of them a better place to live. It was also true that new
settlements would shore up Canadian sovereignty in the face of
Norwegian and other claims to High Arctic islands. In the early fifties

the relocation concept took hold in government circles, even though it was anathema to an Inuit to leave the all-important *nunatuarigapku*, or homeland, imbued as it was with ancestral spirits. Josephie Flaherty had always lived and hunted in the area known to outsiders as The Hunger Coast.

It was not an exclusively Canadian story. Government agents were relocating Arctic peoples across Greenland, Alaska, Russian Lapland and Siberia. Tobias Holzlehner had witnessed the abandoned camps in Chukotka to which pining hunters returned occasionally, in flight from crumbling Soviet new towns. Civil servants like settlements

because they facilitate governance; there is little place within such systems for concepts of emotional topography. Relocations hastened the end of Arctic nomadic life as it had been lived for centuries.

As for the residential schools to which Inuit and other indigenous children were routinely despatched, words almost fail the writer who tries to convey their horror. 'I went to the principal's office and got strapped for using our own language,' a Nisga'a man from British Columbia told the anthropologist Hugh Brody. The Nisga'a had been sent to a school miles from his home when he was eight. 'My heart was beating very fast at that time,' the man recalled of this, the first of many strappings. 'I didn't understand what the meaning of the principal's words were. But a few minutes passed after I got strapped. I didn't want to go back to the classroom. I sat in the hallway until after dinner. I sat there for about two hours. I didn't want anybody to see me cry. So they – sometimes they'd send you into this little room where they, I guess, where you could go and cry, I guess. Very quiet little room ... That's when you get strapped by a strange person in strange surroundings. It's very difficult to grasp what the, what they really wanted you to do.' Whistleblowers vanished. Possessions vanished. Siblings vanished. Minor transgressions earned beatings. Boys and girls were regularly raped. It was a regime of torture. Mary Carpenter, an Inuk from Banks Island, attended a mission school in Aklavik for twelve years, and during that time staff did not allow her to return home, even once. 'I remember when I was six,' she told another writer in 1966, 'there was a girl near me who was so miserable she often wet her bed, so the girl who was boss of the dorm made all the rest of us line up and pee in her bed, then this girl had to sleep in it ...' Tuberculosis was prevalent until after World War II; they called it the White Killer. Doctors sailed north and carted the most serious cases back with them to sanatoria in the south in a vessel known to government officials as the Shakespeare Ship – TB or not TB. Many Inuit died in sanatoria, without anyone with whom they could speak their own language in their last hours. Well-meaning healthcare initiatives regularly fell foul of the law of unintended consequences. In the spring of 1961 a government plane landed at Perry Inlet with an X-ray machine and a posse of nurses. They X-rayed everyone, finding them clear of TB. But the nurses brought the flu virus, and six Perry Inuit died. It is easy to spot the mistakes of an earlier generation. But cultural allegiance blinds us to our own errors, as we march on armed with the same old conviction that we must be right. The ghost in the machine is always invisible.

The fierce sense of self-preservation required for survival meant that Inuit were routinely brutal to one another. There were no noble savages, although there was quite a bit of savagery. It was not some icy utopia. The American visual anthropologist Edmund Carpenter, a deeply sensitive scholar of Inuit culture, left an account of an eight-year-old orphan he came across cowering in a *qarmaaq* in 1951. The unwanted boy was left to sleep on the snow floor rather than on the furs with his foster family. He caught pneumonia and was made to stand all day, terrified, half-frozen and abused, until he died. Myths half-sung in sealskin tents encapsulate the sense of suffering intrinsic to the human condition. *Ayornamut*, the Inuit say; it cannot be otherwise.

According to one critic 'the best known Canadian writer of all time', Farley Mowat remains one of the most compelling white chroniclers of the realities faced by Arctic peoples in the modern age. In 1952 he published *People of the Deer*, a book in which he informed his countrymen of the lamentable circumstances of their northern races. Readers woke up to the predicament of their compatriots, and the awakening unleashed a tidal wave of guilt. A fugleman for the dispossessed, Mowat became an instant and controversial celebrity. The book was to the cause of northern peoples what Rachel Carson's *Silent Spring* was to the environmental movement a decade later.

Mowat was born in Ontario in 1921, spending his teenage years in Saskatchewan, where he kept company with boys from the Dundurn Indian Reserve. He first went to the Arctic aged fifteen with a great-uncle, learning of 'ways of life that were old before ours were begun'. On that journey he saw the multitudinous herd of caribou that migrates through The Barrens, that immense expanse of largely unmapped wilderness extending from the treeline to the Arctic Ocean, and from the Mackenzie River to Hudson Bay. A hunter might sit outside his tent for nine days watching a continuous tide of caribou rush past on either side. The herd became, for Mowat, 'a spiritual talisman', and, instilled with an intangible longing for the Arctic, after serving in World War II he became a biologist of sorts and returned to The Barrens to spend two years with the inland Ihalmiut. Mowat grew familiar with the ghosts and spirits who shared The Barrens with the people and the caribou, among them Kaila, god of weather and sky, Hekenjuk, the sun, and Taktik, the moon. People told him the stories through which they looked back across the void of the years that had passed since their ancestors first trekked into The Barrens. But as trading posts opened, guns had begun to replace bows and spears; first the single-shot loader, then the magazine rifle. When bullets were scarce, a good hunter lined up two caribou for a single shot, so that a bullet going through one animal would also strike a second. Centuries of history had disappeared with the ancient weapons. It was the story of the buffalo on the southern plains, but it was and is close enough in time to see it happening. Mowat watched the Ihalmiut as they waged a war of attrition against extinction. Their lives had always been a chiaroscuro of feast and famine: a healthy hunter could eat fifteen pounds of meat a day in times of plenty, and go without for weeks when he had to. The rivers of tightly packed caribou that surged back and forth across The Barrens had always been, for the Ihalmuit and the forest peoples to the south, a bulwark against starvation. But when the guns came, men lost the old knowledge, and as they became enmeshed in the infamous 'debt system' at the trading posts, they could not afford a single bullet. Even police reports acknowledged that traders had made the plight of Arctic peoples worse by encouraging trapping and discouraging hunting.* 'I was very deeply disturbed', Mowat wrote to the editor of *Atlantic Monthly* in the cover letter to a short story he submitted in 1948, 'by seeing the havoc that can be wreaked on the interior peoples by the passive stupidity of an avowed friend – the white

---

* In addition – and as in Arctic Alaska – people were soon perilously dependent on fur fashions in a southern world of which they knew nothing. When the price of white fox plunged in 1931–2, nearly three-quarters of the children born in one coastal district died of malnutrition or a disease associated with it.

man. It wasn't the sort of picture I expected to find in my own land; it is a damned ugly picture, and rightly or wrongly, I feel impelled to do quite lot of talking about it.'

People of the Deer is a lament for a group the author regarded highly. He had found in the company of the Ihalmiut 'a communization of all material things in the most real and best sense of the word'. Yet the Ihalmiut story, Mowat said, was one of 'disintegration and degradation'. After he left The Barrens in 1949, starvation struck again. Fewer than forty Ihalmiut now lived. Mowat ends his book with an impassioned plea for Arctic peoples, imploring his government to restore food supplies that had been diverted by fisheries and whaling plants, and to curtail the power of commercial interests to hijack economic independence. Many balked at his message, and some objected to his methods ('Fuck the facts!' the author once yelled at a journalist). A restless, buffoonish figure with a beard like an Old Testament prophet, Mowat churned out many books with the flavour of the potboiler (detractors refer to him as Hardly Knowit), but in his old age he produced the remarkable *High Latitudes*, in which he recorded a 10,000-mile odyssey across northern Canada in 1966. Booze and decay had taken hold and, as Mowat saw it, 'almost the entire region was undergoing seismic change' in consequence of a campaign launched in 1957 by the Conservative government of John Diefenbaker to 'enrich the nation by making available the Canadian Arctic's golden cornucopia of minerals, fossil fuels, and other valuable resources'. It was called the Northern Vision, and it was to ensure that the twentieth century would belong to Canada. (It was Prime Minister Diefenbaker's scheme that targeted Iqaluit as First City of the North.) The agonising process of the 'Canadianisation' of the Arctic necessitated (people thought) the integration, if not assimilation, of the peoples who hunted there into the wider Canadian framework. Government policy fell little short of the Soviet insistence, in the twenties, that 'One should simply tell the nomads, "Enough of this wandering around".' 'All us young people are a lost generation,' a young woman told Mowat in 1966. 'Most of us have lost touch with who we used to be, and with our own land . . .'

By the early 1970s, almost all Canadian Inuit were living in prefabricated housing in invented villages with a school, a clinic and a general manager, or *inulirijik* – 'one who fixes up the Inuit'. I saw many settlements of this kind, little changed in a generation. Scheduled air services arrived at about that time, as did the skidoo, or snowmobile. Planners created a new kind of Arctic community for what they called 'refugees from the Stone Age' (the Bone Age would be more accurate). As a result, Inuit began to grasp the way things were done in the white man's world. Their spokespeople started to make representations to the government on the grounds that the relocations had been against their will; that they had not been starving at their old homes – in fact they had suffered at the new ones due to lack of country food; that they had not been allowed to return to their ancestral land, despite promises that they would. Supported by white activists, they said the relocations had taken place solely as a means of asserting Canadian sovereignty, and that Inuit had been used as human flagpoles. Grise Fjord had been (they said) the most northerly gulag in the world, a frozen penal colony. At first, nobody took any notice. But in the more sensitive political climate of the early nineties, descendants of relocated Inuit formalised a compensation claim for Can. $10 million. The Federal government commissioned a blizzard of reports, set up a parliamentary standing committee and established a Royal Commission on Aboriginal Peoples at which Inuit testified in the ballroom of Ottawa's Chateau Laurier. For months, newspapers and broadcast media all over Canada led with the hearings. Two different stories emerged. Police reports from the thirties onwards revealed appalling hardship at Port Harrison, as did Inuit accounts of starvation on The Hunger Coast when people lived on 'nothing but lemmings'. 'You see a small person,' one hunter said at a Commission hearing held not in Ottawa but in Inukjuak itself, 'because during the age when I should have been getting bigger, I was always hungry.' Documents indicated that, rather than wanting to return to their old homes, settlers had applied to have family members travel north to join them. But in 1993, Inuit queued up to say the reverse.

The object of the expensive Royal Commission was reconciliation. The result was the opposite. There could be no reconciliation between two versions of history. Personnel from the Department of Northern

Affairs and the police, the two agencies involved in the relocations, continued to insist that the moves had taken place to safeguard the well-being of the Inuit, and indeed evidence indicated that food scarcity at the new settlements had not been as bad as 'witnesses' suggested.

Declassified material in the National Archives of Canada marked 'Secret' and 'Top Secret' failed to reveal the smoking gun that would prove the human flagpole theory. The relocations were an experiment, those on the government side assented, but not Nazi-style, as others stated during the interminable hearings. It also emerged that many Inuit had changed their stories once the smell of money wafted north. A few independent Inuit-supporters who had been on Ellesmere and Cornwallis Islands during the early fifties had visited the new settlements and expressed satisfaction, among them Bishop Donald B. Marsh, a pro-Inuit Anglican who spoke fluent Inuktituk. (He signed official correspondence 'Donald the Arctic'.) Letters written in Inuktituk syllabics by relocated Inuit at the time contradicted allegations of systemic abuse by police officers. On the other hand, how could a victim have voiced protest? Minutes of Prime Minister Louis St Laurent's 1953 cabinet meetings did reveal sustained unease at the role of the US in the Arctic, and a desire to bolster the Canadian presence. When incompetence emerged, the Department of Northern Affairs and the police blamed one another. And anyway, there had always been cycles of abundance and scarcity, just as there had always been starvation: Inuit sang of it in their myths. I am not convinced that a paternalistic motive was at work in the relocations. The issue of sovereignty must have played a role. But neither was the 'trial' fair. By the time the Commission sat, the liberal public perceived northern indigenous peoples as passive victims of colonial forces. In the years since Flaherty made his film, the dynamics of the Inuit image in the public mind had shifted from blithe spirit to welfare-dependent victim. The notion that white ways threatened native well-being was irreversibly entrenched, and collective white guilt, stoked by the media, conditioned the public to accept revisionist claims of injustices put forward by Inuit activists and their white supporters even if the evidence didn't stack up. Politicians in Ottawa in 1993 would have leapt into the Arctic Ocean rather than take an anti-Inuit stand. The Commission awarded the ten million. The money went to a Heritage Fund for housing, travel, pensions and compensation for the descendants of relocated families.

In 1999 the groundswell of guilt culminated in the creation of a new Canadian Territory owned by the Inuit (it had been a lengthy process; negotiations started in 1976). The Federal government sliced the new administrative region of Nunavut off the east of the Northwest Territories and designated Iqaluit territorial capital. In return for the land, Inuit formally relinquished their right to the other half of the Northwest Territories. In case the point needed reinforcement, the name Nunavut means 'our land'. Extending over two million km², an area five times the size of California, the territory occupies a fifth of Canadian land surface, with between 25,000 and 30,000 citizens – in comparison with thirty-three million Canadians who live in the other four-fifths of the country. Like Chukotka, Nunavut still has fewer than fifty kilometres of road.

The good intentions of liberal Canadians continued to sail on a raft of unintended consequences. Often, issues revolved around food, drink and drugs. Of the three, alcohol enjoyed the highest profile. Most communities of the Canadian north are officially dry, but regulations achieve little beyond the enrichment of those smart enough to smuggle booze and flog it to their neighbours at grotesque prices – either that or the abuse of vanilla essence. When it comes to drugs, traffickers profit from a lively trade funded by institutionalised handouts. When I was in Iqaluit waiting to depart for the field camp *Nunatsiaq News* ran a story about a drugs haul worth $800,000 in Salluit, a community of just 1,200. How, I wondered, could so few largely unemployed people generate such high disposable incomes? It turned out that Salluit had been flooded with cash that month following the Raglan Mine Profit Sharing Agreement, which in June 2007 paid out $4,800 to each Salluit resident. I began to understand that wherever the state intervened in the Canadian Arctic, which was almost everywhere, the mechanics of the system moved in an arbitrary, aimless fashion, like the hands of a clock disconnected from the machinery behind the face.

The battle for the Inuit diet had been fought since traders stimulated economic dependence on the white man by introducing flour, lard and baking powder at the stores, along with tea, all of it available on credit, or in exchange for coloured tokens Inuit received for fox pelts. The abandonment of country food left the Inuit without a major component of both diet and rituals. (A single bowhead produces in excess of 60,000 lbs of meat, and communities celebrate the hunt in the major festival of the indigenous calendar.) The next generation of southerners began to argue that Inuit should stop eating country food altogether, in order to save the whale. 'In support of the decimation of the mammals in the Arctic', they declared, '... the Eskimos and Indians must, in the long run, learn to eat our food if they are ever to become part of our way of life.' Regional authorities introduced quotas, strictly limiting the number of beluga and bowhead which could be hunted.*

That was all well and good (or wasn't), until Inuit began to develop health problems associated with a processed-food diet, and southerners began to feel guilty for the way in which they had imposed religion, money, boarding schools, fixed accommodation, the English language, and pizzas. Tradition, it turned out, was good after all! Civil servants from Health Canada flew north to advise Inuit to stop eating hamburgers and drinking Coke. Then something happened which turned everything on its head. It was one of the most agonising episodes in the baleful saga of relations between the peoples of the circumpolar north and their colleagues from lower latitudes.

In the late 1980s researchers studying the effects, sources and

---

* In 2008 public radio crackled with stories debating the possibility of a collective legal action against Health Canada for 'loss of nutrition' on account of controversially diminished beluga quotas.

pathways of toxic chemicals discovered that because of bioaccumulation (poisons stored in animal fat increasing as they move up the
food chain), and the Arctic's position as a sink (the result of patterns
of long-range transport by air, water currents and river outflow), seal
and whale blubber contained high concentrations of pesticides and
industrial pollutants. When clinicians tested indigenous peoples, the
results sent shock waves through the municipal corridors of Ottawa.
Virtually overnight, Arctic contaminants turned into a crisis for the
Canadian government. This was the Arctic Paradox: the most contaminated people are the ones who live furthest from the polluters. POPs
– persistent organic pollutants – attack the human immune system,
and Inuit children were already experiencing higher than average rates
of infectious diseases (this was only one of the deleterious effects
linked to contaminants). So should Inuit eat less traditional food, or
more? Health workers found themselves in a quandary, stranded
between the need to educate and the risk of frightening people by
driving a wedge of fear between them and the land that sustained
them. Inuktituk lacks the appropriate vocabulary, to start with, so
white speakers and their interpreters facing worried Inuit in community halls had to invent words to describe the contaminants and their
effects. The noun they chose for the toxins in country food, *sukkunartuq*, 'something that destroys or brings about something bad', introduced a note of supernatural mystery, leaving people confused and
fearful. In some cases the distress the information caused was worse
that the potential risks of contaminants, with the result that health
workers dropped the new policy. The situation was a paradigm of
the way in which scientists struggle to send a cohesive message amid
uncertainty, and it marked a new phase in the advance of western
culture into the Arctic, as well as providing a fresh problem for
modern Canada as it tried desperately to do the right thing by its
northern peoples. In the words of Marla Cone, a leading Arctic environmental writer and academic, 'When it comes to protecting Arctic
people from contaminants, no other country has tried so hard,

agonised so much and stumbled so many times as Canada.'* Russia had not agonised at all. It had effectively kicked the Chukchi onto the rubbish heap of history. America had thrown money at the problem. Studies of the mental health of circumpolar peoples in same period reveal serious decline, with increases in depression, suicide and related issues.

The race to extract natural resources continues to dominate the agenda, and the hydrocarbon and mineral potential of the Hudson Bay region has become an investigative industry of its own. Of the 130 companies exploring in Nunavut at the time of my visit, thirty-two were looking for uranium, the rest for gold, diamonds, silver, zinc, nickel, copper, iron ore and sapphires. A gold mine in Nunavut is scheduled to go live in 2010. Canada is a relative newcomer to the murky world of diamond plays but interest in Nunavut quadrupled overnight after a diamond rush in the Northwest Territories in the 1990s following a strike under Point Lake. The little-travelled Barrens, still without year-round access roads, suddenly thrummed with choppers, and in the winter convoy headlights bored into the darkness of the ice roads. Stock market analysts began to compare the Barrens to South Africa, or Botswana. The joke used to go that a typical Canadian-Inuit family consisted of a father, a mother, two children and an anthropologist: now a geologist has replaced the anthropologist. The irony of this latest chapter of the Inuit story is this. Although they have consultation

* Yet in September 2007 Canada was one of only four countries to vote against the UN Declaration on the Rights of Indigenous Peoples. (One hundred and forty-three voted in favour, and eleven abstained; the other three to oppose were the USA, Australia and New Zealand.) Spokespeople said that the Declaration contained elements that were 'fundamentally incompatible with Canada's constitutional framework'. In particular, the Canadian government had problems with Article 19, which appears to require governments to secure the consent of indigenous peoples regarding matters of general public policy, and with Articles 26 and 28, which could allow for the re-opening or repudiation of historically settled land claims.

rights defined in Section 35 of the constitution, and title to 350,000 km², Inuit own mineral rights to only 10 per cent of their land, those rights in Canada normally belonging to the Federal government. So just as circumpolar peoples win a measure of self-government, the Arctic emerges as the last energy frontier and the lower latitudes need it as never before. A warming climate has also stoked the wider debate over sovereignty, as minerals previously locked under ice thaw with lascivious promise. In August 2007, Russian parliamentary deputy and Arctic brave Artur Chilingarov drilled his flag into the bedrock at the North Pole 4 kilometres below the ocean surface. 'The Arctic is Russian,' the bearded one claimed once he resurfaced, 'and we should manifest our presence.'

Meanwhile in Kingston, Jamaica, somnolent bureaucrats woke from a long slumber. They were the mandarins of the International Seabed Authority, an independent body incorporating the UN-hosted Commission of the Limits of the Continental Shelf. The five Arctic nations must lodge a claim with the commission if they wish to prove that their shelves, and therefore their territory, extend beyond the statutory 200-nautical-mile limit. Mr Chilingarov's flag supported the first ever claim, and, bemused at this unexpected turn of events, perspiring commissars told him to go away and produce more data. As for the Canadians: they were prepared to give territory to the Inuit, but they weren't going to let the Russkies have any. Prime Minister Stephen Harper announced plans for a deep-water port on the northern tip of Baffin Island for both military and civilian use, as well as the deployment of six new armed ice-breakers and the opening of an army training centre for cold-weather warfare. The episode provoked a British newspaper to run a story headed, 'Canada Uses Military Might', a candidate for one of the least likely headlines ever to appear in the western media. 'Canada's new government understands', declared Harper, 'that the first principle of Arctic sovereignty is: use it or lose it.' That same month, Denmark too elbowed its way forward, introducing a programme of research aimed at an international legal claim to more

Arctic territory. The mix of panic and confusion implicit in the political grandstanding reflects the unanticipated speed with which the ice is melting. But it also reveals how many issues remain unresolved.

The double engines continued to drone over the Foxe channel, the inky water reflecting little, even in the westering evening sun. The pack ice had gone, but white dots flecked the coasts of the swirled espresso islands. The leaders of the geoscientific mapping project on Southampton Island had chartered the Twin Otter on a resupply mission from Iqaluit. The other three passengers were geologists. I had talked at length to one of them during hours of delay at Iqaluit airport. Doug was a senior scientist from the Canada Geological Survey of Canada, a branch of Natural Resources Canada, not an insignificant government department in a country with more natural resources than it knows what to do with. A rangey Englishman in his sixties who had made Canada his home several decades earlier, Doug had only picked up the trace of an accent. His first field camp in the Arctic had been on the site of a former DEW line station. Like the conflicts before it, the Cold War had hurried Arctic science forward, opening up ice landing strips and stimulating investment in cold-weather technology. Since those heady years, Doug had spent hundreds of months tramping over Arctic tundra looking at rocks. He was phlegmatic about the aesthetic appeal. 'You always think from the aerial photos that it's going to be different and interesting,' he had said as we drank bitter airport coffee from polystyrene cups bearing the image of a polar bear. 'But it never is.'

Shaped like a sea lion sniffing the air, Southampton covers 15,700 mi², or 41,439 km², and with a cluster of smaller islands corks what is in effect Canada's fourth ocean – Hudson Bay and its drain-like appendage James Bay. The earliest known residents of Southampton, the Sadleirmiut, called their island Shugliak, which means puppy suckling (or island-puppy suckling mother-continent). The Sadleirmiut died out at the beginning of the twentieth century when they contracted an unknown disease from some whalers. In the 1920s the Hudson's Bay Company built a fur post on the island and shipped in Aivilimmiut and Uqqurmiut from Baffin Island and elsewhere to service trade. The descendants of these two groups still live in Coral Harbour, the only settlement on Southampton, situated on an inlet on the south coast.

The camp clung to the west bank of the Kirchoffer River. As we approached, a rope of caribou spooled away from the din of the engine: from the air, you could not see the gallop. The Otter bounced hard before ramming itself to a stop, and the four of us climbed down the ladder into sheet rain that fell horizontally. Instead of good old clean snow, sharp air and zero precipitation, one had to contend with mud, fog and drizzle. Washed of all colour except dun, the landscape could not have looked bleaker. 'Told you,' Doug shouted at me over the competing roars of wind and engine. Later he recounted the story of a student who did years of fieldwork in Arctic Canada. 'When I looked through his logs, I used to read SOS a lot. I eventually found out that it stood for Same Old Shit.'

A figure taped in dripping Gore-Tex appeared dragging a banana sledge. Four sodden kitbags sat on it, with our tents in them. There was nothing to be done but put them up. So we battled with water-logged canvas (was this the only camp in the world still deploying actual canvas tents?), arcing poles and semi-freddo soil in driving rain and wind, all four of us casting longing glances at the Otter as it taxied away, leaving us in that wind-blasted, soaking, cold place at the end, as it seemed to us, of the known world.

Much later on that miserable first day, the rain stopped. The sun came out, spangling the river, and I sat on an empty fuel drum watching geologists return from the field in the two camp helicopters. On one side a semi-circle of low hills protected the small camp; along the other, the river ran fast. Camp consisted of twenty Logan tents that had once been white, two lavatory tents positioned at a safe distance, a shower tent deploying a Heath Robinson-Rube Goldberg system of pulleys and buckets to empty an old fuel drum of tepid water over one's head, a gabled cook tent and an identical 'office tent'. The two helicopter pilots each occupied a cabin-sized, standard 'prospector's tent' of the north, their spacious quarters reflecting their elevated role in the mapping project (actually, it reflected the fact that they weren't really part of the team, and that they had to be kept happy, despite the fact that theirs was a rubbish job). Three Inuit 'bear monitors' recruited from Coral Harbour brought the head count to twenty-four, and if we were all in the cook tent together, steam began to rise from the many layers of our garments, as well as an eloquent smell. The bear monitor positions were rotated between any Coral Harbour man who fancied the job. It was a token gesture, as the monitors never really did anything, but they were a friendly presence in camp. The Inuit owned the land, not the geologists, and in effect, the monitors' wages represented blood money. And why not?

Don James was head of the Canada-Nunavut Geoscience Office in Iqaluit and the most senior scientist in camp, as well as an articulate and friendly individual whom everybody liked. I asked him why so much public money was being pumped into mapping an almost empty slab of rock and tundra. 'We're assisting', he said, perching on an oil drum next to me, 'the mineral exploration companies by gathering data so they know where to start looking. The end product of a season of traverses and months of processing work in the labs will be a map of the bedrock of the island on a scale of 1:250,000.' I asked if the team were looking for oil and gas. One was inured to the irony of searching for more hydrocarbons when everyone knew they were contributing to the destruction of the Arctic. It was a kind of Emperor's New Clothes scenario. Nobody mentioned it.

'Basically, yes,' Don continued. A powerful smell of aviation fuel was seeping from the welded seams of the drums. 'The geologists concerned might not have oil and gas in mind, but those using the data later will interpret it for that. We're hopeful that there might be diamonds and base metals here too. Exploration companies analyse the till [glacial deposits] a lot, but they are often not sure where to look, or what to do with the information when they get it. They need start-up data to keep costs within reason. We map, assess, and test rock.'* The Arctic was beginning to shed light on a human capacity for sacrificing the long-term future of the species for the short-term benefits of the individual. We could keep going, throwing the best of ourselves into finding – and burning – more oil, while fully understanding how little time it had taken to destroy an indigenous culture. Climate change suddenly wasn't an abstract issue, because human beings had to solve it – untrustworthy, venal, loveable humans.

Each night before supper, the geologists gathered in the office tent for a group assessment of the day's work. It was called Rock Talk. They went out on foot traverses every day for the whole ten-week season, if the weather let them, and at Rock Talk described what they had observed, passing round lumps for inspection (someone described one rock as 'maple-sugary bronze' – a nice Canadian touch, that), speculating on the rocks' origins and evaluating the implications of what they had found. After Rock Talk, and dinner, people pored over aerial photographs in the office tent while planning the next day's traverses. In the middle section of the tent a bristling bank of charging satellite phones and radios took up one whole canvas wall, each device plugged into the rack of power bars that sucked energy for the eight hours each day that the generator was operational. The students shared a pair of tables in this middle section. The six of them, mostly undergraduates, constituted a distinct group in camp, treated by the senior scientists halfway between slaves and pets. They rotated chores, from washing up to burning trash, according to a pie-chart with revolving arms pinned on the canvas wall.

On the way to one of many traverses, over the chopper headset I heard the others talking about 'the coast', and pointing. I peered out,

* In February 2009, Anglo American acquired fifteen prospecting permits on Southampton Island. The same month, Vale Inco, the nickel and metals division of mining giant Vale, acquired three prospecting permits on the island.

squinting at a jellied sun in a failed attempt to spot any sea, any beach, anywhere where land might conceivably end. Later, I asked Doug about it. 'We were talking about the coast 7,000 years ago,' he said, as if that were a normal activity, which in fact, for them, it was. But in the end we did arrive somewhere recognisably coastal. It was the top of the cliffs of Duke of York Bay, looking out at a crescent-shaped beach. Doug strode around the outcrops brandishing his Brunton compass, eventually homing in on a patch of whaleback rock formations. 'These', he told me, kneeling to scrape off lichen, 'are illustrative of former glacier-covered land. And these' – he pointed at a set of parallel lines etched into the rock – 'are striations.' Formed when debris at the base of flowing glacier ice scours the bedrock, striations reveal the direction in which a glacier moved. 'If we can provide that directional information for mining companies,' Doug continued, 'they have more of an idea of where to look.' So the rocks spoke a language of their own. Unlike the other languages of Nunavut, this one brought development, and wealth, and other things that wreck a landscape.

After an hour logging information, we took off again to pick up two students whom we had dropped off on the slope of a valley earlier. Their role, every day for ten weeks, was to fill large plastic sacks with soil, or till, that had at some point been conveyed by glaciers. They had to dig it up, sieve out the rubble and bag the soil for repatriation to a laboratory in the south where it would be analysed for kimberlite, the crumbly grey-green rock that transports diamonds, and for heavy metal tracers. The work was a kind of rite of passage for prospective geomorphologists, and it was important not to complain about it.

It was 7°C when we gathered for breakfast the next day, and the bugs were dense in the fresh morning air. Ah yes, the bugs. The pages of my notebook tell their own story, encrusted with flattened mosquito and blackfly corpses and splodges of my own blood. The bugs bit us even as we wore jackets with full-head net hoods and peered out at the landscape through a veil of brown mesh. Everyone had his or her own system which created the illusion of small victories in the eternal battle against the mosquitoes. A student had a lamp on her desk in the office tent, and when she switched it on at about nine o'clock at night as the light failed, the insects would arrive in squadrons. When they fell, the student swept them into heaps and kept a chart of nightly kills, adjusting the angle of the lamp head to optimise slaughter. Someone else kept a specimen jar in his parka pocket and raced himself each day to see how fast he could fill it with corpses. A pilot devised an outfit without a single unbattened edge of fabric, thereby exposing not a square millimetre of skin, and he challenged the bugs to get one bite in a twenty-four-hour period. I doused myself in 95 per cent deet, which melted part of my Ziploc sandwich bag and bled black dye out of my notebook cover. But the mosquitoes always won. Their victory was made more bitter (for us) by the knowledge that the female of the Arctic mosquito species, unlike her southern counterparts, does not actually need a blood meal before she can lay eggs. Due to the absence of life in many parts of the Arctic, she has evolved a system of autogenous egg-making using food reserves stored up during the water-borne larva phase. High Arctic blackflies have gone one stage further in the evolutionary plod north. There are no males at all. The lucky females reproduce parthogenically.

We sat on fuel drums swatting mosquitoes, waiting for the choppers' purr as they returned from the first drop-off of the day to pick us up. I was going out on a bedrock traverse with Joyia, the project co-leader, and Joe, another old hand from the Geological Survey of Canada. Joyia was a sanguine figure who looked younger than her thirty-two years. She exuded serenity, perhaps a legacy of her South Indian heritage, and she had welcomed me warmly to camp; we often stood on the tundra and had a talk last thing at night over a final cigarette, if the bugs weren't unduly menacing.

At about ten o'clock we put down a couple of miles to the southwest of camp and started out across a plain surrounded by low hills and glacial outwash deposits. The sky was flawless, and mist rose from a livid blue lake. We had walked a kilometre from our first station and just arrived at our second. It was hot, and our backs had been sweating under the packs. As we began getting out the observational instrumentation, Joyia stiffened. She said, 'Bear'. I tasted again the coffee I had drunk at breakfast. Eight hundred metres away, a polar bear was loping up an escarpment. We had been downwind of him for an hour, so he must have smelt us, and after a few minutes he lifted his snout in the air, and began to circle. Eight hundred metres might seem like a long way to a reader sitting in an armchair. When there is nothing between you and a bear that can outrun you, 800 metres is a very short distance indeed. Joyia cocked the gun, and the three of us loaded the anti-bear firecrackers that allegedly frighten the beasts into running away (an improbable outcome, I always thought). Half the world's polar bears hunt in Nunavut. But only one mattered. We called camp on a sat phone, asking for a pilot to come and get us. The bear completed a quarter circle, and disappeared over a ridge. We kept vigil, and chatted. Joe looked at rocks; it was difficult to say whether his nonchalance was studied. Joyia alternately scanned the horizon with field glasses and fiddled with her Brunton. I tried to think of something to do and failed, my mind fixated on images of my motherless sons. Then we heard the helicopter. It was a good sound. Before we could see the machine, Joyia made radio contact. The pilot had found the bear, and chased him to the other side of a lake. The chopper landed, and dropped off Noah, one of the bear monitors, as he was going to spend the rest of the day with us, increasing our gun quotient. We continued. We had not exactly looked death in the eye as we confronted – with our bare hands – the wrath of Mother Nature in the wilderness, specks of life battling for survival against insuperable odds in the hostile Arctic. But it was going to make a good story at Rock Talk.

Sharp, heavy rain squalls unfurled across the tundra quickly as fog, painting the landscape grey. The horizon dissolved, and the world turned to a miasma of opaque vapour. When the rain cloud rolled back, the distant rocks shone, as though they had been varnished. If that happened in the early morning, our hopes of getting out on a traverse rose, like milk to the boil. But the rain always came back. On my tenth day, it pinned us in camp. The pilots went off to read what they referred to as heli-porn (this turned out to be a stack of magazines called *Vertical*). The scientists retaliated with geo-porn: magazines about hammers, drills, screws and shafts. We mostly hung out in the office tent. Doug put his head out of the door during a lull, withdrew it again, stood up and announced, 'Here's the next bit of crud coming in.' He was the most phlegmatic, as he had so many seasons under his belt: shutdown conditions were an integral part of the Arctic experience. After a week, I had the measure of the weather. The temperature ricocheted between +5°C and, exceptionally, +21. More significantly, the pendulum swung between freezing wind, and warmish calm inhabited by dark billions of mosquitoes. For a few heavenly moments every day, the pendulum looped through the midway point, and there were no bugs, no lacerating wind. But you couldn't really enjoy the interlude, because you knew what was coming next. I can't say it was ruinously grim, because I enjoyed those weeks in camp. But in comparison with the luminous dry air of the Brooks Range in Alaska, say, it was – well, it just wasn't very pleasant on Southampton Island.

The bear monitors Chris and Noah came with us on traverses. Once, when I was with them, we put down next to a pair of rounded, symmetrical hills hunters had named The Buttocks. Throughout the Canadian Arctic one comes across Tit Hills, Shit Brooks, Dog's Balls Lake – you get the picture. Names also record the places where things happened. They do in most languages, but Inuit have no misgivings – thus Pisspot, or Where Robert Broke Wind Loudly. A bull caribou raced up and down behind us, his harem of splay-footed cows and their calves observing from a safe distance. The Buttocks region was noted for its hunting, and Noah and Chris speculated on the high-summer availability of caribou. Noah was thirty-two, and the taller, less confident Chris twenty-eight. Neither had ever been outside Nunavut. They both loved talking about hunting. They kept, cooperatively, nine working dog teams in Coral Harbour, but most people went out on snowmobiles instead of mushing; either that or on ATVs (all-terrain-vehicles, or quad bikes). Noah and Chris shot bearded seal, walrus, narwhal, caribou, hare, tundra swan (the ones with black beaks and feet), snow geese, sandhill cranes, eider duck and king eider. 'My freezer is full of caribou jerky,' said Noah. 'My eldest son loves it.' Everyone's favourite hunt was the polar bear. 'Our community quota for bears', Noah continued, 'used to be sixty-five a year – and we would catch them all, too. Three years ago it was cut to thirty-seven. Our branch of the Hunters' and Trappers' Association picks numbers out of a hat to decide whose turn it is to hunt a bear. When it's my turn, and I get one, I get home and cut it up and make an announcement on the local radio, telling people to come and get some meat for free. In an hour, it's gone. We throw away the neck and most of the innards. The liver's too strong even for the dogs – if they eat it, they go bald. We all have cabins out on the land, and if we have free time we go out there for a few days on the ATVs. My kids love that.' His eight-year-old son had recently shot his first narwhal. But someone stole the tusk.

Buried amid restrictive quotas, alternative food supplies, the economic demands of a family and the blandishments of the Internet, the dream of the Arctic hunter still flickered.

Every year, Noah took his children over to family in North Baffin, driving his snowmobile over the sea ice with a sledge attached. The freeze usually came in time for the caribou hunt on the mainland in the fall, and for the opening of the polar bear season on 1 October. 'But last year it was the end of December before the sea froze,' he told me as we moved along the bank of a creek, following the tap-tap of a geology hammer. 'My grandfather told me he always used to travel over sea ice in the first week of December. Hasn't been possible for a decade.' Close contact with ice meant that modern Inuit were in touch with the repercussions of a changing climate. But they were struggling to stay connected to the value systems of their ancestors. 'Fifty years ago,' Noah told me later as we waited for pick-up at the end of a long day, 'outsiders kicked my grandparents off the land. They never went to school. My parents did, even though the adults in the family said they should be out hunting instead.' It was already frosty, and the air was sharp, but the sky seemed to be sinking into the earth. The only movement in the air was the soft downward drift of microscopic beads of drizzling mist, and, on the low hills, smoky plumes of snow crystals. 'I don't think', Noah continued, 'that education has really worked its way through our collective psyche yet – there are still conflicting values. It's too big a leap for just fifty years. But it will work. I feel we at least have a voice now, and some political power, so we can express our position.'

Despite the hopelessness I observed in many settlements, expressions of self-belief occasionally surfaced. Noah was a keen blogger on an Inuit website called Igloo Talk. I followed this site when I got home. At one point bloggers were posting candidates for the longest word in any Inuit dialect. (Inuktituk is a polysynthetic language in which words are added together to form compounds that are neither verbs nor nouns.) Someone had put forward *Sikusiilarmiutaviniuniwrarpalauqsimammijuillittaungugaluaq*, a useful locution meaning, 'Indeed, they used to say they were from Sikusiilaq originally'. But it didn't win: it was thrashed by *ilinniatulirijijjuakuniiniatugivalausimangikaluamijungalitau*, 'I never thought I would be at the board of education', and by the Kalaallisut word *Nalunaarasuartaatilioqateeraliorfinnialikkersaatiginialikkersaatilillaranatagoorunarsuarooq*, the meaning of which is too complicated for these pages.

After we had returned to camp from The Buttocks, the others got out while I stayed in the chopper, as the pilot was continuing to a pick-up on the west coast. Scattered lakes lay flush, with no lip onto the tundra. As we approached the delta streaming back from the Bay of God's Mercy, it was as if the inanimate rock had dissolved into an eddying flood, for the south-west corner of Southampton Island is one of the world's great waterfowl breeding grounds, a bubbling sea of hundreds of thousands ('perhaps millions', according to Noah) of lesser snow geese, Atlantic brant, oldsquaws, tundra swans and more. It was a spectacle so overwhelming in its magnitude that it was as if a living entity had possessed the land. Whistling swans colonised the tidal flats, still in breeding pairs, while recently hatched snow geese streamed from the wetland tundra towards feeding meadows beneath the limestone plateaux that absorbed the last trickles of the delta. Dark clouds of herring gulls billowed from the coastal cliffs, melding into swarms of plovers, their iridescent breast feathers flashing intermittently, like Morse, as the helicopter wove among the sun's late afternoon rays. Yet by the time the waters froze in October, every bird would be gone. A large biomass and few species distinguish polar ecosystems at both ends of the planet. Extreme environments require huge numbers of individuals in order to secure a viable survival rate (and even so, populations can crash disastrously), and low temperatures inhibit mutation, as opposed to the teeming tropics, where organisms mutate crazily in a riot of moist biodiversity. Neither Darwin nor his brilliant contemporary Alfred Wallace would have had much to go on up there. But I love the ponderous plod of the polar regions, processing in dignified slowness to what might be a better world.

After the west-coast excursion, the fog that follows rain pinned us to the ground for two days in a row. The entire camp repertoire of music started its second cycle over the boom boxes. We listened to the music libraries on everyone's laptop. By the end of the first day, we were listening to Christmas carols. Someone got out a set of electric hair straighteners and we all had a go. The students started a moustache-growing competition (who said Canadians were boring?). Chris appeared offering everyone a cube of *maktaaq*, a delicacy of whale-skin with blubber attached ('Higher in vitamin C than oranges and lemons!'). Noah was desperate to get back home to Coral Harbour. For the hunting? 'No, for the Internet, and Poker Stars.' Conversation turned to horror scenarios of polar lore. The camp in which two senior scientists argued so bitterly over who was in charge that one set out for Ottawa in his snowshoes, returning three days later with a letter confirming his authority. The two bored Russian engineers who went blind drunk – literally – after glugging liquor distilled from brake fluid. Or the Antarctic Soviet station in which, during the long dark night, a man killed a colleague with an ice axe during an argument over a game of chess. (To prevent recurrence, the Soviets banned chess.) To lighten the mood, Joe gave a talk on crustal formations on a Baffin Island batholith, with PowerPoint. I sat through it, but he might as well have been talking Inuktituk.

On the third day we woke yet again to fog, but got ready to go out on our traverses amid the familiar flurry of sandwich-making, waterproofs and rifle checks. An early frost starred the pools alongside the river. The first load left in a chopper at nine, but by ten they were back. Mosquitoes crouched in the lichens, taking a cue from the pallid sun. An hour later, the storm broke. Black clouds uncoiled from the horizon, and the freezing, musky smell of the darkening shores intensified over camp. The low hill behind turned purple, the sky a layered, frowning grey, and the river ran fast. Outside the office tent, Canada and Nunavut flags flapped from their poles with insane gusto. But it didn't close in, so we all went out. One group returned with stories for that night's Rock Talk of a browned circle that was once an Inuit tent ring. Don reckoned it was 5,000 years old. Alongside it lay a flinty limestone tool someone had once used for scraping. Nobody seemed surprised. The past was not a foreign country to them; it was somewhere they visited often.

It turned out that the weather really had cleared. One or two people went for an evening swim in the river, and the bugs came back. I went fishing with Noah, and got two landlocked char which he threw back in, claiming that only the ocean-going variety are worth eating. One of the fish caught on a *saputit*, a stone weir built in shallow water by some ancestral Inuk to catch char, or the sardine-like *angmagiaq* which make an annual spawning run up the inlets. When we walked back, half the camp was in shadow. In the other half, evening sunlight intensified the tundra colours on the ground, deepening the tents to French grey.

'Fuck OFF!' A student hurtled out of his tent like a limbed missile. I knew how he felt. It was impossible to keep the bugs out of the knackered tents, and as the early morning sun warmed the air inside through the canvas, the mosquitoes focused on the fleshy contents of the sleeping bags.

Don was off to Yellowknife on geology business, and I took the chopper with him to Coral Harbour, where he was picking up a commercial flight. John the pilot departed to move some traversing groups, leaving me and Wayne, the helicopter engineer, to spend the afternoon 'in town', where Wayne had to acquire lubricating fluid. The airstrip, built as one of the Second World War staging depots, was 18 kilometres from the settlement, and at first Wayne and I sat in the small terminal building, apparently waiting to see what was going to happen next. A couple of First Air Otters gleamed on the strip. Wayne eventually commandeered transport in the back of a small pick-up which we shared with a pile of plastic chairs, and we set off for Coral Harbour, speeding past the urban dump dating from Coral's origins as a US base and now a registered archaeological site.

'See SNAFU?' shouted Wayne, pointing at pyramids of tyres and wood at the dump.

'Is that an Inuktituk name?' I shouted back.

'No,' yelled Wayne. 'It's from the military phrase, *Situation Normal – All Fucked Up*.' In fact, the distinguishing feature of the whole of Coral was rubbish, as there was a lot of it everywhere, including piles of once-decent timber planks freighted in from hundreds of miles away (possibly thousands) and left to rot in someone's front yard. The harbour itself was almost attractive. Every house and cabin had at least one dog chained outside as well as an all-terrain vehicle and a skidoo parked in the yard. There were two supermarkets, and Wayne selected Northern for the purchase of our picnic lunch. The spacious, windowless aisles pumping out music composed to engender a mood of high-spending relaxation could have been anywhere in the developed world. But fresh food was limited to Californian peaches so withered that it seemed inconceivable anyone would ever buy them, coal-black bananas in a similar condition, shrivelled grapes, mouldy cheese and cartons of milk well past their sell-by date (at least they were half price). There was no bread. Of processed food, there was an abundance. Gloopy cheesy dips in plastic tubs, packets of flavoured sugar crystals for the preparation of fizzy drinks, pot noodles, instant mashed potato, snack-size 'pepperoni' sausages, lurid Miracle Whip, fluorescent candies, and more, much more. It seemed to me that every processed item in the world had made its way to 63°N, up across the latitude lines and the treeline, over the tundra and the pack ice, over the wastes of Hudson Bay, through the indigenous settlements battling for dignity, down into the overheated, lino-floored, echoing corridors of a giant supermarket provisioning the 800 residents of Coral Harbour. And as if that wasn't enough to make them obese, close to the checkouts a worker was unpacking a consignment of LCD screens the size of caribou and marking them with prices that were double or triple those below sixty.

After Wayne had acquired his fluid, we repaired to Leonie's Place, a guesthouse known to him where we were invited to share tea and bannock. Installed in the lounge, we sat on velour sofas among a display of gewgaws, knick-knacks and framed photographs of graduating children and men holding waist-high char, as well as a plasma television. Leonie herself was a large and genial Inuk clad in a spangled top. She must have been about sixty, and she and her husband ran their profitable fifteen-room guesthouse and its adjoining shop for the stream of Federally-funded visitors who serviced the northern communities. Many of her guests, she said, were construction workers and doctors from Winnipeg. At this point, as if the scene were scripted, a guest ambled in. A healer from Pond Inlet, Ootu was a small, owlish man wearing glasses, a grey toothbrush moustache and smartly pressed leisure trousers. He had been flown in by the government to teach public seminars in the art, or was it a science, of healing. With Leonie as translator, I strove to find out about the healing. There was talk of plant roots, then the Church, and then the conversation petered out, resisting my efforts to revive it. Leonie had the idea of turning on the huge television. Images from an amateur DVD revealed a church meeting in Rankin Inlet at which Leonie had preached. Crowds of obese people were laying hands on one another and speaking in tongues (I knew it was tongues, not Inuktituk, because Leonie told me), dabbing their eyes and writhing on the floor. The meeting apparently went on from nine in the morning till six at night. An Inuit quartet from north Quebec sang into microphones and played guitar and drums. 'Four evangelical movements are going strong in the communities around here,' said Leonie, beaming at this outstanding civic achievement and fingering the remote control like a secular rosary. 'Our church in Coral belongs to Glad Tidings. But we all try to get along.'

V

Beautiful Routes to Knowledge

Greenland

In Breughel's *Icarus*, for instance: how everything turns away
Quite leisurely from the disaster; the ploughman may
Have heard the splash, the forsaken cry,
But for him it was not an important failure; the sun shone
As it had to on the white legs disappearing into the green
Water; and the expensive delicate ship that must have seen
Something amazing, a boy falling out of the sky,
Had somewhere to get to and sailed calmly on.

From W.H. Auden,
'Musée des Beaux Arts'

NORTH POLE

100 200 300 400 500 miles
0
0   500 km

Ellesmere
Island

80°N

Uummannaq-
Thule

Baffin
Bay

GREENLAND

Greenland
Sea

Summit
+Station

Ittoqqortoormiit

CANADA

Davis

66°32'N

King Christian
X Land

ARCTIC OCEAN

• Ilulissat

• Kangerlussuaq

Baffin
Island

Arctic Circle

ICELAND

• Reykjavik

Strait

• Tasiilaq
(Angmagssalik)

• Nuuk

NORTH ATLANTIC OCEAN

In 1993, cores pulled from Greenland ice awakened the world to the speed of contemporary climate change. Teams of corers drilled out almost two miles of ice, the end section 110,000 years old. At the time, they were the deepest cores ever recovered. Bella Bergeron was one of the drillers. 'We drilled for four years,' she told me in a Mississippi purr, 'and halfway through, we started realising it was a big deal. Basically, the cores showed the anthropogenic impact on atmospheric composition – a big increase in sulphates, for example, from 1900 onwards, and a leap in nitrates starting in 1955.' She was about the size of my ten-year-old son – an elf – and it was hard to imagine her manhandling a telegraph pole of ice.

Bergeron was back in Greenland working on a shallow-core environmental chemistry project. Cores contain excellent records of slow, orbitally-caused climate change (temperature fluctuations caused by orbital wiggles). They also yield information on specific events that drive the climate system, like volcanic eruptions. The six-strong Summit team were looking at volcanic ash layers to establish what happened to the sulphur deposited after a 1454 eruption on the South Pacific island of Kuwae: the event appeared in the ice at a depth of about 145 metres. They had been slugging it out for three weeks when I arrived. The landscape around their camp was entirely without topographical features: a glittering white plain that thrummed with energy as it batted back the sun's heat. But there is nothing quiet about a coring camp. A generator roared away behind the two drillers, one of whom sat in front of a control console while the other stood in a pit manually manoeuvring a drill into a borehole. It was a 10 cm drill suspended inside an 8 m pole, and it was attached to a motorised pulley. After it had drilled out a 1 m core, the pulley hauled the pole out of the hole and a graduate student wielding a long-handled lavatory plunger prodded the core out onto a table. Another student moved it to another table, sealed it into a tubular polythene bag and packed it into a box. Each individual core had already cost several thousand dollars to extract. 'It's a delicate business,' reported one Greenland corer. 'A nose drip has more of some of the contaminants under examination than many metres of core.'

Condensed in the air as aerosols, the tiny sulphate droplets from volcanic emissions cool the earth by reflecting sunlight back into space, a countervailing force to greenhouse warming. After the 1815 eruption of Indonesia's Mount Tambora, farmers in North America and Europe dubbed the following year, 'the one without a summer', and the crops failed. Over a mug of tea in a tent, the generator off, Bergeron expanded on what her cores might reveal. 'The stuff comes out of the volcano as sulphur,' she began. 'It ends in the ice as sulphate or sulphuric acid, and it's that chemical transformation that interests us. It's the same process as the oxidisation that occurs when you burn coal and get acid rain. We are using the Arctic as a litmus paper for the planet.' Earlier she and I stood alongside the pile of cores. 'Snow that fell during the American Civil War,' she noted, pointing at one plastic tube. 'Battle of Hastings era,' she said as she tapped another.

Bergeron and her co-driller spent the rest of their tea break extolling the new flange-type apparatus at the end of the drill. It had recently replaced the old 'drill dogs', and the drillers were ecstatic. Ice coring is a complex enterprise fraught with operational hazards. I had seen hot-water drillers at work on the West Antarctic ice sheet, and it seemed to me it was the hardest kind of science that there could possibly be, from a practical point of view, that involving extra-planetary travel excepted. It made the celebrated cores from the nineties even more impressive. The project was called GISP-2, which stood for Greenland Ice Sheet Project, and one day forty-one-year-old Bergeron took me to see the original borehole. Topped with a bulbous pole resembling a parking meter, the hole constitutes the most sacred monument in Arctic science. 'We couldn't get accurate dates beyond 110,000 years because of flow distortion,' Bergeron explained as we crunched around the tubular temple to technology, 'but we think we went roughly to 200,000 years.' They worked underground, in a drill dome, and were sprayed constantly with butyl acetate, the chemical used to prevent the borehole from collapsing under the weight of the ice. Worse, a sound system played Pink Floyd. Off shift, the recreational folklore was legendary. It ranged from the Spear-Throwing Olympics to a murky scandal referred to as Gispgate and a diesel-powered sauna built from surplus construction material (it was still there, and I used it). Twenty-eight kilometres to the west, another drill mission, the Danish Greenland Ice Core Project, ran simultaneously with GISP-2. The two teams produced exact replicas of one another's data. It was one of the most fruitful endeavours in the history of science, and it ushered in a new era of palaeoenvironmental investigation.

Over the course of GISP-2, military aircraft flew 83,800 pounds of ice out of Summit. The National Ice Core Lab in Denver stores the unanalysed portions, and anyone who wants a bit is able to go before a panel to make a case. 'We only stopped when we came to silty ice and rock that turned out to be a boulder,' Bergeron concluded. 'And we also analysed that.' Later, when I watched her working, I noticed that when a core was fractured at one end, she took it as a personal failure. 'I perceive the Arctic', she told me, 'as a beautiful route to knowledge.' Admirable: but not if we use the knowledge to bolster our own particular certainties. We carry on as if we live at the end of time, but, as cores graphically reveal, we actually exist in a continuum, and are less important than we care to think. The awareness had survived among the Inuit, people who live peacefully with the certainty of their own cosmic insignificance – not something that could be said of Robert Peary. But the greatest explorers knew it. Failure, Fridtjof Nansen acknowledged, would bring 'only disappointed human hopes, nothing more'.

I had flown to Greenland from Copenhagen, over the ice cap and down to the west coast, where aquamarine pools flecked the rucked glacier ice. I was heading for Kangerlussuaq, but over the tannoy the pilot said we were going to Søndre Strømfjord, the old Danish name. We followed the brown sinews of the fjord deep inland. On decanting into the airport terminal, everyone hurtled into the airside duty-free store. I followed, thinking this must be the route out, into the free open air of Greenland. But no. People were stocking up on vodka.

It was June, and the sky the fabled Arctic blue. It was my first trip back to the north after a winter's hibernation in lower latitudes, and I had beaten the mosquitoes to it. The temperature was 15°C, the air suffused with renascent clarity. I was a guest in Greenland, bizarrely, of the American government. Its National Science Foundation supports a research station at the top of the ice cap, and I had been invited as a writer-in-residence. The Greenland ice sheet is a protagonist in the ongoing drama of climate change: with more ice than anywhere other than Antarctica, the speed of its melt is a critical factor. If the drain proceeds at its current lively rate, thousands of tonnes of fresh water will flood the oceans, reducing salinity, raising sea levels and disrupting currents. I was keen to see the famous ice sheet before it vanished, even if I couldn't see anything happening (it was not yet melting that fast). Ed, whom I had met fourteen years previously in the heavy shop at McMurdo Station, the main US Antarctic base 12,000 miles away, welcomed me warmly outside the terminal building of the Kangerlussuaq airfield. He had fixed a fuel pipe on a stove for me, and we both remembered. Ed was now working on Arctic logistics, and he and his colleagues at 'Kanger' – horrible American abbreviation – organised transit arrangements for Summit Station. We tossed my bags into the back of his pickup and drove to my billet, the promisingly acronymed KISS (Kangerlussuaq International Science Support). On the way, Ed revealed that my flight to Summit had already been delayed for three days.

Back already at the polar waiting game, I settled into KISS, a functional two-storey facility on stilts on a long sloping road among half a dozen other buildings of the same persuasion. My room had a small window, two single beds and the kind of self-assembly wardrobe that could be despatched with one angry slam of its plywood door. Inside the wardrobe, someone had left a set of golf clubs. Almost all the other bedrooms were empty, as it was still early in the season, but a few wanderers prowled the corridors, waiting to depart for their field camp. I found the arrhythmia of constant daylight disorientating, and woke in the middle of my first night in Greenland when a layer of dark nimbostratus split down the middle, pouring sunshine through the curtainless window. Sledge dogs were howling in their pens near the airport perimeter fence, as welcome as the Canadian dogs which serenaded me through my first night in Iqaluit.

Originally a seasonal Inuit hunting and camping ground, Kangerlussuaq had developed as an American airbase in the Second World War. (After the German occupation of Denmark in the spring of 1940, the US military took over responsibility for the defence of Greenland. They were worried that the Germans would use the island as a military staging area, or cannibalise its cryolite, a crucial component in the manufacture of aircraft aluminium.) US Bluie West Eight became a refuelling station for bombers and cargo carriers headed for the fronts: at one point, it soaked up 8,000 personnel. In the fifties, Bluie metamorphosed into a supply base for the four DEW line radar stations in Greenland; this was when the Arctic took on the mantle of imperial frontier. The base closed in 1992. In truth, Kangerlussuaq was still little more than an airfield. There were no roads to other settlements. The community consisted of several dozen houses, a couple of airline office monsters, an arc of warehouses, a post office, a shop and a pizza parlour. Kangerlussuaq was not run down and depressing, like Iqaluit, nor an identikit of southern cities, like Fairbanks. Nor was it an ill-fused coupling of old and new like Anadyr. It was a transit camp in a spectacular setting. The sallow saffron hills of Mount Hassel overlooked the settlement to the north; more mountains loomed to the north-east; and in the south stood the cliffs of Black Ridge, where I hiked every day beyond the Watson River while I waited for my military flight up to Summit.

I saw musk oxen there, on the slopes above the shining eye of Lake Ferguson. They were truffling for lichen and sedge in a small herd, relics of the ice ages blinded by curtains of chocolate guard hair. The broad, flat bosses of their horns, pressing on the brow, swept down and out in a low, wide curve that ended in lethal tips. A polar bear resembles a grizzly and a caribou looks like an impala, but a musk ox only looks like another musk ox. It is the only Arctic mammal that sits out a winter blizzard: besides the ground-length outer hair, the musk ox has a thick wool fleece of exceptional warmth-to-weight ratio. The mountains behind rose in a crescendo, peaks sharp against the sky. The air tasted pure and sharp. Millions of tiny flowers swirled over the foothills: purple saxifrage, white Lapland rosebays and pink willowherb, known to Greenlanders as *niviarsiaq*, 'the young girl'. When I strode around the scarps with their tight carpets of crowberries and fireweed the exhilaration of the moment carried everything before it: *nuannaarpoq*, the Inuit say, *to take extravagant pleasure in being alive*. Late one evening, squinting in buttery light, I sat down on a slope, watching a musk ox downwind rake its horns over a circle of earth that once was a tent ring. Prehistoric immigrants from North America followed musk oxen migration routes down the Greenlandic coasts. One only had to look over the berry-bearing hills with their shards of bone and feather to glimpse a heaped-up past. The musk ox looked at me sceptically. Cliffs dark as pitch frowned towards the Davis Strait, and Canada, and on the other side, far off, the ectoplasmic fog of the ice sheet blurred the horizon. Straight ahead, airstrip and fjord blended into a single caramel agglomeration. The carmine Greenland Air Otters and Cessnas were parked near the terminal, but the hulking National Guard C-131s were out at the western end of the strip. From where I was, they looked like ships coming up the fjord, tail fins rising like a mast.

Erik the Red invented the name *Grøn-Land* after sailing his long-boat from Iceland in 982. He wanted to make the place sound fertile to potential settlers. In fact, crops couldn't be grown anywhere, and still can't, though around the modern capital Nuuk the government subsidises a little sheep farming (the animals must remain inside all winter). As for Erik, when his friends arrived he had to brazen it out. Half of those who had survived the journey went back, some to one of the dismal shipwrecks that darken the sagas. The others persevered, facing the unknown.

Denmark laid claim to Greenland, a landmass fifty times its size, under Christian IV in 1605.* Missionaries, trade monopolies and general attrition notwithstanding, Greenland Inuit experienced less interference than their Canadian neighbours and had not been comprehensively outnumbered like their American ones. Avanersuaq in the north-west actually managed to remain outside Danish control until 1937, making the Inuit there the last group of all the world's Arctic peoples to live as subjects of a nation state. The spirit of another age, however, moved to the far north. In 1979, Greenlanders won Home Rule. Greenlandic Inuktituk staged a revival in schools, though linguistic differences pointed up less tractable cultural divides: numbers in Greenlandic only go up to twelve – after that you use the word for 'many', which is *amerlasoorpassuit*. Six years after Home Rule, following the disappearance of the cod when the ocean cooled, and then the

---

* Denmark was acting within the political framework of the Dano-Norwegian union until 1814, when the latter was dissolved, and Denmark gained total control of Greenland.

arrival of a foreign fishing armada trawling for other species, Greenlandic politicians managed to wrest their country out of the EEC, to which Denmark had been admitted in 1972. While I was in Kangerlussuaq, the main national radio station broadcast a speech by foreign minister Aleqa Hammond in which she explained, 'We do not feel ourselves part of Europe – we are an Arctic people.'

Hammond is an Inuit, like most of the 57,000 Greenlanders, and majority status has allowed her people to march forwards with a greater degree of cultural integrity than the Chukchi and the other Russian herders. Greenlanders have made the leap from subsistence hunting to a developed, technology-dependent society in two generations. On

the radio Hammond went on to express the wish that independence would one day follow Home Rule, a hope shared by most Greenlanders, Danish subsidies amounting to a third of GDP notwithstanding. A midwinter referendum in 2008 moved the country closer to this goal when an overwhelming majority approved a system of increased local control and the replacement of the subsidies with a share of oil revenues, following the Canadian model (hopefully with more success). In one of the many ironies of a warming climate, the loss of ice that has deprived many Greenlanders of traditional hunting grounds may yet usher in foreign investment, and jobs, as newly exposed rock yields up its minerals. A trial dig by Hudson Resources of Vancouver recently unearthed a 2.4 carat diamond at Garnet Lake in west Greenland, prompting the arrival of diamond hunters from all over the world. Exploration companies have also located sources of gold, zinc and lead, and oil multinationals are negotiating licences to explore vast tracts of open water around the coast. The story already had a familiar ring.

From Kangerlussuaq I eventually made it up to Summit with the New York Air National Guard 109th on a ski-equipped C-130 4-prop Hercules. It was a two-hour flight, and once we had crossed the coastal margins the glaciers stretched out like paws. The active faces were blue and creamy, and rolled into vertical folds, curtain-style. Then it was corrugated ice and more green pools until the dark tops of the coastal mountains disappeared below the encircling horizon and we looked out from the plane over hundreds of miles of flat and hypnotising white simmering in refracted sunlight. The pools are moulins. A moulin is a tubular chute that travels all the way to the bedrock at the bottom of the ice sheet and carries the meltwater to the ice edge: it is part of the complex internal plumbing system regulating the volume of the ice cap. The water acts as a lubricant, speeding up the flow of the glacier to the ocean. In an attempt to assess the speed of the flow, in 2008 NATO scientists threw several hundred yellow rubber ducks down a moulin, each stamped with an email address and the offer of a reward in three languages, one of them Inuktituk. In places 3,000 metres thick, Greenland's frozen coating covers 80 per cent of a country four times the size of France. Like the musk ox, Summit ice really is a relic of the last ice age. The ice has survived because its volume sustains its own climate. It reflects light and heat, its elevation keeps it cool, and it is too large to be dented by warm weather systems from the south. Its mass is even likely to protect it from substantial diminution as the climate warms, largely because increased melting at the margins will be offset by a rise in snowfall in the interior.* Glaciers, on the other hand, are more sensitive to climatic shifts. The four-mile-wide Jakobshavn glacier near Ilulissat has doubled its speed in a decade, flowing towards the coast at about 7 kilometres per year and annually discharging in excess of 10 million cubic miles of ice. As flow accelerates, tongues shatter and retreat (the remains of the Jakobshavn tongue retreated more than 6 kilometres between 2000 and 2006). There is nothing new in climate variability. During a medieval warm period, Britain exported wine to France and vintners harvested grapes in southern Norway.

Suddenly – we must have reached 72°N – a handful of tiny buildings and a few dozen orange pyramid tents appeared below. Then we landed, the door of the Hercules opened, engines still thundering, and I stepped out in a tumultuous rush of thin air, diamond dust swirling above my head and the snow crust friable beneath my boots. Camp manager Cathy Young was waiting to meet me, shouting indecipherably against the engines. I piled my gear on a banana sledge and we rode a snowmobile to the Big House, a structure bristling with antennae that resembled a rectangular sputnik. Inside, four long tables and three

* But satellites have revealed a weakening of Greenland's gravity, apparently a result of the loss of tens of thousands of tonnes of ice. So perhaps the ice sheet is vulnerable. NASA specialist Waleed Abdalati recently stated categorically, 'The ice sheet is starting to stir'.

sofas separated the galley at one end from the communications room at the other. A disco ball and lines of cut-out snowflakes dangled over a small library. While I was waiting for Cathy to start the safety briefing, I pulled out a volume. It was a guide to the Bahamas. After the briefing, Cathy and I stood on the Big House deck and watched the C-130 that had brought me making three attempts to take off again. Before the fourth, a crewman got off and fixed up rockets to give it an extra boost. It was called Jet Assisted Take-Off.

Cathy had nine staff, including two cooks and a paramedic. Polar environments attract the type of support staff that used to be called 'alternative', and at Summit you could barely move for ponytails swishing in the Arctic breeze (that was the men: the women favoured Number 2 cuts). The carpenters met for yoga in the recreation tent before going on shift. The Arctic drew in not outsiders but misfits, as I had seen in Alaska: people who wouldn't submit to the routines of the south. It was not a place for the indolent. The ice cap in partic-ular was inimical to life. To manufacture water, Cathy's team collected snow and melted it with heat expelled from the generator shed. Regulations required residents to husband water: one short shower every four days. You could tell how far someone was into the four. The staff lived in the Greenhouse, another stilted sputnik, but the twenty-three scientists and visitors camped in Tent City. The tents were called Arctic Ovens. They were standard double-wall pyramids adapted for the polar regions with a dark lining designed to absorb solar radiation and therefore heat the interior. Over the course of a long first night, I had time to reflect that the name was misleading and the theory flawed (the tent was too big for the radiation to heat it). The temperature subsided to a demoralising -27. I couldn't get warm, I couldn't sleep, and, much the worst thing, I couldn't find a way of reading without my hands freezing. Camp was at 10,500 feet, but the effective pressure altitude was between 12,000 and 13,000 feet, so I also experienced the tight-headed feeling that precedes altitude sickness. I had been guzzling Diamox, a prescription prophylactic; but when I was still, I could hear the beats of my heart as the blood rushed past my ear drums. I lay awake for many hours, convincing myself that I did not need to go to the lavatory (actually a pee-flag), which of course I did, as I had been drinking water by the bucketful in order to stave off altitude sickness. And so the first night passed with many rueful thoughts. I was no longer the carefree young traveller who lived in a knackered text in the -30s for months on end, shampooing my hair in washing-up liquid or not at all, and going home when I felt like it (or not at all).

Crawling out from the Oven each morning like a creature at some key stage of evolution, the first thing I could make out, through the iced-up fringe of my eyelashes, was the opaque glow of Sat Camp huts half a mile away. Named for its satellite status, the small camp was the domain of a multi-institutional, multi-year atmospheric science project led by Jack Dibb from the Climate Change Research Center in New Hampshire. When I first met forty-eight-year-old Dibb he was wearing a T-shirt printed with the legend, *Mall Wart: bringing you cheap plastic crap*. He had a round belly, a short dark ponytail and a grey beard, and when he wasn't doing science he raised alpaca on his New Hampshire farm.

The Sat Camp team had already been working for a month – they had set up in temperatures of -50 in the first weeks of summer light, and were finding the minus tens we were currently enjoying too balmy. A fortnight before I arrived, they had made a discovery. Their instruments had detected bromine oxide and short-lived acidic bromine gases just above the snow, with evidence that the acids were enhanced in the air filling pores in the snow pack. Yes! Dibb and his team were convinced that the bromine could unlock some of the complexities of the photochemical cycling that controls the earth's atmosphere. Now they had to work out where the gases were coming from.

The fifty-foot-long Sat Camp tent became a haven for me, a Greenlandic home where I scribbled in my notebook while members of the team scrutinised columns of data on screens, checked instruments, analysed snow, weighed glass bottles, pored over satellite images, threw around theories and drank sachets of revolting latte tea. Sometimes I was allowed into the meteorological suite to change the ionised water and triethanolamine in the test bottles.

Bromine is a member of the halogen family, a group of highly reactive elements that includes chlorine and iodine. Scientists first realised that halogens play an important role in atmospheric chemistry in the seventies, when Mario Molina and F. Sherwood Rowland deduced that fluorocarbons – halogens with carbon attached – were responsible for the stratospheric ozone hole in the polar regions (a discovery for which they won the Nobel Prize in Chemistry in 1995). Since then, a few small groups of crusading chemists have found that surprisingly small amounts of halogens strongly perturb chemistry in the troposphere (the lowermost part of the atmosphere) as well, but mainly in unusual places like polar sea ice, salt flats in desert regions, and some volcano plumes. A vocal subset of the group suspects that bromine oxide and other halogens may be present at just a few parts per trillion throughout the troposphere. If they are correct, the impact on global ozone and the oxidative capacity (the ability to break pollutants into smaller molecules) of the atmosphere would be significant, and would radically alter understanding of both climate change and pollution.*

A passionate commitment to the secrets locked in halogen particles motivated everyone at Sat Camp, from Dibb and his senior associate Greg Huey, a professor from Georgia Tech who wore Carhartt dungarees with one strap undone in homage to the good old boys of the south, to Katrine Gorham, a Californian graduate student and the only female, and Tony, an undergraduate who attracted accidents. On his first day Tony had gone outside to the lavatory tent (it was strictly for solids only: liquids were deposited directly onto the ice). Mistaking the tent window for the door, he got stuck halfway in, remaining

---

* Basically because none of the current models include widespread halogen chemistry, so even the best must be getting something wrong.

stranded for some minutes with his legs scissoring in the breeze. Compulsive bloggers to a man and woman, Tony's colleagues stampeded outside to get the best shots. They competed both for the most hits on their sites, and for scoops, though the latter was a tough business in a place where little happened, and a trawl through the blogging season revealed reiterated comments about how well the instruments were running and photographs of the thermometer registering -25. An engineer uploaded a fresh photograph of himself each day to illustrate the progression of his beard. My arrival had precipitated a frenzy of mendacious reportage of the 'Famous Writer Visits Sat Camp' variety accompanied by voluminous pastings from Amazon.

Once every three days, Dibb changed his T-shirt. Next up, after Mall Wart, was *Protons have mass? I didn't even know they were Catholic.* A global thinker with a truly speculative mind, Dibb had demigod status at camp despite his logos. He had been working in Greenland for two decades, and explained that non-scientists and non-crew, such as visiting dignitaries, journalists and spare parts like me were known as Useless Eaters. There were many logistical challenges to polar atmospheric research, and the concentrations of gases the team were detecting were crazily small: they were measuring some in parts per trillion. But Jack believed he was onto something. 'In 1998,' he explained over a nalgene flask of black coffee, 'we had a eureka moment. A bunch of us discovered that nitrogen oxide was coming out of the ice. That was the smoking gun. Nitrogen was being photolysed in the snow, kicking off the kind of smog photochemistry we see in LA: it was the first time anyone realised things were going on actually in the snow, rather than stuff just falling on it. Follow-up studies showed that the fast chemistry at Summit was not quite like standard smog chemistry, leading us to wonder if halogens could be playing a role.'

Like the author, the reader perhaps finds the complexities of snow chemistry challenging. But these are the issues under scrutiny in the Arctic today; they are hard for the uninitiated, and not easily reduced to sound bites. Screaming headlines about impending catastrophe and images of orphaned polar bear cubs have not yet solved many problems.

I was out checking the instruments with Dibb one afternoon, struggling to keep up with a lesson in the periodic table, when a wind swept across from the east, whipping up snow crystals which swirled around camp. Dibb hurried back to the tent, me panting in pursuit, and we found everyone in a state of febrile anticipation. It turned out that the crucial bromine discovery earlier in the season had followed a wind event (it was never windy at Sat Camp – there were just 'wind events'), and the team were hoping that this new wind might produce more bromine. But it didn't. 'This makes things more complicated,' said Huey. Every day they came up with new theories and tossed around hypotheses. Their collective and as yet unproved hunch was that the newly detected halogens were mixing down from the troposphere, and were indeed ubiquitous in the global atmosphere. And that could affect lower latitudes, as models show that even very low levels of halogens shake up ozone distributions. 'This one would make us famous, if it's true,' said Dibb. 'But it's going to get more complicated before we understand it. It's a mess. It's a wonderful mess.'

As a guest of the US government in an extreme environment I had endured a round of medicals before my appointment as writer-in-Greenlandic-residence. It was a requirement of the organising institution. The dental regulations alone were too agonising to warrant repetition here. I made fiscal history once again (as I had done many years ago, when I went to the Antarctic) by claiming a syphilis test against tax. TB, Hepatitis B & C, excess cholesterol, mammograms – at least prophylactic surgery had been abandoned. Until a few years ago the Australian Antarctic Programme required winterers to submit to an elective appendectomy. But at Summit I discovered that preventative hazard removal has not vanished entirely from polar medicine; that scientific advance has unintended consequences; and that Americans are sometimes too clever for their own good. Doctors at the National Science Foundation still insist that visitors to Summit have their wisdom teeth removed prior to arrival in Greenland (mine, fortunately, came out years ago). The week after I arrived, a graduate student contracted a jaw infection following the removal of his wisdom teeth prior to deployment. It was his first field trip. Tyler, the Summit paramedic, prescribed antibiotics, but the bacteria failed to respond. Doctors back in America examined the infected area via satellite video link. Tyler installed the patient in his cupboard-sized surgery in the Greenhouse, and began to look haggard himself. He was a remote region specialist, but hardly relished the prospect of lancing an abscess at the back of a throat and securing the wound, especially as the doctors coaching him disagreed on point of entry (one favoured oral entry, the other wanted go in through the cheek on the basis that it would be easier to guide the operation on a screen). On the third day the spreading infection looked as if it might close the patient's wind-pipe. The rest of us waited in the Big House for updates. Early in the evening, we heard there was going to be a medivac. The patient was to be airlifted to Thule Airbase, where the Twelfth Air Command maintained an operating theatre. Cathy chartered a Twin Otter from Nuuk, but when the weather closed in there, it couldn't take off. The patient's face ballooned and he was put on an intravenous drip. Tyler looked hunted. The hours ticked away in the Big House, and the cloud layer came down to meet us. People talked in low tones, waiting for the next volley of static. But at four in the morning the weather began to clear, and at 5.15 the scarlet Greenland Air livery appeared in the pale blue sky. We heard later that a Thule doctor had stabilised the patient, and that he had returned to the US and made a full recovery. But we all knew that the dangerous and ferociously expensive medivac had taken place as a result of an unnecessary procedure that was designed to obviate – a medivac. The bloggers went wild.

An African in Greenland was first published in Paris in 1981, a period in which Lévi-Strauss and exotic ethnology had captured the imagination of French intellectuals. In this book they got two for the price of one, for the first chapters deal with the author's childhood in rural Togo. It was a long journey from Togo to the Arctic Circle.

The author, Tété-Michel Kpomassie, records how as a small child he fell out of a tree while gathering coconuts and, following a purification ceremony by the High Priestess of the Python, was destined to be initiated into her cult. The prospect was so terrifying that he dreamt of escape – to Greenland, which he had read about in a missionary bookshop in Lomé. Greenland was, to the young Kpomassie, the antithesis of the jungle – white, frozen and python-free. When he was sixteen, he took off. The journey to the distant unknown is among the oldest stories ever told, but in his book the self-educated Kpomassie makes it his own. It took him eight years to get to Greenland, working his passage up the west coast of Africa port by port and taking jobs in France and Copenhagen. But his real break came when he found a wealthy mentor in Paris.

In 1965, aged twenty-four and an Arctic greenhorn, Kpomassie arrived at Julianehåb, known to Inuit as Qaqortoq, on the southern nose of Greenland. Even at five feet eleven he towered above the Inuit, and of course, he caused a sensation. The national broadcasting station announced his arrival on the evening news. 'I had started on a voyage of discovery,' he wrote, 'only to find that it was I who was being discovered.' *An African in Greenland* – which I found in a bookshop in Brighton rather then the tropics – did what I most like a travel book to do. It held up a mirror, and the Arctic reflected back the world.

Kpomassie was a man for whom the interior and the exterior life converged, and he recorded his observations and responses with the same artless ingenuity, combining comicality, like all the best writers, with a sense of the sad absurdity of life. As an African, he did not carry the white man's burden, and it would not have occurred to him to romanticise Inuit lives. He describes a baby suffocated by drunken parents; a meal of rabid dog; a group conversation in someone's front room which continued as each person took his or her turn

squatting over the shit bucket. More significantly, he notes more than once 'the crying lack of mutual help in a Greenland village, and the villagers' profound contempt for their poorer countrymen'. But he took everything in his long stride. When his drunken host pissed in his rucksack, soaking all his clothes, he was unperturbed. The Inuit competed to host him, and he immersed himself in their lives, learning both language and customs. Greenlandic society was on the cusp in 1965 – or rather, had just teetered over the edge of the slope that led to westernisation. Qaqortoq already had a cinema, though the projectionist halted the film every ten minutes for a muffled voice to translate the last batch of Danish subtitles into Inuktituk over a tannoy. (There was still no bank in the country, however.) In the populated south the old customs had already vanished. 'Children are sent to school,' Kpomassie observed, 'but are not taught anything about the traditional activities. Even worse, that way of life is disparaged to their faces, although it is their own. When they grow up, they can't even paddle a kayak.' Like many white men before him, Kpomassie relished the Inuit Greenlanders' enthusiasm for casual sex, and for loaning out wives. Until, that is, he found his special girlfriend snuggling up with another. 'I was quite willing to share other men's girls,' he notes, 'but not my own'. Endemic boozing and gonorrhoea eventually lost their appeal. 'Greenland morality was beginning to disgust me,' he writes, and so he made his way up the west coast in search of the pure white land he had read about in the Togolese jungle.

As he moved north, Danes faded away. He wintered in a turf hut entered through a tunnel on all fours. 'The house', he wrote, 'vaguely reminded me of an African mud-walled hut.'* His host was Robert Mattaaq, a destitute paterfamilias who wore trousers tied up with string that he did not take off for the entire winter. Mattaaq had papered the walls of his igloo with pictures torn from magazines; he referred to the collage as his library. Under his supervision Kpomassie drove dog sleds, perched alone in the darkness on a mound of frozen fish, and he came to see the patterns that had governed Inuit life for centuries. Even wife-loaning had a practical significance – if a man was killed hunting, his wife's lover provided for the dead man's family (so there was some mutual help after all). It was a survival mechanism. Above all Kpomassie immersed himself in the spirit world. In the inner life of the Inuit, not only did all living creatures have souls, but so did inanimate objects. Each rock, lamp and sealskin had its *inua*, or owner: 'These *inue* [plural form]', he writes, 'are not exactly souls but manifestations of the strength and vitality of nature.' They are spirits that walk around at night, and talk. For the Inuit, it made their empty land less lonely. Rituals

---

* In fact, it was an *iglu*. Contrary to western belief, an igloo is a traditional, turtle-shaped house made of stone and peat, entered by a tunnel (*katak*) and ventilated by a hole in the ceiling (*qingaq*). Sometimes it was clad in an extra insulating wall of snow blocks (*torssusaq*) which did make it look like our idea of an igloo. The window (*equut*) was made of seal gut. Glass was already available in the sixties, at the Danish trading stores, but it cracked in severe cold.

designed to appease the spirits governed every aspect of life, from hunting to mourning the dead. 'In the eyes of an Eskimo hunter,' marvelled Kpomassie, 'the Arctic world with its vast, frozen expanses, its barren, snowy peaks and great bare plateaux – all that drab, white, lifeless immensity of little interest to an African like me – becomes a living world.'

Alaskan road-builders and pipeline engineers had the opposite relationship with the environment. It was they who invested it with meaning, not the other way round. Once the dismantling of Inuit culture began, there was little chance for those myriad spirits that had been roaming the hunting grounds for two millennia. In Kpomassie's time there were still only three Catholic priests in Greenland, but their Protestant predecessors had effectively turned the entire population into Lutherans. The first pastor, the valiant Norwegian Hans Egede, who arrived in 1721, kick-started mass conversion when he translated 'daily bread' as 'daily seal'.

In the 1950s and 60s the Danish government pursued the now infamous G60 policy. To facilitate administration, civil servants decided to concentrate Greenland's population in the bigger communities of the south, and as a consequence they relocated the occupants of villages with fewer than 500 inhabitants. In larger settlements the Grønlandsk Teknisk Organization bulldozed turf dwellings and replaced them with flimsy wooden houses. At the time of Kpomassie's visit, Robert Mattaaq lived in the only turf home left in Upernavik. Danes were trying to transform the Greenlanders from hunters to fishermen in order to create a commercial fishing industry in the south from which they, the Danes, would profit.

Kpomassie found the Greenland he sought in Mattaaq's turf burrow. Had pack ice not prevented him from travelling further north, he would have discovered whole settlements even more deeply involved in the old ways. Still now, fifty years on, in Siorapaluk, the northernmost natural settlement in the world, a few dozen families survive by fishing for halibut or by hunting seal, narwhal, walrus,

Beautiful Routes to Knowledge

birds and polar bears. Siorapaluk is 500 miles from Avanersuaq and the isolated Uummannaq settlement, called Thule by westerners.* Uummannaq-Thule was one of the oldest indigenous polar sites east of Canada. At about the same time as Kpomassie, another French speaker fetched up: Jean Malaurie, author of *The Last Kings of Thule*, one of the best books ever written about the Arctic. He knew the southern fringes of Greenland well before he left to spend a year in Uummannaq. 'The Arctic in 1950', Malaurie wrote of that area, 'was a living Lascaux in some ways,' its inhabitants 'witnesses to what the postglacial era may have been in Europe and Asia'. In the course of his demographic research the twenty-eight-year-old Malaurie lived in his own igloo, learned to hunt, to speak the dialect of the Inuhuit, the Arctic people of the north-west, and to practise the rituals of the *pulaar*, or social visit. In the winter, certain Inuhuit (and some dogs) suffered *perlerorneq*, a kind of polar hysteria that strikes in the dark months. Everyone was hungry then, and often the only food available was *kiviaq*, a rotted and fermented guillemot dish. 'I pulled a leg,' wrote the gallant Malaurie, 'and the carcass slipped free of the skin and feathers . . . Flesh, heart, coagulated blood, and fat virtually ran into my hand. I let the meat melt slowly in my mouth.' Citing Montaigne, 'Every man calls barbarous that to which he is not accustomed,' he nonetheless drew the line at *oruneq*, a gourmandise of warmed partridge droppings.

---

* It was the Danish-Greenlandic ethnologist and hero Knud Rasmussen who brought the name Thule to Greenland. He founded a trading station next to Uummannaq and named it Thule; soon the toponym was being applied to the region. The name was apparently first bestowed on an unidentified northern land by the Greek geographer and explorer Pythias in the fourth century BC. The notion of a mysterious sub-Arctic Thule has recurred ever since then in myth and magic. Louis XIII's cosmographer described the people of Thule as 'pygmies who hiss like geese'. The name also featured in fantasies of Nordic-German idealised societies in the Weimar Republic. In 1916 Hitler joined the closed organisation *Thule Gesellschaft* as a *gast*, or visiting brother.

The 300-strong community at Uummannaq had not seen wood until 1818, when the English explorer John Ross appeared among them – their first contact with the white man. A Greenlandic Inuk who had gone to Scotland on a whaler and returned home with Ross famously painted the encounter. John Sacheuse's 'First communication with the natives of Prince Regent's Bay' reveals Ross and his second-in-command wearing cocked hats, tailcoats and white gloves and shaking hands with fur-clad figures half their size. Malaurie lived with descendants of the same people in the dying days of their isolation. As he saw it, 'In that pure state, the Inuit built his sense of self only through the group and through being one of the group.' Out harpooning walrus one day, a hunter told him, 'The more I think as an individual, the less I feel I exist.' The Frenchman found the experience deeply uplifting. 'It obliged me,' he wrote, 'to discover in depth my own identity. They [his Inuhuit neighbours] reminded me that a man's life should be a constant challenge that enables him to become what he truly is.'

The Thule airbase where our medivac patient recovered went up in a hurry close to Malaurie's adopted home in 1951, a Cold War bomber installation which cost a reported $800 million. To describe its effect on the hitherto isolated Inuhuit population as seismic would be an understatement. Nobody had consulted or informed the Inuhuit: plans had been kept secret from them. From their igloos, reported Malaurie, who saw it all, they watched a fortress rise. In 1954 the Minister for Greenland, speaking in Copenhagen, announced that the Thule Inuhuit 'had decided' to move 125 miles north to Qaanaaq, on the edge of Murchison Strait.*

Before the bombers came, the north-west of the island had already found a man to express its bleak landscapes in paint. Greenland discovered its Gauguin in Rockwell Kent, the early American modernist who saw his Tahiti in the starlit winters of Igdlorssuit. Kent, or Kinte as he was known to his Greenlandic neighbours, twice spent a year in the north-west of the island, in flight, as he said, from the chaos of 1930s America.

Born in 1882 in Tarrytown Heights, New York, Kent had an appetite for geographical extremes: besides Greenland he painted in Newfoundland, Alaska and Tierra del Fuego. Uncluttered landscapes allowed him to reflect on mystical aspirations. Besides 'the warlike glamour' of the beluga hunt, the challenges of his dog team and the pleasures of the *kaffemik*, or coffee ceremony, Kent wrote of the rewards of Greenland – 'the contentment of merely *being*'. He was an accomplished writer as well as an artist and printmaker, and his Arctic books include *Salamina*, the story of a year spent in the care of his eponymous *kifak*, or housekeeper. The 'moral' of *Salamina*, according to the author, is that 'people don't need gadgets to be happy', a message that would be easy to dismiss as a truism, if only contemporary culture didn't remorselessly reinforce the opposite message. Regretting the inroads made into traditional life by western ideas of progress, especially the introduction of a monetary economy that encouraged Greenlanders to buy unnecessary items, like we do,

---

* Malaurie continued to visit the region, witnessing the old ways growing weaker. Productive life dwindled, as working as a cleaner at the base brought in more cash than hunting. 'The decline of this plurimillennial hunting society', he concluded, 'has derived more from an economic system and from the civil law that sustains it than from any so-called culture shock. It was not Danish culture or Christianity that initially undermined it, but rather the capitalist system of exchange.' But in the late seventies, he saw a measure of Inuit power become a reality.

This is Salamina — apparently hanging out nothing but a clothes pin. If I had given her wash it would have covered up her hands. She always tried to cover them, for they were working hands. This book permits of no concealment

Kent concluded, 'What do men need? Who knows? And anyway, it's too late now.'

Often he camped out on the sea ice to work for days at a stretch. 'In Greenland one discovers, as if for the first time,' he wrote, 'what beauty is. God must forgive me that I tried to paint it.' The stylised portraits that emerged, in the form of woodcuts or pencil drawings, depict broad-chested, heroic figures with high cheekbones and seal-skin *kamiks* that come to a point at the toes. In fact, the graphic art tradition in which Kent worked was quite English – one thinks of Hogarth and Blake. His superb skills as a draftsman had already brought him worldwide fame as a book illustrator. At one stage, he was the most popular artist in America. But post-war abstract expressionism left no room for figurative and landscape compositions. More seriously, Kent's outspoken leftist beliefs led to trouble in the McCarthyist

fifties – there was no 'contentment of merely being' in that bitter landscape – and although he never joined the Communist Party, the State
Department revoked his passport. He went on to ally himself with
Stalinist Russia, won the Lenin Peace Prize, and bequeathed much of
his work to the Pushkin Museum in Leningrad. In 1969 his home in
the Adirondacks was struck by lightning and all his notebooks and
canvases went up in flames. Fortunately, many paintings had already
gone to market. Kent's stock is again high. In 2003 Sotheby's in New
York sold *Blue Day, Greenland*, for $232,000. So perhaps his message
wasn't too late after all.

The Guard came to Greenland from their base in Scotia, New York
for ten-day stretches, and the next flight period was approaching. Jake,
one of the pony-tailed brigade, began grooming the ski-way in his
Caterpillar tractor, trundling up and down for twelve hours, then leaving
the ice to cure for two days before starting again. Discussion dragged
on in the Big House about how we were going to haul the cores out
from their storage chamber under the ice in preparation for their
journey to a laboratory in South Dakota. (Retrograding ice cores was
a notoriously hazardous business, and every ice scientist had a story
about faulty refrigeration, soggy cardboard boxes and a million dollars
down the drain.) People started pulling gear on banana sledges to the
cargo berms on the outskirts of camp. Empty hydrogen cylinders from
Sat Camp stood lashed together, like comrades in a doomed adventure. I started packing up my Oven, as I was leaving with the ice cores.

Those last days were luminous. I hiked the ski-way under blue skies
until a white-out swallowed Tent City in a cosmic gulp, and I was
obliged to follow the flag line home. Ice prairies bent in every direction, edging towards the margins, where they curdled into glaciers and
flowed across the tundra to the ocean. Far from tiring of the intimacy
of camp, I had grown accustomed to it. It seemed normal to be
flossing one's teeth while talking to a stranger, or to drop one's windpants at a pee-flag without checking who was around. A number of

people were leaving with me, and camp life took on a valedictory tone. On the day before the last one, the chemists scheduled their traditional football match, Over 35s (Old Pirates) against Under 35s (Snow Bunnies). It was English football, but, in deference to the altitude, we played four seven-and-a-half-minute segments. Or rather, they did. I was too frightened of falling over. Guile prevailed over fitness and the Pirates triumphed.

The morning of departure, everyone gathered in the Big House waiting for an Off-Deck time from Kangerlussuaq. Cathy chaired a meeting to coordinate activities and allocate jobs. I was on the team getting forty-six cores out of storage. We used a snowmobile to tow out boxes four at a time, loaded thirty-two boxes per pallet, and threw cargo nets over the pallet mountain. Jake appeared on a Cat forklift, and we watched with trepidation as his clumsy machine tottered over ice ridges, a pallet of almost priceless ice cores quivering in the air. It was a painfully gorgeous day. Then the wait – the endless waiting of a polar camp. We sat around the coffee urn listening to Huey, still with one dungaree strap down, retailing the already familiar story of how he once waited three days on account of cross winds. But we did leave that day, with the assistance of rockets. It was a Cold Deck flight, which means that for the benefit of the cores a crewman keeps the temperature well below zero. So the cores stayed frozen. And so did I.

As I shivered in the Oven in high-tech fabrics, sustained by plentiful American provisions, I wondered how the Norse Vikings had survived 450 years in Greenland. And why they had eventually failed, after such remarkable success. The story of the explorer Gino Watkins, another outsider who had challenged the Greenlandic environment, complemented the Norse saga, as taken together, the two raised questions about individual versus collective effort; about adaptation versus reluctance to change; and about a climate that can cool or warm in a slow, devastating trend.

'Exploration is the physical expression of the intellectual passion.' The sentiment of Captain Scott's sledger Apsley Cherry-Garrard lies buried beneath the shoe-eating to which exploration often descends. In Greenland the nobility of discovery fuses with heroism and tragedy in the dashing figure of Gino Watkins, a young Englishman, beloved by his countrymen, who took on the ice sheet and pioneered jet routes across the Atlantic. In the 1920s, politicians and businessmen agreed that commercial air travel held the key to economic development. It was known that the shortest distances between destinations did not follow lines on maps, but traversed the curve of the earth, which meant that the shortest air route between Europe and North America would cross the Greenland ice cap. After refuelling in the Faroe Islands and Iceland, experts argued, planes could stop again at both east and west Greenland before proceeding to Southampton Island, where I had so recently stayed with Noah and the Canadian geologists. Pan Am sent Charles Lindbergh to investigate a northern route. A Swedish pilot made many much publicised attempts to fly to New York via the Arctic. The Canadian government invested in air travel north of sixty. It was the space race of the age, and a major topic of public debate, like climate change today. (History has a killing sense of humour sometimes.) The least known portion of any putative polar route was the east coast of Greenland and the central ice plateau, and much had to be learned of their topography, weather and magnetic effects. Watkins realised that if he could prove that the most difficult section of the Arctic air route was viable, and that passengers and mail could therefore reach Vancouver from London in five days, airline operators would open their wallets to fund exploration. Like Erik the Red, Watkins wanted to make Greenland attractive, not to settlers but to aviation chiefs. Like Kpomassie, Malaurie and Kent he embraced the Inuit (in some cases literally) and lived at least partly off the land, learning to kayak and eating what he hunted. Like Jack Dibb and the corers, he wanted information.

Watkins was one of a group of Britons who came to embody the marriage of intellect and action that characterised exploration in the twenties and thirties. Mallory, Tilman, Shipton – all exemplified the romantic metaphor of travel as a personal quest, a pure and idealistic pursuit that transcended war and economic depression. In addition, in 1920 it was only eight years since Captain Scott perished on the Ross Ice Shelf, and the jingoistic British public were still gasping for polar heroes, especially since ideals had perished by the million in the Great War. Explorers were knights errant who enabled national self-belief, and Watkins was the man for the hour: the perfect pin-up. In 1935 the Prime Minister himself, Stanley Baldwin, ended a warm and fulsome tribute, 'They talk of decadence in this country!' Watkins emerged as a male version of the aviatrixes of the period: Amelia Earhart, Beryl Markham, Amy Johnson, Jean Batten – glamorous figures who hogged the front pages in goggles, flying suits and sexy rubber headdresses.

Watkins grew up in a grand house in London's Belgravia at a time when the battle between horse power and the internal combustion engine was at its most intense, and in Grosvenor Place, close by the Watkins' family home, motorised taxis competed noisily with horse-drawn growler cabs. Like many men of action, as a child (he was born in 1907) Gino was considered sickly; as an adult, also like many explorers, he played hard and worked hard, seeking out what a friend called 'a life bright with contrasts' (who doesn't?). He had beautiful manners and looked the part: there was a touch of the matinee idol about him. He wore his custard-coloured hair parted on the right, had clear blue eyes, a delicate straight nose and a small gap between his front teeth. He was strong and athletic and eager for adventure, and when selected to lead a university expedition while he was at Cambridge, he grasped the opportunity. The team made the first crossing, and the first charts, of Edgeøya off the east coast of the Spitsbergen archipelago 500 miles north of Norway, and Watkins revealed a flare for communication: according to a team-mate he never gave orders, 'it was more Gino's house-party style of leadership'. The fact that the others called him by his first name speaks for itself.

In 1928, before he had ever been to Greenland, Watkins set out on a nine-month exploration of Labrador to map the head waters of the Unknown River. He had put a brilliant proposal to London's Royal Geographical Society, arguing that mapping might lead to the discovery of minerals, or of hydroelectricity to power British wood-pulp plants. The three-man team travelled steerage to St John's in Newfoundland and from there, with a year's stores, continued on a mailboat to Rigolet on the Labrador coast. There they discovered how Labrador had acquired its sinister reputation as an impenetrable wilderness where game was scarce and the remote settlements infested with TB (one of them called his book about the expedition *The Land that God gave Cain*).* The team paddled canoes and portaged for the first 100 miles, battling mosquitoes and eating muskrats. Most of the time they were really hungry, as the hunting was poor. When winter drew in they switched to dog-teams and sledges, struggling through deep, soft snow and sleeping in sodden bags. The scientific results justified the cost of the expedition, and stoked Watkins' reputation when they were published in *The Times*. The Arctic pulled him back: he had an emotional connection with the elemental landscapes of high latitudes. 'It is queer how it gets hold of one,' he reflected. 'The call of the North.' There was something of the poet in him. He now prepared a plan for Greenland, calling his project The British Arctic Air Route Expedition. Dog sledges on the ground and planes in the air: in future years many were to call Watkins' era the golden age of polar exploration. BAARE was Watkins' biggest and most ambitious expedition to date, and in the search for fresh sponsors, he turned to industry. He befriended Augustine Courtauld, youngest son of the textile dynasty. Courtauld was not an intellectual, but he too had

---

* 'The Land God Gave to Cain' was how French navigator Jacques Cartier described the north shore of the Gulf of St Lawrence when he spotted it from his ship in 1534.

a poetic imagination. His mentor was Peter Rodd, the handsome delinquent and adventurer on whom Evelyn Waugh partially based the character Basil Seal. Unlike Watkins, Courtauld looked a mess. He was also courageous and introspective, characteristics upon which he was to draw deeply in the ordeal to come. Watkins took him on, and although Courtauld's father refused to bankroll the expedition, aunts and cousins gave generously. The rackety Prince of Wales (the future Edward VIII) agreed to become President of the Committee: flying was his latest craze, and he had recently bought a Gypsy Moth, characteristically failing to grasp the point that he was not allowed to fly in his own plane or anyone else's. Besides Courtauld, Watkins recruited twelve men including an army doctor and two pilots. The average age was twenty-five. Fifteen years ago I met one of them, by then a sprightly nonagenarian. Alfred 'Steve' Stephenson had joined the expedition as chief surveyor straight from his finals at Cambridge. I went to his home in the New Forest to interview him about another, Antarctic, expedition. But he showed me photographs of Greenland, and reeled off the name of each of the fifty sledge dogs.

Watkins chartered Shackleton's old ship, the 125-ton *Quest*, a sealer with her bow sheathed in greenheart. He purchased two De Havilland Gypsy Moths and a pair of motorboats and travelled to Copenhagen to make arrangements with the Danish government. He signed up an exclusive newspaper deal with *The Times*, explaining his plans to the public in lengthy news columns. 'By the iniquity of Mercator's projection,' he began, 'Greenland seems to hang like an enormous tongue of ice and snow far above the trade routes of the Atlantic ... Actually it droops its pendulous snout straight between England and Canada.' On 6 July 1930, the *Quest* left Gravesend after hoisting the expedition flag, which depicted a polar bear with wings. A man had gone ahead to Jakobshavn in west Greenland to purchase sledge dogs. He took them on to the Faroes, and waited on a lighter till the *Quest* arrived to pick them all up along with a ton of whalemeat. Then it was on to Iceland, and a last bath in the hotel. Approaching Cape Dan in Greenland, Watkins decided to head up the bottle-neck fjord leading to Angmagssalik (now Tasiilaq), the chief settlement on the east coast. After landing thirty miles to the west, the men worked twelve-hour shifts to unload and erect their prefabricated hut on a spur at the foot of Sulusuk (Shark Fin) mountain. The weather was fine, but not the mosquitoes. Besides the hut, they put up two 70-foot wireless masts

and built dog pens and a hangar for the planes, which had been fitted with skis. Crowds of women and children searched through the rubbish for empty baked bean tins with which to sole their boots. The East Greenlanders had had little contact with the outside world, unlike their neighbours in the west whose largely ice-free coast had facilitated trade for two millennia. Every two or three years they journeyed down the coast to Auarket to trade with West Greenlanders, bartering walrus and narwhal ivory for tobacco, rice and tea.

A year after my trip to Summit I returned to Greenland on a Russian ice-breaker and saw for myself the remarkable isolation of the east coast even today. There was no land access to almost a million square kilometres. The ship sailed south alongside King Christian X Land, a lonely, uninhabited coast carved out with intricate fjord systems and deep channels scoured of ice by 140-knot katabatic winds racing off the glaciers. The light was diaphanous, lacquering the high mountains with sucrose sheen, and rockfaces bounced back booms of calving glaciers. It was a landscape of ancient resonance; one could imagine a Viking longship rounding the headland. I had my eldest son Wilf with me. At Ittoqqortoormiit in Scoresbysund, the most isolated settlement in Greenland on the biggest fjord system in the world, he made friends with small boys who ran down to play jumping games on our zodiac boats, the linguistic problem mediated by references to the Manchester United line-up. On Sabine Island in Hochstetter Forland we hiked for three hours across plains so boggy that Wilf sank up to his thighs. He was happy, as he had just found a caterpillar of the Greenland moth. In a typical example of Arctic adaptation, this furry brown larva spends thirteen years growing two centimetres, producing its own antifreeze so it can essentially go into cryogenic suspension every winter. When it turns into a moth, it lives for just one year. In the case of both the caterpillar and the musk ox we had also seen that day, Wilf failed to identify which end was the front and which the back and was obliged to photograph them from two directions.

To facilitate access to the interior, Watkins set up a base fourteen miles from the hut at the top of an icefall that the men christened Buggery Bank (in the official, published account, it appears as Bugbear Bank). He was keen to locate a depression Nansen and two other explorers had reported running across the interior: he hoped that by following such a depression, a plane might be able to fly lower, and more safely. Sledging parties went out to gather weather records, and men went up in the planes to use aerial photography to map. They ate what they killed and picked, from ptarmigan to crowberries, augmented by porridge, treacle, boiled beef and jam from the stores. Watkins favoured simply consuming supplies till they ran out rather than imposing rationing ('If it was worked out by slide rule that each man had 0.65 ounces of jam per day, it seemed to take its flavour away'). The cosy hut had electricity, a proper curtain at the window and live-in Eskimo staff. The kitchen maids had to be reminded to wash up after dinner every single night, as it seemed to them such a waste of time. Watkins had an affinity with native Greenlanders and enjoyed their company as well as appreciating their skills. They, in turn, revered him. Knud Rasmussen, who knew the land and its people as well as any outsider, later wrote that Watkins 'was almost a God to all the Eskimos from Alaska to Angmassalik'. Some of the girls were pretty. Percy Lemon, an army captain, was the first to take an Eskimo mistress. Watkins followed. The lover of F. Spencer Chapman, the ornithologist and ski expert who went on to become one of the most distinguished expeditioners of the era, had a son before the men went home. This kind of behaviour did not suit the public image, and so the public never knew of it. (The moral superiority of the explorer had long been another polar myth.) Some of the team disapproved. Army man and surveyor Martin Lindsay expressed outrage on practical as well as moral grounds: all winter he had a woman climbing over him to get at Watkins in the bunk above.

They established another station actually on the ice sheet. The upward haul through soft snow was hell, the terrain hatched with crevasses. On 10 October, Chapman noted in his diary that he had 'never felt as miserable', and that it was impossible to get any colder. But everyone who made the journey to the station was overawed. 'From now on', wrote Chapman in his diary after leaving Buggery Bank, 'the scene changed to what most of us will carry with us always as the most intense and lasting memory of Greenland . . . No rock or patch of earth nor any living thing broke the monotony of this featureless plain of dead white.' The interior of an ice sheet is the most mesmerising of all polar landscapes. People marooned at southern latitudes think an absence of mountains and valleys renders a landscape monotonous. But in the polar regions the opposite is true. Courtauld referred to 'the ascetic nakedness' of Greenland. The otherworldly emptiness ushers in a transcendent calm that stills the spirit. The coastal landscapes of Greenland reveal the potential of man's symbiosis with nature. The abiotic inland ice is beyond nature.

Up on the ice cap everyone acknowledged the ghostly presence of Nansen, who had died suddenly a month before the expedition left England. It was he, along with five companions, who had made the first crossing of Greenland; according to one polar historian it was 'the first great geographical goal since Stanley settled the sources of the Congo and the Nile eleven years before'. The people of Christiania (now Oslo) lionised their modern-day Viking on his return, thousands crowding the quayside to catch a glimpse of the conquering hero. Oscar II, the king of Sweden-Norway, concluded that Nansen's status was a consequence of 'the ultra-Norwegian mania for a "great man"'. By 1889 Nansen fever had spread beyond the Nordic lands. His double-decker tome recounting the ski trip across Greenland, published simultaneously in English and Norwegian in 1890, brought alpine-style skiing to the attention of the outside world. Nansen was the intellectual giant of polar exploration. Among many other accomplishments he was a founder of neurology. Initially a zoologist, he had gone on to study the central nervous system, discovering that nerve fibres, on entering the spinal cord, bifurcate into ascending and descending branches. They are still known as Nansen's fibres.

Watkins enjoyed similar status in Britain, and modern polar aviators continue to venerate him for what he achieved in Greenland. One of the helicopter pilots at the geology camp on Southampton Island often talked of him, always in reverential tones. But perhaps the laurels should go to Courtauld. When one man was required to stay alone on the ice cap to keep records going during the winter (there was insufficient food for two to stay), it was he who volunteered, arguing that as long as he had enough tobacco, food and books, he would relish his solitude. On 6 December 1930 the others sledged off to the coast leaving him in a double-layered dome-shaped tent entered by a tunnel beneath the snow. It had a chimney-like ventilator, which gave the whole construction the appearance of an upturned umbrella, and a large Union Jack flapping on top. 'There is nothing to complain of,' Courtauld wrote in his diary on his first night alone, 'unless it be the curse of having to go out into the cold wind every three hours to observe the weather.'

Back at the hut, the others settled into a winter routine. They skinned bird specimens, ground rocks for the microscope, repaired sledges and spent a lot of time charging batteries, as others still do everywhere in the inhabited Arctic. The gramophone was popular among both expeditioners and Eskimo, as was the wireless, that symbol of the interwar years, especially when it was able to pick up the BBC – on a good evening, at 9.30 men listened to Big Ben striking midnight. Besides that there were moonlit skiing parties followed by dancing at Eskimo settlements to the light of seal-blubber flares. At the end of February they started catching shark, and a week later dynamited holes in the 4-foot layer of ice over a lake to fish out trout. In the middle of February, a message crackled over the wireless from a German science party 350 miles to the north. The leader, Alfred Wegener, had brilliantly produced the hypothesis of continental drift in which he argued that continents had gradually moved laterally, crashed into one another and partially fragmented (eventually proved correct, continental drift led to the science of plate tectonics). Wegener's peers, all 'fixists' who maintained that continents did not move, reviled his theory, setting earth sciences back fifty years. Now, according to the message from his coastal base, Wegener and an Eskimo assistant had failed to return from Eismitte station, their ice-cap camp. Their colleagues concluded that due to the lateness of the season, Wegener must have decided to sit out winter at Eismitte with two scientists already there. In which case, the party would be running short of food. Could Watkins send supplies? Watkins said he would go as soon as the weather improved. But before it did, they heard from the wireless that two bodies had been found. Wegener and his companion had not remained at Eismitte. They had tried to ski to their coastal base. Down in the British camp, the disaster raised anxieties about Courtauld. Until this point the others had not been unduly worried, though they knew their colleague would be busy shovelling snow. But Watkins had been sending regular wireless despatches back to England, and the Courtauld family had begun to panic. Now, in response both to the German news and to pressure from England, Watkins ordered a relief party to set out earlier than planned. Men spent a month criss-crossing the plateau in a fruitless search for the flag above Courtauld's tent. One concluded that snow must have buried the tent ('And people who are buried are generally dead'). By the middle of March, anxieties took hold. Had fumes from the primus suffocated Courtauld? Or did he walk off to tend the instruments and get lost in a sudden blizzard?

The second relief party left on 21 April. On 5 May, Watkins spotted the top of the ventilator shaft. 'But as we got near,' wrote Chapman, 'we began to have certain misgivings. The whole place had a most extraordinary air of desolation. The large Union Jack we had last seen in December was now a mere fraction of its former size . . . the vast snowdrift submerged the whole tent with its snowhouses and surrounding wall. Was it possible that a man could be alive there?' Courtauld had been alone for 140 days. Watkins approached. He knelt in the snow and shouted down the ventilation pipe. 'August! August!' A sheet of coppery cloud rippled across the sky. From the depths, they heard a voice. 'He looked as if he had stepped straight from Ober-Ammergau,' wrote Chapman when they had dug out their man. Courtauld's hair and beard were knotted and matted, his face was stained with smoke and grime and his cheeks hollow. The instruments outside the tent revealed that over the course of his incarceration the temperature had fallen to -53°C.

Courtauld had read *The Forsyte Saga*, played chess against himself and planned a yachting tour with the help of *Bartholomew's Touring Atlas*. He had drawn up table plans for banquets, and menus, including the wine for each course and the vintages of the port and brandy to be served. He had sipped lemon juice to ward off scurvy, and planned where in Suffolk he was going to buy his house ('Fewest possible servants'). But he had thought he would be relieved in mid-March. He began to go very short indeed. His toenails fell out. He had barely any fuel left, and by Easter he was lying in darkness all the time. 'If it were not for having you to think about as I lie in the dark and can't sleep,' he wrote to his fiancée Mollie Montgomerie, 'life would be intolerable. I wonder what you are doing.'* By mid-April he was smoking tea and eating uncooked pemmican. He could no longer heat the tent. He did not despair: quite the reverse. He wrote of 'the curious growing feeling of security that came to me as time passed . . . while powerless to help myself, some outer Force was in action on my side, and I was not fated to leave my bones on the Greenland ice cap'. To a man who had grown up surrounded by luxury (the Courtauld London town house is now the Dutch Embassy), he coped well. He had eventually trapped himself inside the tent by leaving the spade outside, and he disliked no longer being able to take weather observations (though he estimated wind speed from what he could hear, a practice now known in polar regions as 'taking tent weather'). Extraordinarily, the relief party arrived a few minutes after the primus died.

They had a hard sledge journey back down to the coast, disorientated by sun dogs and other polar mirages. But there was something more peculiar. A Junkers monoplane flew over and dropped supplies they didn't need. This was an inexplicable development – perhaps another as yet undocumented mirage? – until letters that descended with the food revealed that news of Courtauld's disappearance had

---

* Courtauld married Montgomerie. After his death in 1959, she married Rab Butler. She died in 2009, aged 101.

ignited a conflagration of anxiety at home, where newspapers were bored with the Budget and the king's bronchitis.

In spring, with saxifrage and alpine azaleas blooming around the hut and Arctic terns streaming over the fjord, Watkins ordered all hands to learn to kayak. It was the only efficient way to hunt seal. On viewing the ciné film of the expedition the following year at London's Plaza cinema, the *Times* reviewer wrote, 'To see Mr Watkins and his men, strapped into native canoes, turning turtle in the icy water so that they may learn how to right themselves without assistance, struggling with their tents in the teeth of a blizzard, and practically lifting heavy sledges up steep, endless slopes by means of pulleys pegged into the ice is to realise that the Arctic explorer is born, not made.' By the summer, the team had successfully mapped a US-European air route and located positions for fuelling stations. 'It is quite clear that this route will be used,' Watkins wrote. He thought he was doing what was right, like most people, and in the context of air travel, he was. His work mapped the century, in aviation terms. Technology failed to reveal what was going to happen when hundreds of thousands of contrails dissolved in Arctic skies – just as it failed to reveal that the nurses accompanying the X-ray machine brought a killer virus, or that prophylactic tooth extraction would lead to a full-scale evacuation.

When Watkins reached England in November 1931, the king heaped him with medals. Reports of his success were bright spots in newspapers dominated by the ongoing economic chaos that followed Britain's disastrous departure from the Gold Standard in September. Facing strikes, unemployment, shortages and an austerity programme, the public greeted Watkins, their golden-haired hero, with adulation. When Jacopo Bassano painted him, London's National Portrait Gallery hung the picture. Meanwhile, on the ground, cars had won the battle for the streets of London, and horse-drawn cabs had vanished from Grosvenor Place, and from everywhere else. It was air travel that now gripped the public imagination. The First World

War had pushed aerial technology forward, and throughout the twenties flimsy biplanes set the records. Daily flights had been in service between London and Paris for a decade, in 1929 an RAF man made the first non-stop flight from Britain to India in a Fairey long-range monoplane, and, on the day Courtauld emerged from the deep, the first airmail service was on its way from England to Australia. (It took twenty days.) Pan Am offered Watkins £500 in return for a further year of meteorological data. He set about raising the rest of the cash while simultaneously seeking funds to pay off the debts of the last expedition. He was allocated an office on the second floor of the Royal Geographical Society, opposite Hyde Park, and received a telegram there addressed WATKINS EXPLORER ENGLAND. At the BAARE welcome home party he had sat next to a tall, fair-haired pilot called Margaret Graham, and before Watkins left for Greenland again on the Pan Am mission the couple announced their engagement. Margaret travelled with her fiancé to Copenhagen. 'She was wonderful, but it was hell,' Watkins wrote of the moment when she stepped off the pilot boat – the final farewell. 'Ten months seems a long time.'

Watkins' second expedition to Greenland was leaner than the first, and as the four participants could not afford to charter a vessel, they travelled across to Greenland in a Danish government ship. At Angmagssalik news spread that Watkins had come back, and a hundred kayaks and *umiak* raced through the fjords to find him. After three days, the team proceeded 120 miles north-east to a Y-shaped fjord, where Watkins selected a section of dry ground above a river mouth and erected a dome tent. When it was clear there, the skies frosted the mountains in pastel pinks and blues. A 100-foot wall of ice longitudinally streaked with lines of moraine debris stopped the northern head of the western prong of the lake, the debouchement of an active glacier. They began work immediately, preparing weather charts in the areas where Pan Am planned to build fuelling depots. On this trip Watkins intended to keep both men and dogs supplied with seal meat: it had meant more room for surveying equipment on the ship. It was therefore vital to lay in sufficient supplies before the winter set in, so Watkins himself left camp each day at dawn, and after four or five hours, or sometimes six, he returned with a seal.

By late August the film of grease ice that forms before the sea freezes was growing thicker every day: in the polar regions the freeze and thaw of the sea replaces the rise and fall of sap. On the 20th, while his companions skied north to collect data, Watkins set out as usual in his 18-foot kayak to hunt seal. He travelled east towards the middle of the lake. Wisps of mare's tail cirrus pencilled the sky. Seals broke the surface of the water, the ripples spreading into concentric circles, but Watkins waited. Neither he nor the seals heard the faint crack from high above that signalled that hundreds of tonnes of ice were about to calve from the glacier. When the berg fell, the displacement of water created waves twenty feet high. Watkins capsized, losing sight of both kayak and paddle. He got back to his kayak, the harpoon still held in place by a small string of ivory beads. His gloves were tucked under the sealskin line, and the hunting line itself was coiled on the kayak tray. But by that time, Watkins was too numb to haul himself up. He drifted peacefully down the slender lake until his fingers uncurled from their holding on the lashings and he slid quietly into the friendly Arctic waters. He was still only twenty-five. 'That he should be dead now', Courtauld wrote when he heard the news, 'is the worst blow for England that I can think of.'

The blithe spirit of early aviation laid the foundations for what might be the next in a long line of climate catastrophes for humanity. But climate is rarely the only factor. The 5,000-strong Norse Viking colony that flourished for 450 years lit the way to its own demise even as it endured a certain degree of climatic shift. The hopelessly conservative settlers failed to learn to fish or to make skin boats in which to hunt whale or spiral-tusked narwhal like the Inuit with whom they shared the island; they did not even eat fish. A damaged environment was a second factor in the collapse. Norsemen cut down all the alder and willow, because unlike the Inuit they never used blubber for heat and light. As a result, they were always short of fuel, and as they cut turf they were short of land too. The mantra by which they lived – 'We are Europeans!' – meant that they starved in the presence of abundant food resources. They clung to Christian images of home with a tenacity that killed them, using precious wood to roof a church rather than manufacture a fishing rod and fretting about the fashions of the ancestral homeland rather than making friends with the Inuit. When a ship brought news that Viking belles had switched from hair combs with tines on one side only to a double-sided variety, Greenlandic settlers set about procuring up-to-date combs with which to pin up their own blonde hair. A changing climate also played a role in the abrupt failure. Erik the Red established his colony in a period propitious – by Greenlandic standards – for growing hay and pasturing animals. (Our own civilisation, similarly, arose during an anomalously stable interlude.) In about 1300 the climate began to cool and become more variable, heralding the Little Ice Age. Inuit thrived in the colder conditions, as ringed seals were plentiful. Hay was not.

In the words of the brilliant ecological geographer Jared Diamond, 'The environmentally triggered collapse of Viking Greenland and the struggles of Iceland have parallels with the environmentally triggered collapses of Easter Island, Mangareva and the Anasazi, the Maya, and many other pre-industrial societies.' Whole civilisations, especially complex ones like ours, do not fail solely as a result of environmental damage or the failure to manage environmental resources. There are always contributing factors. The Norse colony in Greenland was a small, peripheral one in a fragile environment, wholly different from a twenty-first-century industrialised behemoth. But after listening to Jack Dibb and watching cores slide out of the ice, I wondered if we could dismiss its relevance. The Norse example shows how the deadly nature of a slow trend (cooling, in their case) can be concealed by wide fluctuations, and that in some circumstances failure is the only alternative to adaptation. Remember that Inuit living on the same island as the Norse did not fail. As Diamond concludes, 'Greenland history conveys the message that, even in a harsh environment, collapse isn't inevitable but depends on a society's choices.'*

Halfway through my circumpolar journey it was clear that conditions in the Arctic that could lead to a major climate shift were more significant than I had anticipated, and more directly linked to fossil fuels and greenhouse gases from industry and agriculture. The Norse colonists revealed the human propensity to sacrifice the long-term interests of the species for the short-term gain of the individual. Just as the Arctic shows what we are good at – individual endurance, initiative and dogged investigation as demonstrated by Watkins, Courtauld, Dibb and the corers – it also reveals what we are bad at, which is collective, preventative action. I do not think one could spend long in the Arctic without concluding that the present way of the world is unsustainable and that many chickens will race home to roost in the lifetime of our children, if not in our own. Like the Viking chieftains, we in the developed world might find that we have merely bought ourselves the luxury of being the last to starve. But contrary to what many claim, there is no single most important problem. All environmental challenges are interconnected, including those resulting from an unsustainably swollen population. In the words of James Lovelock, sanest of Cassandras, in some respects the Earth functions as a single organism and regulates itself, and will go on regulating itself with scant regard for humanity. Of course, we are part of the system, and although we will never be able to control it, it would be in our own long-term interests to reduce our impact on it. What we could learn from the

* Recent scholarship suggests the plague back in Norway brought the colony to an end: a reduced population boosted the availability of farming land, so the Greenland Norse went 'home'. So was this the choice they made?

Norse, as Diamond has pointed out, is the necessity of 'long-term planning and willingness to reconsider core values'. These he recognises as 'crucial in tipping outcomes towards success or failure'. In the case of Watkins, a Greenland glacier calved and killed an individual. A changing climate converged and interacted with a range of other factors to kill 5,000 Vikings. Was there a lesson? Or was it just a foreshadowing of what John Updike described as 'the blood-soaked selfishness of a cosmic mayhem'? I was to reflect on this during the months after my Greenland travels. The Arctic was present in our house in London – in maps on the wall, in talk of trips, in the 18-inch Siberian walrus penis bone with which my children regularly brained each other. It was hard not to wonder if they would talk to their children's children about the Arctic as my generation speaks of black-and-white television and tinned spaghetti. That summer I read one of my sons *Gulliver's Travels*. The day after we finished, he asked, out of the blue, 'Which are we, Mummy – the giants or the little people?'

VI

Watchdogs and Whales

Svalbard

Ice across its eye as if
The ice age had begun its heave.

Ted Hughes,
'October Dawn'

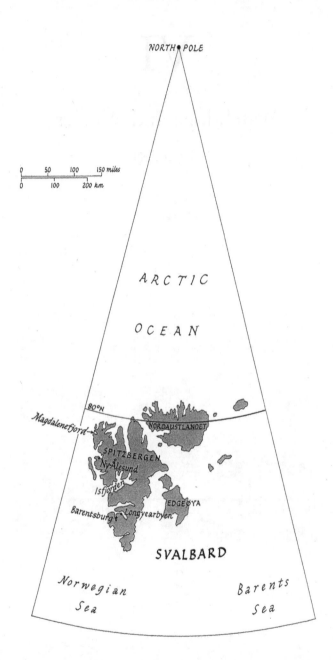

NORTH POLE

0   50   100   150 miles
0   100   200 km

A R C T I C

O C E A N

80°N

Magdalenefjord →

NORDAUSTLANDET

SPITZBERGEN
Ny-Ålesund

Isfjorden

EDGEØYA

Barentsburg → Longyearbyen

SVALBARD

Norwegian
Sea

Barents
Sea

Beyond the window, rain fell more heavily, puddling on the paths and whipping the fjord into millions of minuscule peaks. Geir Wing Gabrielsen took a swallow of instant coffee and watched water pearl off the feathers of a barnacle goose. A boyish fifty-four-year-old with Hollywood teeth, Gabrielsen has worked twenty-eight Svalbard summers, a decade of them testing birds for contaminants; colleagues carry out similar work on bears. Their findings lay at the heart of the agonising confusion over the Inuit diet I had heard so much about in Canada. Sitting out the rain at a research station in Spitsbergen, Gabrielsen had been reflecting on damage still being done by chemicals banned for a generation. The villainous molecules simply refused to go away, flourishing in the marine food chain as if they had never been outlawed at all, another poisonous legacy of well-intentioned technological innovation.

With no indigenous population and no permanent settlers, Spitsbergen and the other islands of the Svalbard archipelago present the biologist with unique opportunities. So remote that migrant Palaeo-Eskimo stopped before they reached it, the Norwegian-owned group lies off the western flank of the Barents Sea, a brisk 500 miles from the tip of Norway proper. Gabrielsen, an animal physiologist at the Norsk Polarinstitutt in Tromsø, was working out of the Ny-Ålesund station in the north-west of Spitsbergen, and we were talking in its mess hall. I had just returned from a hike up a glacier in the course of which I had got so wet and cold that my many garments, exposed now to central heating, were emitting jets of steam. 'Fat', Gabrielsen explained above the quiet sound of a person hissing, 'is more important to Arctic animals than to those of lower latitudes, as they need more energy and insulation. That's why a ringed seal pup is 50 per cent fat at the time of weaning. But pollutants passed up the marine food chain tend to be stored in fat – they are often lipid soluble, but not water soluble. Polar animals are therefore especially exposed to pollutants. We are finding that Svalbard bear cubs absorb high levels of industrial pollutants from fatty maternal milk. The marine food chain passes some of the deadliest of these upwards, so species near or at the top, like bears or glaucous gulls, are the most affected.' Elsewhere in the Arctic, human beings top the food chain. 'Bioaccumulation', Gabrielsen continued, 'occurs when an organism begins to build up contaminants from its environment. And a process of biomagnification happens as chemicals move up the food chain. Here in Svalbard we are seeing the effects of both.'

Polychlorinated biphenyls (PCBs) head a freakish catalogue of marine-borne contaminants. First manufactured in 1929, the nearly indestructible PCBs made ideal coolants, insulators and hydraulic fluids. Although the majority of countries blacklisted them in the seventies, their most baleful components are still hard at work. Researchers list PCBs in a Dirty Dozen, along with DDT (the synthetic pesticide dichlorodiphenyltrichloroethane) and chlordane. Other scientists go further, identifying a Dirty Sixteen. All these legacy contaminants (known as POPs – persistent organic pollutants) are bio-accumulative, toxic and susceptible to long-range transport. In some human populations of the Arctic, POP levels are the highest anywhere on earth, and it is POP toxins that are attacking Inuit infant immune systems in Canada. In addition, new contaminants are constantly joining the squad, and as concentrations of some PCBs decrease, others are increasing. 'We are finding flame retardants in glaucous gulls' eggs,' Gabrielsen went on. Some investigators consider the polybrominated diphenyl ethers (PBDEs) in flame retardants the most troubling toxic chemical in use in the world today. First detected in Arctic wildlife in the mid-1990s, traces of flame retardant have been found in every species tested, including whales, seals and seabirds. A toxicologist at the Norsk Polarinstitutt recently concluded that concentrations in the environment are doubling every five years. Flame retardants have saved lives, like our old friend the X-ray machine. Who knew the cost?

Above the oceans, wind transports many of the same chemicals north (along with plenty of others). The Arctic has become a sink for globally migrating airborne mercury, a heavy-metal neurotoxin released by coal-burning power plants and chemical factories. Unlike many toxic particles, mercury remains in the atmosphere long enough to travel thousands of kilometres, and as a result of high emissions in lower latitudes, wind-driven acid rain currently circulates freely through the Arctic. Acid rain deriving from sulphur and nitrogen oxides is or has been the main issue in transboundary pollution. Outside the window, an arrow of male eider headed towards the eastern mountains through invisible clouds of heavy metals. We both watched them until their outlines dissolved against the snow. 'The Arctic is supposed to be pristine,' Gabrielsen observed ruefully. 'But it's becoming a drain.' Marla Cone, the American environmental writer, recently investigated the effects, sources and pathways of toxic chemicals in the Arctic. 'Never before', she wrote in the conclusion of her revelatory book, *Silent Snow* (the title pays homage to Rachel Carson), 'has the Arctic had to weather so many concurrent pressures from outside forces – contaminants and climate change and modernisation . . . The stresses of the Arctic are supposed to come from the harshness of nature, the brutality of its weather and terrain, not from the careless hand of man.'

The clouds had moved off, exposing periwinkle sky. The tundra sparkled with the clarity that descends after rain. Sensing my gloomy mood, Gabrielsen salvaged a hopeful conclusion from his revelations. 'When I tell my story it is pessimistic, but my government is using what I do – we in Ny-Ålesund are watchdogs and thermometers. I put evidence on the table, and the government takes decisions.'

Centuries before the developed world unleashed the first pesticide in order to develop it that little bit more, the Svalbard archipelago was once the most active whaling ground in the world. In the beginning only Basques knew how to catch big whales, and when they had ransacked their own Bay of Biscay from St Jean de Luz to Santander, they headed north-east. By the end of the sixteenth century others could also wield a handy harpoon and Basques lost the big-whale monopoly – especially after Frisian navigator Willem Barentsz sighted uncharted landfall while searching for a route to the east. Thinking he had found a hitherto unknown region of Greenland, Barentsz named the land *Spits-Bergen*, 'sharp mountains', and continued on his way. But it was not Greenland. Barentsz had made the first confirmed sighting of Svalbard, a 24,300 mi^2 archipelago edging towards polar fast ice.

After he had seen the *spits bergen* (until after the Second World War the name of the archipelago; now the name of its largest island), pack ice swallowed his ship, and Barentsz and his crew were obliged to winter on Novaya Zemlya at 76°N, further than any European before them. Barentsz died in an agony of scurvy on the open boat journey out of there, leaving his colleagues, who struggled down to the White Sea, and rescue, to report their new land to the Delft magistrates. Within two decades of Barentsz' discovery, systematic whaling boomed in Svalbard. One captain said there were so many whales in the fjords that the waters were solid, and ships had to break through them.

In Magdalenefjord, close to the monumental tidewater glaciers on the Gravneset peninsula on the west coast of Albert I Land, the bowheads bled dry. Seventeenth-century Europe was hungry for lantern fuel, soap, and bone for corsets. When news reached the ports that the waters of Magdalenefjord were rich in living tankers agglutinated with blubber, ships raced north in pursuit. When I was there, the bay that had been alive with blood and whaleships was glassy calm, platelets of candled ice murmuring in the shallows. Deposited from the ship in which I was travelling into a zodiac and onto a beach, I was dive-bombed by squadrons of Arctic terns, tail streamers shooting skyward. (Terns migrate between polar summers: Arctic to Antarctic, and back.*) Fending them off, I walked over to the remains of brick try-works where whalers boiled blubber. On the mountainside beyond, a bear stood on its hind legs, bent croupier-style at the waist, peering into a gully.

Once a ship had anchored, its crew spent many hours harpooning before rowing ashore in shallops towing a floating corpse that might

---

* Although few individuals besides terns migrate between the Arctic and the Antarctic, several hundred marine species have made the journey over many generations, drifting on deep currents. A round trip can take a species 1,600 years. Successful transpolar travellers include a snail that spins a net of mucus to catch algae.

be 18 metres long. Bowheads, which swim slowly, are among the easiest whales to harpoon. They do everything slowly, even living: some carry on for two centuries, placing them among the longest-lived known species. In their relationship with ice they are, according to one biologist, 'outliers on the curve of mammalian evolution'. The bowhead exemplifies the Arctic: pushing the boundaries of the biologically possible, it is an outlier on the curve of civilisation itself. Elusive, hyperborean, freighted with mystery, the bowhead, not the polar bear, is the Arctic made flesh. But they were floating gold mines. A medium sized bowhead yielded 20–30 tonnes of oil, as well as hundreds of the horny keratin strings called baleen that hang in its mouth to filter food (they made ideal corset stays). Such a glittering prize justified huge risk. A hundred graves hummocked the unvisited shingle at the back of the beach: no wonder that in the minds of the whalers, the Arctic was a satanic place. An advertisement in a Bristol newspaper recruiting for a voyage in 1757 noted optimistically, 'Only one Man died a natural Death and but two accidental, of 90-odd Men on board our Ships, for Six Voyages running.' Scurvy was so prevalent that a whole mythology grew up around it. Veterans used to say that the disease walked about in human form on Spitsbergen: that of an old woman who was the eldest daughter of King Herod. She and her eleven beautiful sisters appeared to whalers and trappers in foul weather, chanting through eddying snow. Those who survived scurvy might drown when tow ropes tangled round a shallop, or a thrashing bowhead struck out with its tail. In addition, flensing harpooners, according to master whaler William Scoresby, 'not unfrequently fall into the fish's mouth', there to drown in briny saliva. Despite the perils, ships kept coming until whales vanished from the fjords, hunted without pity, like the walrus. Once the business moved out to the open sea, Svalbard lost its pre-eminence. The decline of whaling meant that nobody felt the urge to claim Svalbard – and this in an age when nations were fighting over every useless atoll in the Pacific.

Russian fox and bear trappers arrived on the tail of the whalers.

Between about 1720 and 1740, a cottage industry arose round the coasts. Svalbard was perceived as an extension of the Russian Arctic, and the largest camps were permanent, men going up one year relieved by a fresh crew the next. The majority of Russians were Pomors, a seafaring people from the White Sea coast whose homeland straddled the Arctic Circle. Usually despatched under the auspices of a trading company or private individual, or, as demand declined, by the powerful Solovki monastery, each sailor was paid with a share of the bag – if he ever got home to claim it. Pomors were often tempted to winter, risking everything for richer pickings, as bears are easier to kill on land (in summer they prefer to hunt on retreating sea ice), and Arctic foxes more valuable in their cold-weather coats. Others were forced to winter after becoming separated from their ships. The chronicles of those years are rich in stories of winterers dying of scurvy or trichinosis or some other unspecified disease, the deep-frozen corpse of the last survivor discovered the following summer in the foetal position on the floor of his frigid hut, scratchy pages of a diary on the table and the graves of companions outside in the permafrost.

A ship that went down in 1743 left four Pomors from Mezen stranded on Edgeøya, Svalbard's third largest island (and the one the young Gino Watkins was to map). Starting off with little more than twenty pounds of flour, an axe, knife, tinderbox, musket and gunpowder, they established themselves in a hut abandoned by earlier trappers, lit clay lanterns and ate reindeer, fox and bear (lying on a major maritime migration route, Edgeøya has one of world's densest populations of polar bears). One man died. The other three lived in the kippered hut for six years, until a rescue ship finally appeared. Their record has never been equalled in the Arctic. Perhaps stranger still, it turned out that those long years had not extinguished the lure of the wilderness. One of the three survivors returned to winter on Novaya Zemlya. But his luck had run out. That time he died, together with his two sons, who had gone with him.

In the nineteenth century, trippers glided by on pleasure yachts.

Léonie d'Aunet almost fainted clean away in the Magdalenefjord grave-yard, though at least she turned the experience to her advantage by publishing a book about the trip which made her famous in Paris. Called *Voyage d'une jeune femme au Spitzberg* (Travels of a Young Woman in Spitsbergen*)*, it recounted, in whimsical prose, a sailing trip in 1853 that lasted almost a year. D'Aunet was travelling on a pre-marital honeymoon with her fiancé François-Auguste Biard, a painter of note twenty years her senior. She was enchanted by Magdalenefjord (*'cela halucine l'esprit'*) but took fright when obliged to pick her way through a carpet of seal bones on the beach ('long fleshless fingers like those of a human hand'). Continuing to the human graves, she found many in the process of disgorging semi-decayed contents. It was, she wrote, *'une cimetière sans epitaphes, sans monuments, sans fleurs, sans souvenirs, sans larmes, sans regrets, sans prières . . . une solitude terrible'*. The imagination that can wrest prose like that from a Svalbardian beach is primed for grand-scale romance. Léonie went home to a passionate affair with Victor Hugo, in 1843 regarded as the world's greatest living writer.*

Deep in the sheltered waters of Kongsfjord, a posse of Norwegian sailors tossed cables onto the Ny-Ålesund jetty. Nick Cox was waiting for me on the wharf wearing brown galoshes and holding the long metal handle of a cargo cart. Nick spent every summer in the Arctic, like a tern. He was in charge of the British hut at the multinational Ny-Ålesund research station, and I had met him earlier in the year at his office in Cambridge. An intensely practical figure who started his polar career as an Antarctic boatman, Nick's role was to facilitate

---

* Biard was suspicious, and the rotter hired a private detective. One day a posse of policemen surprised the naked lovers in the bedroom and duly arrested them. Léonie was carted off to Saint-Lazare prison, but as a *pair de France* (a peer), Hugo was immune from prosecution. He began writing a novel called 'Jean Tréjean', about a convict and an abandoned woman. It was a plea for natural justice, the title soon changing to 'Les Misères', and subsequently *Les Misérables*.

science. His short Cumbrian physique was well adapted to trekking over glaciers to help a meteorologist who couldn't fix the transformer on his weather station. One had the impression that there was no Arctic crisis he could not handle, and if other groups at Ny-Ålesund had concerns about personnel in the field when the weather turned foul, they invariably turned to Nick to coordinate the rescue. He was a martinet when it came to safety and procedure, but loved a laugh, and never stopped talking. I came to cherish Nick's company. He was immensely considerate to his greenhorn charge and did everything he could to ensure I saw as much as possible while I was at Ny-Ålesund. Having spent all or part of the year in the Arctic or Antarctic for thirty-four years, he loved the polar regions with affecting intensity. In Cambridge he was like a fish thrown out of the water onto the muddy bank.

We pulled the cart loaded with my bags up from the wharf and over an incline. A man was cycling round the perimeter fence of a dog yard, pedalling furiously to keep up with a husky on a rope. Founded as a coal mine, since 1963 Ny-Ålesund has functioned as a scientific station owned and managed by the Norwegian King's Bay Company. Ten nations maintain a permanent presence, the British one consisting of a stilted prefab with seven bedrooms, a suite of labs, a large storage facility and a communal lounge. Once we were inside it, Nick showed off the washing machine. It was a long way from bivouacs in a blizzard. Installed in my room, I watched a family of Arctic foxes outside the window. A vixen and six kits had set up home under the Dutch cabin. The vixen was watching out for the return of her food-bearing mate, while the stub-tailed kits rolled in a single furry ball. The tall Dutch scientists going in and out of the hut above the foxes stooped to vanish through the tiny door like characters in Alice in Arctic Wonderland, abandoning yellow clogs to the fox kits. Beyond the Dutch hut, the fjord narrowed towards a glacier blockade: Kongsbreen and Kongsvegen, with the distinctive Tre Kroner peaks, named after Norway, Denmark and Sweden, rising behind. Up in the northern edges of the settlement, a pair of stone lions flanked the entrance to Yellow River, the Chinese Base otherwise distinguished by a plastic azalea in each window and a faulty drain that leaked sewage onto the permafrost in a yellow Yangtze of its own. In their steady pursuit of world domination the mandarins of Shanghai and Beijing had not overlooked the Arctic. Their scientists were bent over laboratory benches inside Yellow River measuring the long-range repercussions of the coal-fired power stations that were going live across China that year at the rate of one per day.

The season was not yet fully underway, and there were only two other residents in the British hut. Both were crustacean biologists from the University of Bangor. They were planning on dredging amphipods from the fjord and measuring their metabolism. The shrimp-like crustaceans are at the bottom of the food web (I soon learned), and population variation has a significant impact on their many predators. There was a lot of baffling talk about taking a molecular approach to link genotype to phenotypic plasticity, but on the whole I found it hard to get interested in the amphipods, a tankful of which were already paddling innocently in the lab. Half of the project cargo had failed to arrive, an occupational hazard in the polar regions, and the other half wasn't working (likewise). Nia, the more senior of the biologists, remained sanguine, but Sam, her PhD student, was close to nervous collapse. He did not know – fortunately – that science cargo sometimes arrives at Ny-Ålesund a full year late.

The Norwegian King's Bay Company ran the research station with a light touch and, like everything Scandinavian, its influence was civilised and benign. The self-service mess hall, which catered for a summer population of 130, occupied a purpose-built facility with windows on three sides. When Nick, the two unhappy biologists and I arrived for breakfast on the first morning, our Norwegian neighbours were already washing down their *Geitost* cheese with spoonfuls of cod liver oil from a glass jeroboam in pole position on the serving counter. After the meal, Nick gave me a tour of the mess complex, at every stop launching into a lengthy anecdote that did not end until a fresh one took over the baton. In one wing, he revealed the Byzantine waste disposal system. It represented a new art form, but even these complexities could not compete with the arrangements I remembered with agonising clarity from McMurdo station in the Antarctic. There a maniacally ecological management had come up with so many different categories of waste that I once stood in front of a row of bins having a breakdown as I attempted to dispose of a Pringles tube. The lid had to go in Plastic, the paper wrapped round the cardboard tube had to be peeled off and put in Printed Paper, the tube itself went in Thin Cardboard, the foil inner lid in Foil, the metal rim at the bottom in Light Metal, and the remaining Pringles, accidentally contaminated with Avgas, in Food Waste. The polar regions, invested now with sacerdotal status in the race to save the planet, foreshadowed waste-disposal governance coming soon to a kitchen near you.

Before I was allowed to walk beyond camp alone, I was required to take a rifle course. This, Nick assured me, would save me from the jaws of one of the many polar bears in the vicinity. (Not them again.) One end of a gun was much the same to me as the other, and I had little appetite for learning the difference; but the alternative, being crushed to eternal oblivion between the tobacco-yellow henges of a polar bear, attracted me even less, especially after my near-death bear experience on Southampton Island. The first component of the course consisted of two hours in a seminar room in the new marine biology lab. The teacher, Terje, was a ruddy-faced Norwegian in his twenties, and I was his only pupil. Sun poured through plate glass windows, varnishing the long blue desks, and in the room next door, vast marine specimen chest freezers hummed in unison. Terje began with the demoralising news that in Svalbard the average male bear weighs in at between 400 and 600kg (though it could be worse: elsewhere they swell to 1,000kg). 'He can run at 40 kilometres an hour, which is 11 metres per second,' Terje continued with pride, as if he had trained the beasts personally, 'and unlike a tiger, he will never try to hide.' It was also disheartening to learn that bears are moody, wayward and unpredictable. The most dangerous ones are the two-year-olds who have just left their mothers, as they are inexpert hunters, and hungry. 'So you might want to avoid those,' said Terje. Old and sick bears are also best avoided, as they can no longer hunt. 'If he's smacking his teeth' (Terje demonstrated), 'he is already annoyed, so get ready.' Spring was apparently a risky time to travel as mothers protect new cubs by attacking. So it was important to bugger off if you saw any cubs at all. Nor was summer a season for relaxation. Here on the ice-free side of Spitsbergen, bears might be hungry due to a lack of pack ice on which to hunt. Terje illustrated each of his categories with examples of maulings somewhere in the archipelago, acting out the story by dropping on all fours and straining the hinge of his jaws. In 1977 – this was just one from an extensive repertoire of episodes – a group of Austrian campers at Magdalenefjord heard strange noises outside the tent. When one of them stuck his head out, a bear smashed it with a front paw and dragged the man to the sea ice, where, in full view of the other campers, it ate everything except a section of jaw and a belt buckle. (Terje removed his belt and swung it in the air.) I looked out of the window, certain that I would see a bear speeding towards the glacier with Nick dangling from his mouth, still talking. Finally Terje launched into a story about a bear headbutting the door of a trapper's hut. The scientist inside had a rifle, but it was on the other side of the hut – the bear, who had bashed the door open, was between him and his gun. 'But it was all right!' said Terje, triumphant for once. 'The door was too small for the bear to get his shoulders through. He could only fit his head and neck in.' Silence hung heavy in the lab as I digested this information. 'Surely,' I asked, 'the head is the business end?' 'The scientist hit the bear on the nose with a frying pan,' Terje concluded, brandishing an imaginary utensil.

For the next stage Terje drove us up to the rifle range on one of the low hills behind camp. A cover of grey cloud had moved in, masking the sun. The air was like something paralysed. I struggled through the bullet routines before letting off a succession of rounds at a target, unnerving explosions in unmoving silence. We agreed I was a useless shot, and that was that. The first drops of rain fell, smacking the stones on the hills. Terje took the opportunity to tell me I was not, according to Svalbard legislation, supposed to shoot until the bear was 10 metres away. Ten metres was the length of the zodiacs in which we had been zipping around the fjords. 'But I can't even load in that time,' I whined. 'It is the *sysselman*'s [governor's] rule,' intoned Terje in his metronomically measured English. 'If you shoot a bear, you must inform his office, and an investigative team arrive.' I had the impression that if the bear ate me before I could uncock my rifle, it would be shrugged shoulders all round among the *sysselman*'s filing cabinets.

Our neighbour Maarten Loonen was a familiar figure in Ny-Ålesund. One of the tall inhabitants of the Dutch house, and the chief Dutch scientist on station, he was based at the University of Groningen and had been studying the fluctuating population of barnacle geese in Kongsfjord since 1990. In 1943 fewer than 300 roosted on the archipelago; at the time of my visit, the population had swelled to 25,000. Extreme weather stresses Arctic ecosystems (and they are relatively young: ten or twenty thousand years, following the retreat of the ice sheets, compared with millions in the tropics). An unseasonal snowstorm or big freeze can destroy a whole generation, in turn jeopardising species higher up the food chain. Maarten's geese showed what a changing climate can do – if PCBs don't do it first.

Like many Dutchmen, Maarten spoke better English than me, and with his spiky hair, round belly and smooth skin, I could imagine him turning into a barnacle goose when my back was turned. He invited me to go out observing with him for an afternoon, and so with rifles loaded we started off past the Japanese station, past the airstrip, past the rocket launch pad and over a bridge fording a river bloodied with sandstone deposits. There we reached a pond, and Maarten put up his tripod and telescope. At a distance of 200 metres, he read out information from rings he had put on geese feet three years previously. I didn't believe it, so I looked through the lens myself. 'If the sun is behind me', Maarten boasted, 'I can read them at 300 metres.' We walked on to Brandal Point. The rain had begun to pound down again. All around, goslings had just hatched. Only the female incubates: to facilitate heat transmission, she has a pair of breast patches without feathers. For the first three days, goslings live off absorbed yolk. Then they learn to feed. A strong young goose pecks 120 times a minute when it finds food. But the Arctic fox population had kept time with the geese. 'The average barnacle couple', said Maarten, 'produce fifty eggs, out of which 2.2 chicks reach adulthood.' I had watched the dog-fox opposite my window ferrying goslings to his vixen and kits.

We walked on. 'This grass is too long for them,' Maarten remarked after we had reached stands of wet green at the lakeside. 'In this state, it's like spaghetti for geese, and they can't eat it.' The sun vanished behind a cloud. When it went, the colours went too. 'I see the grass here with my goose mind,' Maarten concluded before stopping to scrutinise a white blob against a patch of scree on the lower slope of the nearest mountain. But it was a boulder, not a bear. After all his years in the field, Maarten had plenty of experience with a rifle, but, like me, he was uncomfortable with the idea of a gun in his hand. 'It's a cultural thing,' he said. 'In Holland you are perceived virtually as a criminal if you hunt. But here in Norway you're almost a homosexual if you don't.'

A finger of land divided two narrow fjords, and the cliff at the end of it attracted birds. Puffin, pink-footed geese, long-tailed ducks, ivory gulls, dunlin, king eider, sanderlings and red-throated divers shrieked and squawked around lime-stained fissures. It was startling to see species familiar in dowdy British winter coats resplendent in summer plumage. Grey phalaropes in Arctic carmine, snow buntings transformed from dusty slate into dazzling black and white, golden plovers with refulgent breast feathers. Guano had fertilised soil cover below the cliff, enabling saxifrage and moss campion to outwit the permafrost,

Arctic battlers that blossom in the short burst of summer. If you're under snow from September till May, you need to grow a lot in the short burst of twenty-four-hour light. (The highest woody-stemmed plant in the archipelago still only reaches 15 centimetres.) Fauna also has to maximise the brief growth period. The flight feathers of a barnacle gosling grow 7 millimetres a day after hatching in Svalbard in June. Lichen approaches the problem from the other end by living so long that it can grow as slowly as it wants. Some patches on the bird cliff were alive before Britain became an island.

The next day a ship brought science cargo, and crates blocked the entrance to our hut. But they were the wrong crates, and Sam stood looking at them with the horror of Lady Bracknell observing a handbag. Another reprieve for the amphipods, but disaster for Nia and Sam. The rain continued to belt down. Nick, buoyant as ever and determined to salvage something from the day, emerged from a storeroom brandishing two raffia-clad bottles of Chianti. It turned out that residents of Ny-Ålesund marked Saturday with a special dinner. They changed out of windpants into civilian clothes, brought alcohol to the mess hall, and proposed toasts. A natural authoritarian, Nick made his team go back if they set out from the hut looking too polar. He himself had a roster of herbaceous Saturday-night ties. On that particular Saturday, the imminent departure of a long-term resident provoked the round of postprandial speeches that are a Scandinavian pastime. Nick told me he once attended a formal dinner at Ny-Ålesund at which he was placed thirteenth out of fourteen in the order of speeches, and that was to celebrate the opening of the new jetty.

To experience the romance of the trapper, I went to stay in the nearest hut. Two new arrivals at Nick's empire were coming along: Antonia, a wildlife watercolourist from Dorset on a mission to paint barnacle geese, and her partner Richard, a landscape photographer. In the mess hall, I ordered a field box of food for three, ticking off items on a printed list. The rain had finally ended, cleansing the air – breathing deeply, it was as if the lungs had been rinsed. The ground beyond the shingle beach was crunchy underfoot when we jumped from the zodiac, as the sun had not softened the fretted ice above the permafrost.

A broadloom of dirty ice and meltwater streams patterned the land around the point. Clouds came and went from the other side of the fjord, and from the interior; but you could see *spits bergen*. Three female geese had set up a crèche in the shallows of the fjord. The hut itself, fifty metres from shore, was made of rough-hewn planks weathered to the colour of birchbark. An anteroom contained a set of bunk beds, and the single inner room a wood-burning stove, a table, two benches, two gas rings and kitchen equipment including a stack of plates welded together by fossilised food items. Remembering Terje's story, I had brought my own frying pan for self-defence purposes. We fired up the stove, which quickly began to draw. Odd gloves dangled from pegs on a line above it, and someone had pinned the skin of a harp seal on the wall over one of the benches, opposite a small window with floral curtains looking out at the Conway Glacier at the southern end of King Haakon VII Land. One particular trapper occupied the hut for many years. He used to return from his annual visit to the mainland with the previous year's supply of Tromsø newspapers. Each day, on his way to his traps, he would deposit a newspaper in a mailbox he had made near the hut. Then he would collect it on the way back, and enjoy last year's news. Trapping flourished until 1940, and the governor still issues permits to individuals keen to live the polar life (or live a version of it. A trapper on Kapp Wijk has a fast satellite Internet connection in his hut). Trappers have been banned from taking bears since 1973, but they still catch eider for down, and Arctic fox in white or – if the hunter is lucky – blue winter coats. It seemed a desperately romantic life, Internet notwithstanding.

The three of us walked along the point. The rubbly strand was thick with Siberian driftwood, swept from the great rivers as they froze and spun in the circular currents of the Arctic Ocean before being blown onto the beaches of Spitsbergen. Antonia already had her sketchbook out, whipping through pencil drawings of a pair of geese on the edge of Brandallaguna, a triangular body of water behind the point. The light was flat. Big windsock-shaped clouds hung in the sky below a layer of cirrostratus. Richard lay down to photograph ribs of driftwood. I picked among beluga tusks and rusted barrel hoops in the metre-high ice foot, a weak and unstable wall of ice and snow left on the shore when the winter sea ice broke up. We looked out for bears, and listened to small waves slap the pebbles. Out in the open sea at the end of the fjord, a dazzling stripe on the underside of distant clouds mapped the sea ice. In a polar phenomenon called ice blink, clouds are lit from underneath by sunlight reflected up from a patch of pack ice in a contrasting dark area of water. When Nansen first came upon ice blink, he wrote, 'I felt instinctively that I stood on the threshold of a new world.' Of all the Arctic landscapes I have seen, this one, without a permanent population, could claim to be the purest. Like the Antarctic, Svalbard was *terra incognita* (or *frigore inhabitabilis*, as it appears on pre-Renaissance maps). No people had invested this land with the spiritual meaning that confers a sense of ownership more powerfully than political foot stamping. Whalers, trappers, explorers, miners and scientists – they were visitors, like me. It was easy to feel at home in a place that was nobody's home.

The portions of food neatly wrapped in the wooden box were moderate, except for a whack of sausages, which was unfortunate, as it turned out that Richard and Antonia were vegetarian. But we also had some pancake mix. Then it emerged that the propane bottle had run out of gas, so not even I could tackle the sausage mountain. We had plenty of bread though, which we could eat with jam and – ham. In the evening we set the kettle on the stove and looked out of the window. Sunlight shone through in moteless shafts. The stove was an efficient heater but a poor boiler: its tower design meant such little heat was coming out of the top that after two hours the water in the kettle was only tepid. The trapper was never in a hurry. Nor were we. Midnight could have been midday – in every sense. Even when the sun doesn't set, at sub-Arctic latitudes a temperature difference distinguishes day from night, because at midday the sun is at the highest point of its trajectory, making the air warmer, and at midnight at its lowest point, thus cooling the 'night'. The difference in the sun's altitude between midday and midnight reduces as one approaches the Pole – and so, therefore, does the temperature differential. (The further north you travel, in other words, the smaller the difference between day and night – a suitable metaphor for the otherworldliness of the polar regions.) Kongsfjord was not far from the 80th parallel, a latitude at which the planet enters the magic zone of day–night equilibrium. But the presence of the frying pan in the sleeping bag was not conducive to sound slumber.

In the morning we were standing outside our front door eating bread and jam when a dog-fox ran by with two goslings in its mouth. Cloud hung low like a lid, and Nick's voice was crackling out of the VHF radio, halfway through an anecdote about a schoolmate whose head was so flat at the back he could stand flush to a wall.

Pole-seekers approached in search of another kind of romance. In 1773 Captain the Hon. Constantine Phipps landed on Svalbard during a Royal Navy expedition in HMS *Racehorse* and the ill-named *Carcass*, both ice-strengthened men-of-war vessels known as 'bombs'. The fourteen-year-old midshipman on *Carcass* was one Horatio Nelson. Phipps was under instruction to see how far he could get to the North Pole (an optimistic coda to the order stated that under no circumstances should he go any further). He nearly got both ships terminally stuck in ice, and the navigational chart he brought back was, according to Sir Martin Conway, doyen of Svalbard historians, 'a marvel for its extraordinary badness'. But Phipps also returned with useful observational data, as well as an important natural history log (it was he who gave the polar bear its scientific name, *Ursus maritimus*). At 80°N, a wounded bear had almost changed the outcome of Trafalgar. Or so Nelsonian mythology would have us believe. The account of the plucky little sailor engaging in full-frontal combat with a monster bear has played an important role in the sedulous creation of the Nelson legend and its knightly progression towards apotheosis at Trafalgar. A fixated public endlessly recycled the image of the encounter (still do): Landseer engraved it, Southey popularised it, souvenir manufacturers stamped it on plates and pamphleteers, novelists and poets enshrined it in prose and verse. The *Eagle* comic worked it up for the schoolboys of the 1950s and in the 1980s Ladybird immortalised it for the succeeding generation. Only the historical record makes little of the episode. Awkwardly, it reveals that young Nelson was stalking the bear, rather than the other way round. Nelson is not a figure whose accomplishments require embellishment. Yet the Arctic even fictionalises him. The truth was that he wanted to give his father a bearskin. When his flintlock musket flashed in the pan, he slunk back to the waiting *Carcass*. There is something fine in the fanciful story's origin in a key voyage of the Enlightenment, an age devoted to the eradication of myth and ignorance.

A century after Nelson was not attacked by a bear, the possibilities of floating over the North Pole in an air balloon captured the Scandinavian imagination. The strandflats of Svalbard's Danskøya (Danish Island) offered the most north-westerly harbour, and eager balloonists flocked north in the race for primacy. In 1896 Swedish engineer Salomon Andrée planned to set out in his 212,000-cubic feet hydrogen balloon *Ornen* (Eagle). Tall, fat and passionate, and fired by a restless, rigorous curiosity, Andrée had once eaten forty boiled eggs as an experiment. *Eagle* was the world's biggest balloon to date, made of 3,360 squares of pongee silk varnished and sewn together with 86 miles of stitching. The pilots steered with drag ropes. But unfavourable winds aborted Andrée's mission. In 1897, he tried again, returning to his scaffolding and hangar on Danskøya and dyeing Svalbard waters red as he brewed sulphuric acid and iron filings for his gas. The balloon's cargo included Belgian chocolates, four jars of whortleberry jam, a specially designed primus that could hang outside the gondola, thirty-six carrier pigeons and a dinner jacket. The king and queen of Sweden came up for the launch. This time *Eagle* did land: it crashed on the pack ice at almost 83°N, its silken canopy armoured with frost. Andrée, with companions Nils Strindberg (nephew of August) and Knut Fraenkel, had little choice but to set off over the ice and march 200 miles to safety, crossing leads a mile wide in a canvas boat.* The three were never seen alive again. For a generation, their story remained the greatest polar mystery since Franklin. Then in 1930 sealers found their last camp, together with the bodies, undeveloped film and Andrée's flight logs and diary, on Kvitøya, the fifth largest Svalbard island. A recent study concluded the men probably died of bacterial food poisoning such as botulism, but trichinosis has always been a possibility – a disease caused by eating meat, in their case polar bear, infected with the larvae of a parasite. 'We think we can well face death, having done what we have done,' Andrée had written as he floated over the Arctic Ocean.

The ice-damaged prints recovered from the final camp are among the most affecting of any polar images: a study in the unequal battle between man and the Arctic. The photographer was twenty-four-year-

* A lead is a lane of open water between ice floes.

old Strindberg, a university physics teacher. He had designed a special reflex camera for the voyage, in a sealed case. Love and adventure pulled him in opposite directions. He had left a fiancée in Norway, and wrote to her almost every day. 'I am sure that I am laying down the foundations of our future happiness', Strindberg confided in a letter found on his body. Anna Charlier waited for him for thirteen years, then married an Englishman, Gilbert Hawtrey, and settled in Paignton, Devon. But when she died (by which time she had learned the news from Kvitøya), she asked for her heart to be cut out and buried in Sweden with Strindberg. Hawtrey obliged. Perhaps he is the true hero of the Andrée story.

International hopes shifted to the airship, the latest transport sensation. American journalist Walter Wellman stepped forward. He had received a telegram from the editor of the *Chicago Record-Herald* with the order, BUILD AN AIRSHIP AND WITH IT GO FIND THE NORTH POLE, surely a candidate for the most ambitious instruction ever to issue from a newsroom. Wellman duly set out for Spitsbergen with a hydrogen-filled airship three years in a row, each time just failing to kill himself. Then he heard that Peary had made it, and he lost interest in the North Pole, leaving the ice clear for Norwegian explorer Roald Amundsen. In 1925 Amundsen and Lincoln Ellsworth flew a pair of Dornier seaplanes to Spitsbergen to make the first of two aerial attempts over the North Pole. Ellsworth's father, a coal millionaire and numismatist, had agreed to fund the expedition providing Lincoln gave up smoking (he also agreed to upgrade the sewer system in his home town of Hudson, Ohio if the town imposed a fifty-year alcohol ban). Much of the Arctic Ocean remained unexplored, and by crossing from one side to the other, Amundsen hoped he might learn something of the landmass still rumoured to exist in the vicinity of the Pole. But the Dornier engines failed at 87°N, and the aviators only just escaped with their lives. Amundsen and Ellsworth then also decided to try airships. Now called Zeppelins, the best airships were at that time designed and manufactured in Italy (like Germany,

Italy had actively deployed airships in the war, building 20 semi-rigid M-1 class vessels with a bomb load of 1,000 kilograms) and so Amundsen and Ellsworth asked leading aeronautical engineer Umberto Nobile to collaborate in an expedition which would cross the Arctic Ocean from Spitsbergen to North America. All the western governments were busy commissioning airship models, and the press leapt hungrily on every story featuring fresh gondola designs or innovative ballast theory. When Andrée inflated *Eagle* in front of the world's press, balloon technology was as avant garde as that of the wireless had once been, or the motor car. Who could have known that the age of the airship would be fleeting?

Nobile was a slight, hyperactive colonel who knew more about airship engineering than any man alive, and he had piloted a great number, always accompanied by his terrier Titina, who sat alongside him in the gondola. Amundsen and Ellsworth bought the medium-sized, semi-rigid N1, Nobile's latest cigar-shaped Zeppelin. It was inevitable that Mussolini would perceive the expedition as a propaganda opportunity. He was consolidating power in a characteristically Italian rumbustious political setting, and, like any other leader, was on the lookout for bandwagons. Nobile was anti-fascist, but nobody cared about that. Mussolini told Amundsen he could have the N1 free if it flew under an Italian flag. Amundsen refused. The N1, rechristened *Norge*, was to traverse the Arctic in Norwegian colours. The national rivalry played out against the backdrop of an Arctic air race was shaped at least in part by the aspirations of two young countries striving to write their names in the geographical record books. And they did. In April 1926, Amundsen, Nobile, Ellsworth and an Italian-Norwegian crew floated over the Pole in *Norge*. Amundsen and his colleague Oscar Wisting, who had been with him in the Antarctic, were the first at, or over, both Poles. Peary's claim to have reached 90 north in 1909 was almost certainly false, so the *Norge* men were the first human beings to see the North Pole.

But did a balloon count? You decide: it's only a matter of opinion. The conquest of the North Pole has none of the tragic glamour of its southern counterpart – no race to the finish, no definitive record, no household name immortalised in death. *Norge*, the sources agree, made the first of many uncontested flyovers. In 1948, twenty-four Soviets landed near the Pole and walked to the spot: they were the first to stand there. In 1958 the crew of an American nuclear submarine became the first to travel under the Pole, and the following year another US sub surfaced. In 1968 four Americans rode from Canada by snow scooter. In 1969, Briton Wally Herbert and three others sledged from Alaska to Svalbard via the Pole. Theirs was the greatest Arctic journey of our time and has never enjoyed the recognition it deserves, perhaps because Ed Hillary's conquest of Everest the previous decade had shaken all the fairydust over the Himalaya. Herbert, a man with a Napoleonic sense of drama, followed the drift of the ice and together with his companions camped on floes for two winters, drinking Bass bitter, using napkins at table and picking up airdrops of steaks, bottles of HP sauce and eggs that didn't crack. In an agonising summer sledge, degree by painful degree, they made the first surface crossing of the Arctic Ocean. It took 407 days to reach 90°N from Barrow, Alaska, and when they got there Herbert telegraphed the Queen. Trying to stand at the Pole, he wrote later, 'had been like trying to step on the shadow of a bird that was circling overhead'.

The crew of the *Norge*, meanwhile, celebrated with egg nog, and by dropping flags onto the pack ice. To Amundsen and Ellsworth's fury, Nobile tossed out not one but many *tricolori*, all larger than theirs. Like toddlers in a nursery, they all wanted the biggest. *Norge* continued without misadventure to Alaska, landing in Teller after seventy hours aloft. It was the first flight between Europe and North America, predating Lindbergh's trailblazing crossing from Roosevelt Field to Le Bourget by thirteen months, and one of the oldest geographical myths of all time died, as the aeronauts confirmed that there was no landmass in the middle of the Arctic Ocean. (Mercator, the greatest cartographer who ever lived, had depicted, in his 1595 *Atlas*, an exquisitely symmetrical ring of Arctic land with slender passages to an area of water at the centre, allowing the perpetuation of another myth: that of an open water route to the Pole.) But Amundsen and Nobile had clashed from the outset. Both were tricky characters. Each claimed the other had contributed little or nothing of consequence to the *Norge* mission. They were polar opposites: Amundsen the lugubrious Thor of Viking legend, Nobile the operatic, gnome-like figure from southern Italy, and the Arctic amplified their traits into caricatures. Amundsen attacked Nobile publicly, accusing him of being a bad pilot, and of gesturing with his hands while giving orders, surely part of the job description of being Italian. The situation deteriorated when Mussolini co-opted the triumph of *Norge* as a fascist victory, transfiguring Nobile into a national hero. Of the ninety-four pages of Amundsen's autobiography dealing with *Norge*, barely one omits a strike at Nobile, that 'strutting dreamer' guilty of arrogance, incompetence, pettiness, an 'itch for ostentation', lack of self-control, vanity, 'illusions of greatness' and above all determination to claim for himself the leadership of the first expedition to cross the Arctic Ocean by air. 'Fortunately', wrote Amundsen at the conclusion of his 40,000-word tirade, 'I have a sense of humour.'

Public interest in the Pole continued undiminished, and Nobile determined to return to the Arctic. In 1928, in a high-profile mission supported by the Italian government, and now elevated to the rank of general, he took the airship *Italia* up to Spitsbergen to fly to the

Pole and carry out a scientific programme which included a survey of unmapped sectors of the Arctic Ocean. There was to be no Norwegian flag this time. Leaving a ship in Kongsfjord, Nobile again reached the Pole, this time dropping a wooden cross presented by the Pope wrapped in yet another large Italian flag. The crew played 'The Bells of San Giusto' on a gramophone, and set off back to Spitsbergen. At 81°N, the gondola section of *Italia* crashed onto pack ice. Six men in the main part of the airship floated off and were never seen again. The injured Nobile, eight survivors and Titina set up camp on a floe, contriving to make their tent red, and so conspicuous from the air. Radio operator Giuseppe Biagi struggled day and night to send a message to the mother ship moored in Kongsfjord. After hours of crackling, the wireless intermittently leapt to life. But nobody seemed to be hearing the desperate appeals from the floe. Three men set out on a march for help, reaching such a state of exhaustion, exposure and hunger that one died. The others learned from a wireless broadcast that the Italian authorities had announced their deaths. Days passed. Then a farmer in Arkhangel heard Biagi's SOS.

News of the crash went global, initiating the most frenetic Arctic search in the history of exploration. The rescue turned into a race between rescuers, between nations, and between newspapers and radio stations. An armada of vessels and at least twenty planes set out to find Nobile. Before anyone was able to land at the red tent, or manoeuvre an icebreaker within walking distance, planes dropped emergency supplies including laxatives and cakes that tasted of salt as they had been contaminated by seawater. Rescuers crashed and had to be rescued, recriminations fanned across Europe as countries raced to be first at the tent, rumours circulated that the two marchers who had survived had eaten the third, and a sensational news story ran and ran. But all eight men got out in the end, as did the dog. Like the arrest of Dr Crippen as he disembarked from a liner in New York, Nobile's rescue was a landmark in the history of wireless technology.

Amundsen joined the stampede of rescuers. In public, he said it was a gesture of reconciliation. But he had been asked to help, and it was more a case of saving face than saving Nobile. Amundsen failed to engage with life outside the polar regions: he needed a grand obsession to keep him sane. Now in his fifties, he had withdrawn from public life into private bitterness, nurturing imagined resentments against a multitude of former friends, family and colleagues, and against life itself ('the Norwegians, almost to a man, turned on me with unbelievable ferocity', he wrote after going bankrupt in 1924 solely on account of his stubborn truculence). He drowned in self-pity while his mentor Nansen pondered his own insignificance. Rage, prejudice and unhappiness exist in some dark place in all of us, but Amundsen's undignified autobiography, *My Life as an Explorer*, gave them form. Now he took off from mainland Norway, heading for Svalbard in a French seaplane, the first man to attempt a flight over that dismal stretch of water. On this trip, the wintry veteran fought his last campaign. He never made it to Svalbard, vanishing without trace in the Barents Sea. How often reconciliation comes too late. And how little we learn.

Nobile limped back to Norway and a reception almost as frigid as the red tent. In his homeland, he discovered that Mussolini had turned against him too: crashes and foreign rescuers were not what the dictator had in mind. An inquiry followed, then a trial. Officially blamed for the disaster, by 1929 former hero Nobile was virtually a political prisoner, and he remained an outcast for three decades. Arctic authority Vilhjalmur Stefansson concluded he had been 'well and truly railroaded', and Captain Scott's man Tryggve Gran said he was 'a new Dreyfus'. Not only had he failed: he had followed the wrong star. In the year of the *Italia* debacle, Hubert Wilkins and a co-pilot flew a Lockheed Vega monoplane from Alaska to Spitsbergen, and Gino Watkins prepared for pioneering aviation missions in Greenland.

Exploration for its own sake burned out in the years following the wobbly progress of balloons and airships over Svalbard. But a new race had emerged from the wreckage of the gondolas: the energy race. Nobody wanted Svalbard's whales or furs anymore. They wanted its coal.

On the west coast of Spitsbergen volcanic eructations of pitchy smoke off Grønfjord signal the proximity of Barentsburg, a Russian-owned mining outpost exuding, along with the smoke, more than a whiff of the Soviet era.* I saw it all when I left Ny-Ålesund for a week on a ship circumnavigating the island. Barentsburg was an anti-oasis: a grimy human hellhole in an otherwise pristine wilderness. I loved it. The coal company representative waiting on the wharf, a pasty young man in a parka, introduced himself as Slava. He spoke English with a heavy accent and impeccable diction. 'Modernisation this year will improve ecological aspect of power plant,' he said as thirty of us filed past Himalayan peaks of metal leaking toxic substances into the permafrost. We climbed steep flights of steps, past a child's swing with rigid poles, a cat, and a sign in Cyrillic announcing a cafe that no longer existed. At the top of the steps we paused in front of the anchor of the *Hercules*, a Russian supply ship that sank on the way back to Murmansk in 1948 with the loss of all hands. Someone had hooked a bunch of pink plastic roses over one of the prongs. The humanity of the Arctic had a pathos its southern counterpart did not share.

Slava had learned his English at Moscow University. What he liked most was telling jokes, and he had honed his sense of comic timing. Pausing in front of a mural of trees painted on a wall next to the coal-loading pier, he announced, 'This is only forest in Svalbard. Is evergreen.' His eyes scanned the audience, hungry for laughter. Keen to please him, we began to oblige with vigour.

---

* The terms of the Svalbard Treaty, signed by the main powers in 1920 and in force from 1925, permit signatories to engage in commercial activities on the islands. Diplomats had hammered out the details at the Paris Peace Conference – one of the few agreements reached there that still have practical significance. Sovereignty of Svalbard was an easy problem for the Versailles peacemakers to solve, especially as the islands, unlike Kurdistan or Palestine, did not present a human face: there were no indigenous delegations petitioning the conference halls.

In 1932 what was left of Barentsburg passed to the Soviet state. Now run by Trust Arktikugol, the mine produces 120 thousand tonnes annually, most of which goes to Holland and Denmark. Of the 500 Russian and Ukrainian residents, 150 are women. Miners have a two-year renewable contract. 'Some are here five, ten, twenty years,' Slava claimed, raising his voice to contend with the screaming of black-legged kittiwakes, 'enjoying the magic of these wonderful places.' The truth was that Barentsburg had suffered from a critical lack of investment, chiefly as a result of the withdrawal of state subsidies as Russia listed from command to market economy. Outdated safety equipment contributed to an accident in 1997 in which twenty-three perished. And Slava did not mention a murder in 2004, when one miner killed another in a gambling brawl, or the appalling shortages of food and other essential goods during the period leading to the collapse of the Soviet Union. Or the 1996 Tupolev crash in which 143 miners and their families died. When he revealed that there were only fifteen years of coal left, I asked about the future of the mine. 'The leadership', he said, 'have yet to announce plan.' A proper Soviet touch that. Here at Barentsburg the Soviet Union had never collapsed at all.

We walked along mud streets cobwebbed with snow, past folksy wooden buildings with fretwork window frames, though Slava revealed that everyone now lives in monolithic blocks at the back of the settlement. Shrouded figures emerged from doorways, nodding in our direction before hurrying away. Alongside a bust of Lenin, miners had painted more murals, this time of blue-eyed, lantern-jawed heroes of the motherland, fists raised against the tundra. Black replaced white as the default colour in Barentsburg. A fine layer of coal dust rimed everything; one could imagine never getting clean, and coal dust working its way into the very organs. At the end of a street, a herd of pigs huddled in the corner of a blackened pen. 'Most northerly pigs in world!' Slava shouted in triumph. Everything solid seemed to speak of more prosperous times: a Culture Hall with a concert auditorium, a huge school where five children followed the Russian syllabus and a monumental Sports Hall with interlocking Olympic rings above worked-iron doors. Inside, a crystal-studded mosaic of a polar bear overlooked a swimming pool filled with heated seawater which, during the transmission process, had mysteriously turned brown. Snowy mountains glittered dimly through the misted windows, and a pale sun threw shadows over tiers of peeling spectator seating. Silence echoed back from the high ceiling in a lament for something indefinable that had vanished.

It was hard not to sense fear in the wind that chased puffs of coal dust through the streets. It blew in a memory of the gulag. Pausing outside a 100-room concrete hotel in which nobody stayed, Slava announced that passengers booked in for a week if their ship left without them. Nobody laughed. 'It is joke,' he added miserably. At that moment, a limousine with blacked-out windows cruised down the street, turning left at the end, towards the accommodation blocks. A small Russian flag flapped on the bonnet. 'It is Russian consul,' said Slava. 'He lives in big consulate,' and he pointed to an attempt at a concrete mansion. The scale of public buildings at Barentsburg owed everything to post-Stalinist gamesmanship.

Many others besides Russians came in pursuit of minerals, staking hundreds of claims. Foreshadowing superpower conflicts, well-bred Americans stepped from the pages of Henry James novels to establish private mineral fiefdoms that would compete with Barentsburg. In 1901 John Munro Longyear, an industrialist from Marquette, Michigan, disembarked from a tourist ship in Bellsund on Spitsbergen with his wife and five children. He said, 'This looks like gold country.' Klondike was still on the mind of every entrepreneur, and coal was black gold. Returning with two partners, in 1906 Longyear, a Christian Scientist, founded a mining settlement that he named after himself on the west coast of Spitsbergen 55 kilometres from Barentsburg (though the two are not connected by road). Many of his mines capital operational. Today a resident of Longyearbyen – now the unofficial capital of Svalbard – stays six years, on average: when people reach the end of a posting, they return to the mainland to grow old. 'We are not allowed to die here,' a waiter told me at breakfast in a hotel in Longyearbyen, though I wonder how even the omnipotent *sysselman* banned death from his empire.

In her book *North of the Desolate Sea*, Liv Balstad, wife of the first post-war *sysselman*, gives a lively account of life in the Svalbard mining communities in the forties and fifties, emphasising both positive, of which there was some, and negative, of which there was a good deal. A husky nearly killed her baby, the first mail plane crashed on the way back to Norway, everyone squabbled their way through winter as cold and darkness bit deep and her husband fermented fish in a tub under their bed. And then there were accidents. Balstad saw coffins being hauled to the wharf adorned with wreaths made from pot plants. On 5 January 1962, twenty-one miners perished after a seam disintegrated. Prime Minister Einar Gerhardsen resigned amid accusations of inadequate safety provisions. 'When a man comes up here,' Balstad wrote, 'he knows really only what he is coming *from*, not what he is coming *to* . . . for most of them, Svalbard is the solution to a plan, a dream.' She cited 'the power of adaptability and the art of resignation' as the essential characteristics required to survive. Women, who made up 10 per cent of the population, tended to fare better than men in winter. 'Once she [the woman resident] has found the Svalbard melody,' Balstad wrote, 'she knits herself more strongly than the man to the land and all it means.' Communities developed to support the mineworkers, maintaining their own schools, newspapers and ski-jumping contests. Balstad recorded that as the fifties progressed, 'while the so-called Cold War gradually extended its hold on the outside world, the friendship between the Norwegians and the Russians in Spitsbergen became steadily warmer'. The two groups exchanged social visits by boat, with folk dancing displays on either side. In the photographs of these events, the Soviet women are three times the size of their Norwegian counterparts.

A spirit of warmth and cooperation had persisted in the coal towns. A ship's steward told me she had spent most of her childhood in Longyearbyen. Her father was employed by the Store Norske Spitsbergen Kullcompani. 'Fifteen years ago, when I was at school,' she said as we leaned over the bow rail, 'Longyearbyen was even more of a mining town than it is now. There were no food shops. Mum used to fill in an order form, the mine company consolidated the orders and a week later a man came to the door with a box of food with our name on. My father's pay number was also marked on the lid, and the food bill was deducted from his pay along with rent and electricity. Every day we got milk from an Iron Cow outside the company offices. It had been made up from powdered milk.' In winter, Longyearbyen had less snow than Tromsø on the mainland. 'But what falls', Ingrid said, 'stays till May and blows around. Longyearbyen becomes another country in winter. Snowmobiles have the tundra to themselves. We used to say it was a good winter when the snow stayed a long time, not when it went early, like people do down in mainland Norway.' Then she paused, narrowing her eyes and scrutinising the water between ship and shore. She said, 'There's a calf with that beluga.'

At Christmas, one particular trapper always called on the Balstads. For many years he had lived alone at Sassen, a few miles from Longyearbyen, and he came to town at Christmas to send a telegram to his family in Norway. In his twenty-ninth year, he failed to appear, so they sent someone to his hut. He had had a heart attack. But they were able to get him home alive. 'They were diehards,' Balstad concluded, 'these men who would just as soon hunt a polar bear in their bare underpants at 35° below zero . . . as the rest of us go into a baker's shop. And they were artists in life.'

In addition to its cast of lively biologists, Svalbard attracted atmospheric chemists probing the alteration in planetary gases. It was an ironic development on an archipelago with a modern history shaped entirely by the extraction of hydrocarbons, as coal had caused part of the damage the chemists were assessing. Attention in some quarters at least had shifted from raping the Arctic (or conquering it by getting there first) to saving it, and a cosmic dimension had entered the science literature. Like other aspects of the northern polar regions, the proximity of coal mines and cutting-edge climatology in Svalbard highlighted the frailty of human endeavour.

Irish physicist John Tyndall was one of the first to explain the greenhouse effect properly, as long ago as the 1860s. He suggested that slight changes in atmospheric composition could bring about climatic variations. The role of water vapour in the heat-trapping layer of gases was, he said, that of 'a blanket more necessary to the vegetable life of England than clothing is to man. Remove it for a single summer night . . . and the warmth of our fields and gardens would pour itself unrequited into space, and the sun would rise upon an island held fast in the iron grip of frost.' The term 'greenhouse effect', not one of Tyndall's, is a misnomer, as greenhouses work by preventing convective cooling; but it has cemented itself into many languages notwithstanding its inaccuracy. Tyndall went on to identify the relative radiative forcing values of different greenhouse gases, demonstrating for the first time that 'perfectly colorless and invisible gases and vapours' were able both to absorb and to emit radiant heat. Climate change is part of a natural order involving glacial cycles and violent climatic shifts. Ice cores have revealed temperature instability during both ice ages and interglacials like our own: without any human interference, ice ages have always had warm periods, and interglacials cold ones. Factors that vary the amount of received solar radiation include changes in the angle of the earth's axis, the waning of the sun, and, as shown by the Greenland cores, volcanic eruptions. The task facing Scandinavian atmospheric chemists on the ground in Spitsbergen – and others in labs around the world – is to prise apart natural methods of readjusting earth's energy balance from anthropogenic interference in the same processes.

Chemists at Ny-Ålesund had built a laboratory suite at 474 metres, and a cable car to service it. Called Zeppelin Station after the mountain it sat on (Zeppelinfjellet, in turn after Amundsen's airship), it overlooked the whole of Kongsfjord, including the dam of glaciers at the end, as well as the carboniferous uplands. When I returned from my circumnavigation I ascended, in the cable car, with a Norwegian graduate student called Dorothea who went up every day to change the filters in the equipment. Below us on the tundra, a haze of fine drizzle softened the outlines of a lake frozen into a convex bulge. Once we were in the lab, and the freezer entrance doors shut tight behind us, Dorothea unveiled a bewildering array of instrumentation housed in iron cubes, glass cylinders and steel bell jars; some were clicking softly, some described an inky line on a spool of graph paper, and some just sat there looking menacing, coolly calibrated to track some clear, odourless gas gathering to disrupt the energy balance of the planet. Dorothea had a lecture ready. 'The gases we measure here are those that block earth's heat radiation,' she said, 'preventing it escaping into space. Without that natural blocking effect, a sheet of ice would cover the earth. But with too thick a layer of the dozens of greenhouse gases, not enough radiated heat would get out, and the planet would boil, like Venus.' She had the Zeppelin data to hand. 'At the start of the nineties', she explained, 'machines here measured carbon dioxide at one part per million. Last week it was up at almost 3 ppm. This automated gas chronometer' – we paused in front of a white metal box resembling a dishwasher – 'has a flame ionising detector that analyses a sample of methane every fifteen minutes and sends the information to Stockholm. In quantity, methane is the third greenhouse gas, after water vapour and carbon dioxide. It is ten times more effective than CO_2 in absorbing and reradiating infrared energy back to earth's surface – in other words, it contributes hugely to the oxidising capacity of the planet. Levels have rocketed by about one per cent annually over the past two decades, largely as a result of human activity like rice cultivation and modern livestock practices.' Almost all the data yields revealed some kind of correlation between anthropogenic emissions and temperature increase. Dorothea ploughed on. 'Although earth has become dramatically both hotter and colder many times, it has only rarely been warmer than it is now. And the greatest warming', she said, opening the door on another, darkened lab, 'has taken place above 40° of latitude in the northern hemisphere. Sure, the Antarctic is melting. But the Arctic is melting faster. If the modellers are correct and the trend up here continues, life on earth will have a lot of adapting to do.'

There is broad consensus that 'dangerous' climate change means two Celsius degrees of warming above pre-industrial levels.* A layperson might think such a rise relatively insignificant. But only a few degrees separate a warm earth from its iced-up doppelganger. Between the Renaissance and the early nineteenth century, mean temperatures were probably only a degree or two below present levels – but think of all those images of ice skaters and ox-roasts on the Thames. In the thirteenth century, in the region known now as Four Corners in the south-western United States, the entire Anasazi civilisation collapsed as a result of a modest drop in temperature and rainfall. By comparing children's teeth from the year 1100 with those of 1450, scientists at the University of Michigan found that mean annual

---

* There is little consensus on anything else, especially the percentage of energy cuts required to prevent the two degrees becoming reality.

temperatures in western Greenland fell by about 1.5°C during that period. As we have seen, that apparently insignificant drop played a role in the demise of the Norse. As one scientist has pointed out, these abrupt disappearances reveal to what extent humanity exists in 'precarious equipoise between survival and oblivion'. A short act in the drama was being played out in the labs and the mines of Svalbard.

Freak weather has been recorded throughout human history (think of Noah). The twentieth century had its share. In *The Grapes of Wrath* Steinbeck depicts the human cost of the dust bowl experience of the thirties as tens of thousands of Okies trekked west to California in pursuit of a nugatory dream of life. But freak weather tends not to last long. The warming of the past decades indicates that at the start of the twenty-first century even a small change could have a radically destructive effect on the inhabited world. It is not the planet that is at risk. It is us.

In the lab, a man sat in the gloom eating Jammy Dodgers. We walked past him, through another door and down a corridor. Mass spectrometry detectors, condensation particle counters, electro-polished stainless steel canisters collecting air – the battery of multi-million kroner equipment quantifying the imminent big bake queued up for recognition. I was gasping for a Jammy Dodger: it seemed the only short-term solution. A graph on the wall revealed that atmospheric levels of carbon dioxide, methane and nitrous oxide remained approximately constant between 1000 to 1800, then rose; at the end of the millennium the coloured bars shot three-quarters of the way up the sheet. The extent to which man, for the first time in history, has become the central force in shaping both climate and ecosystems is reflected in the term 'anthropocene', coined in 2000 by Dutch chemist and Nobel-laureate Paul Crutzen. His suggestion that the influence of human behaviour on the earth constitutes a new geological epoch is gaining ground.

The early migrants might have stopped in Greenland and left Svalbard alone. But the anthropocene had arrived without them. The latest thing was oil. Like so many places in the Arctic, the Barents Sea south and west of Svalbard had been identified as a potential source of gas and oil. At the time of my visit, Russia and Norway were quietly arguing about where their respective marine economic zones began and ended. Coal had already played a decisive role in shaping Svalbard's environmental history, and now oil was taking on the role. A bell is tolling in Svalbard for the whole Arctic. But as Geir Wing Gabrielsen suggested, it is not too late, yet.

VII

Four Legs Good

Lapland

Far beyond the Germanic tribes lived the Fenni . . . Farther than this every-thing dissolves into myths

Tacitus

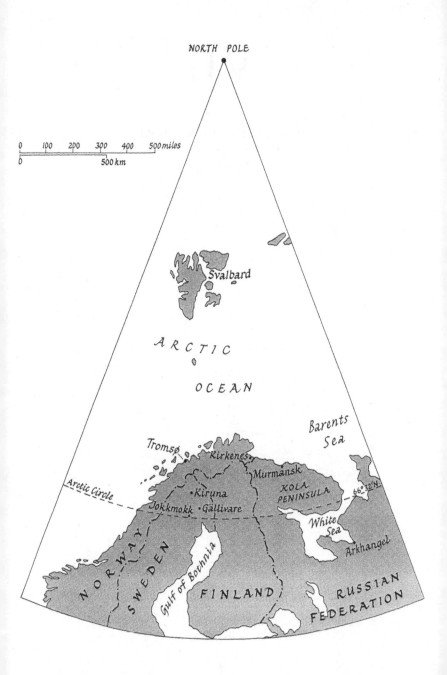

B ack in November 2002, across the fog-bound Barents Sea from Svalbard, I had towed my infant son on a sledge among Sámi herders engaged in the age-old rituals of seasonal migration. In the darkness of a winter afternoon, as pinpricks of light from a distant settlement glimmered across the cold fells and my friends goaded reindeer, it moved me deeply to see a European people so closely in touch with their past living in uneasy alliance with the present, and the experience left unanswered questions concerning the indigenous cultures of the far north. The temperate climate and its husbandry brought the countryside home, and so did familiar faces. Sámi descend from both Europeans and Uralic-speaking Asiatics, and in physiognomy the European dominates. Following the 2002 visit, I pursued my interest in that enigmatic land and its hardy peoples while baby Reg grew into a sturdy boy with no memory of the closing moments of transition and assimilation that we had witnessed together. Quite by chance, I found two writers who brilliantly revealed an earlier phase. They were Johan Turi, the first Sámi ever to publish a book, and Axel Munthe, his magnificent Swedish friend.

Sámi occupy the northern arc of Scandinavia and north-west Russia. The land they call Sápmi (also known as Fennoscandia, after its geological shield) extends north from Idre in Dalarna, Sweden and adjacent areas in Norway – across from Engerdal in Hedmark to the shores of the Atlantic. From there it rises to the top of the Norwegian coast; eastwards Sápmi moves through Finland and across to the Kola Peninsula in the Russian Federation.* The Norwegian seaboard in those regions, deeply indented with fjords and valleys, arches a thousand miles to Kirkenes, a port almost bombed out of existence in the Second World War and so close to Russia that street signs appear in Cyrillic. The stark wilderness of the *Finnmarksvidda* plateau dominates the interior: people call it Big Sky Country. Elsewhere in Lapland, virgin forest and tundra bogs alternate with fell and marshland, gorges and treeless plains, frozen lakes, the eerie Lappish heartland around Kvikkjokk in Norrbotten, Sweden and the Finnish gold pans of the Ivalojoki and Morgamjoki south and west of Lake Inari. Hard by the Russian border where golden eagles fly, wolves and brown bears roam the forest and the softly rounded fells above the treeline. Sámi once had the barren hinterland of Arctic Norway to themselves, as well as high ground unsuited to cattle further south from which they came down only to trade, becoming famously addicted to coffee. But in Finland, which their ancestors once inhabited in its entirety, Sámi have been on the retreat from invading agriculturalists and loggers for two millennia. On assignment for a newspaper, I had joined a group of herding families north of the Arctic Circle in Sweden to find out how they were coping economically with European Union regulations. Few relied exclusively on herding. Some said everything but reindeer had changed out of all recognition. Others were optimistic.

Sámi have been living off reindeer since the Stone Age and began domesticating their own herds in the sixteenth century, migrating as nomads with the animals.† Forest Sámi bartered with mountain Sámi

---

* The word Sápmi occurs in all Sámi dialects and in fact refers to Sámi territory; to one Sámi; to all Sámi; and to the Sámi language.
† In the reindeer world, the line between wild and domestic is blurred; the creatures I saw referred to as *domesticated* looked anything but, and they certainly weren't prepared to footle around in the presence of humanity for a moment longer than necessary.

and both traded with coastal Sámi who lived at the heads of the fjords and followed sea mammals and fish shoals; when the whales came, a *noajdde* or shaman sat on a headland and cajoled them to shore with magic spells. In the winter all Sámi made holes in lake ice with a pick and laid gill nets, threading the nets between holes by using a long flexible wooden strip. Many trapped ermine and beaver, luring the animals into underwater cages, where they drowned. Forest Sámi also hunted brown bear through the low-lying wooded lands with spears and bow. Like other Arctic peoples, Sámi regarded the bear as a sacred messenger between gods and people, and it was important to treat him with respect, even when sawing him up for the pot.

All Sámi traded with the foreigner. The biggest fairs were at Varanger, Alta and Lyngen, three major fjords on the northernmost curve of Scandinavia, and from them Sámi skied away first with bronze, then iron, then salt, coffee, flour, cracked barley and cloth (as well as measles), while a pale-skinned merchant sailed off with a cargo of dried fish and beaver furs. The point of a fair might have been primarily economic, but it was also a chance to live it up away from the wife and Lapplets. Eighteenth-century documents bristle with complaints about Lappish drunkenness at the fairs, and Lutheran missionaries who arrived in 1632 at first made little headway. It took seventy years, but from then on their influence grew steadily, often with baleful consequences for the herders. Missionaries introduced compulsory church attendance, with fines for those who did not appear. It was hard for nomads to follow such rules, though harder for shamans, as they were burned at the stake. As for the non-missionary invaders, fur drew them north, just as it was attracting Cossacks to Arctic Siberia and Europeans to Canada. Then minerals began to glint in the tundra, and by the eighteenth century mines were operational across the region, worked partly by Sámi forced labour. In addition, homesteaders tried their luck, encouraged by the Lapland Settlement Act in force from 1673 to 1873. These people were chiefly Swedish cattle farmers or hay harvesters or Finnish slash-and-burn corn growers who destroyed dry land where reindeer grazed for lichen. None of them admired the Lapps, except in one regard. They were the greatest skiers in the world. They had to be: they needed to keep up with migrating animals. Carbon-dated fragments of a ski preserved in a peat bog in Russian Lapland reveal that the Arctic ski is older than the wheel. Lapps appear regularly in the Norse sagas as skiing stars. 'Lapps', according to one saga, 'are so cunning that they can follow tracks like dogs, both in thawing snow and on hard crust, and they are so good on skis that nothing can escape them, whether man or beast.' Lappish snowcraft reached its zenith in Norway. 'They ski down high mountains and slopes,' reported one eighteenth-century Norse observer, 'at breakneck speed, so that the air whistles in their ears, and their hair streams backward in the wind. Indeed, if you place a cap or something else in their way, they bend down at full speed, and pick it up.' Skiing soon became a symbol of national identity all over Norway but especially in Finnmark, the largest and northernmost province. Every farm boy there made his own skis, planing and chiselling the blanks and steaming the tips, and specialist craftsmen worked them up from birch, pine, hickory, maple or Norwegian ash, impregnating the wood with pine tar under heat to ensure a good glide and even decorating the upper sides. Both Norwegian and Sámi still have over 300 expressions to describe the interplay between snow and ski.*

In his 1910 book *Muitalus sámiid birra* (later translated as *Turi's Book of Lappland*), Johan Turi depicts herding life in the Jukkasjärvi district as it was at the beginning of the twentieth century; and his prose is as clear as the mountain streams where he herded his deer. Like most Lapps Turi was short, with broad shoulders and a narrow waist, black hair, and a face with only a hint of his semi-Asiatic roots. He thought a great deal about the well-being of his people, and had even been to Lulea to lay their grievances before the governor. He wrote in response to what he saw as the imminent destruction of his way of life at the hands of southern settlers, and thought that if incomers knew more about his leaderless people's lives, they would no longer 'come to twist everything round till the Lapps are always slandered'. The volume includes bitter memories of 'the black-clad ones' (the settlers) who pushed Lapps off the land, as well as thoughtful descriptions of what it is like at night when water gets into the tent and the bedclothes get wet. Turi came from around Kautokeino in the Arctic highlands of Finnmark, the area where men wore four-cornered hats. He was a blue-eyed mountain Lapp – a fell Lapp – and a herder, but in his heart he was a hunter, gliding over frozen bogs and mountain ridges on long slender skis, navigating by the stars. 'To chase a wolf on skis', he wrote, 'you must ski till the blood comes into your mouth.' Turi considered

* The Sámi language is in fact three separate and highly inflected Finno-Ugric tongues, each split into dialects, many barely mutually intelligible. About a third of modern Sámi speak a version of it. Strong linguistic similarities between Finnish and Sámi bear witness to centuries of close contact. The word 'tundra' has its origins in Kildin Sámi, entering the English language via Russian.

the wolf the worst enemy of the Lapps; a single animal often killed a dozen reindeer in a night. God, Turi avowed, had created all the animals except the wolf, who was begotten by the devil. He could put to sleep the men who were watching the herd at night simply by looking at them through the darkness with his glowing eyes. Then there was the wolverine, who sprang to the throat of a deer and hung on for miles till the reindeer lost so much blood that he fell down dead; or the eagle who carried a newborn calf if it was left alone for a moment by its mother; or the lynx who crept up to jump at a reindeer who had wandered away from the herd. Turi said he could not understand how his forebears had managed to keep their herds together in the old days, before they had associated themselves with the dog.

Turi tells of the way a mother put a hot stone into the cradle to warm it and sometimes forgot to take it out before returning the infant, with the result that the baby was burned and grew up with a crooked back. In particular he paints a heart-stopping portrait of a *sijdda* – an association of families – on the move, a caravan of men and reindeer that cannot stop for illness, birth or death. Herders on skis preceded the bulky draft reindeer, which were linked by leather thongs into a group called a string. In the rear came the old folk, on foot, followed by the dogs. Children under four travelled strapped in cribs to the side of a draft beast, while older ones rode on top. The migrating herd were somewhere ahead. Turi describes the precarious business of getting the strings across the river (the herd swam).' 'Really', he says, 'the Lapps have almost the same nature as reindeer ... both of them are a little shy, and because of this shyness they have been driven away from everywhere, and so the Lapps must now stop where there are no other folk than Lapps, that is on the naked high fells ...'

When they were following the migration, Turi said, nursing mothers breastfed their babies while they were strapped into their cradles on the side of a reindeer (I tried this when I was among the herders in 2002 and found it an impossible, Houdini-like manoeuvre). And he told of the way settlers deliberately got Lapps drunk on *brännvin* (grain

liquor), extracted all their livestock as payment, then employed the Lapps as indentured herders. In another section of his book he deals with 'the Lappish song', called the *yoik*. It was a way, as he puts it, of remembering specific people and specific reindeer. Yoiking was a kind of humming either with words or the imitation of animal sounds. In origin spontaneous, like all song, it was often improvised, inspired by an especially fine buck or a moonlit night in the forest. As Turi concluded, if it is really clever, yoiking, 'is so wonderful to hear that the listener almost has tears in his eyes, but when it is a yoiker who swears and grinds his teeth and threatens to kill reindeer and their owners too, then it is horrible to listen to'.

Axel Munthe, a Swede famous for his bestselling *The Story of San Michele*, stayed with Turi at the turn of the last century, alighting on Lapland as a personal Shangri-La. He projected his own romantic longings onto the Lapps, perceiving them as antithetical expressions of contemporary society as he observed it in Stockholm and Rome. (He was a doctor for a period to the Italian aristocracy, and remains famous in his native land for his love affair with Crown Princess Victoria, later Queen Victoria, great-grandmother of the present Swedish king.) The beleaguered Lapps already had a troubled relationship with the outside world. But they were still leading a life that would have been at least vaguely recognisable to the writers of the sagas. Munthe describes men returning to camp with lassos swung over their shoulder and women carrying huge birch bowls of milk while a thousand reindeer foraged on the tundra beyond outposts of vigilant dogs. Near what is now the Finnish–Swedish border, Munthe sat in a tent with Turi and his wife Ellekare, hooking slices of reindeer cheese out of the kettle. One by one, wrote Munthe, the dogs 'had crept in and lain down by the fire. Then we drank each in turn our cup of excellent coffee from the two cups of the household and they [members of the *sijdda*] all took their short pipes from their leather pouches and began to smoke with great gusto. The men pulled off their reindeer shoes and spread the tufts of carex grass to dry before the fire, Lapps wear no socks. Again I admired the perfect shape of their small feet with their elastic insteps and strong, protruding heels. Some of the women took their sleeping babies from their cradles of birch bark, filled with soft moss and suspended from the tent-poles, to give them the breast. Others explored the heads of their half grown children lying flat in their laps.' That night Turi was anxious to break camp before the snow became too hard under the birch trees. 'I can hear by the way the dogs are barking that they are already smelling the wolf,' he said. Turi and his wife told Munthe that they had three times tried to kill a bear but he had escaped each time, as the Ulda had befriended him. They were trolls who lived under the earth, and quite amiable as long as you left them alone. If you disturbed them, they strewed a powder on the moss which killed reindeer.

When he left Turi, Munthe walked to Forsstugan through the wilderness of marshes, torrents, lakes and forests which was the home of the Lapps. It was a two-day trek, the first leg of Munthe's journey back to civilisation. His guide was Ristin, the Turis' sixteen-year-old granddaughter. She was on her way back to the Lapp school at the nearest church-village, and she wore a long white reindeer tunic and red woollen cap. Round her waist she had a broad leather belt, embroidered with blue and yellow thread and studded with buckles and squares of solid silver. Suspended from her belt hung her knife, her tobacco pouch and her mug. Munthe noticed a small axe for cutting wood stuck under the belt. She also wore leggings of soft white reindeer skin fastened to her wide skin breeches and carried on her back her *luakos*, a birch-bark knapsack. Agile as a goat, according to Munthe, Ristin sprang through the hip-deep water, only occasionally looking from side to side to establish her position. The pair sat down on soft moss for a meal of rye biscuits, fresh butter and cheese, smoked reindeer tongue and water from the brook. Then they lit pipes and listened to the birds. The Lapps say that the bluethroat has a bell in his gullet and that he can sing a hundred different songs.

As they descended, the solitary dwarf birches of the slopes grew into groves of silver birches mixed with aspen and ash and thickets of willow elder, birdcherry and wild currant. Eventually they emerged on a forest carpet of silvery grey moss in the twilight of the northern summer night and slept on their rucksacks until the sun rose in a flame of golden light and they breakfasted on a capful of bilberries. 'Through the mist of the valley at our feet', wrote Munthe, 'a mountain lake opened an eyelid. I approached the lake with uneasy forebodings of another ice cold bath. Luckily I was mistaken. Ristin stopped short before a small *eka*, a flat-bottomed boat, half hidden under a fallen fir tree. It belonged to nobody, and to everybody, it was used by the Lapps on their rare visits to the nearest church village to exchange their reindeer skins for coffee, sugar and tobacco, the three luxuries of their lives.' The lake was so transparent that Munthe thought he could see the bottom, and halfway across they met two elk, then on the other side got lost in a fog so impenetrable that they had to hold hands. After struggling for an hour knee-deep in icy water, Ristin said they would have to wait out the fog – *rog* – which might take a day, depending on the wind. They sat miserably on their packs for several hours, the *rog* sticking to their skin. Munthe tried to light his pipe, but water had filled his pockets, inundating the matches. 'While I was still staring dejectedly at my soaked matchbox,' he said, 'Ristin had already struck fire with her tinder box and lit her pipe.' Another defeat for civilisation. At journey's end an old Swedish couple offered them hospitality while declaring candidly, in the presence of Ristin, that Lapps were superstitious and ignorant: they were not even Christians, nobody knew where they came from and they spoke a language unlike any other tongue. The old pair failed to grasp that they were hooked on superstition themselves. The man, Lars Anders, told Munthe that the trolls who used to live in a nearby mountain with hundreds of dwarves had vanished when the king had begun to blast the rocks for iron ore and started building a railway. The goblin in the cow stable, on the other hand, was doing well. When Munthe announced his departure, Anders said it was 'an easy and comfortable journey' to the railhead at that time of year, and there was nothing to fear: an eight-hour ride through the forest to Rukne, three hours downstream in a boat, six hours on foot across the mountain to the church-village, two hours across the lake to Losso Jarvi, and from there an eight-hour drive to the new railway station, where in fact no passenger trains ran as yet but the engineer would be sure to let Munthe stand on the locomotive for 200 miles until he could catch a goods train.

A committed misanthropist and cultural conservative, Munthe empathised with the Lapps' lack of engagement with the modern world. His attitude had resonance as I struggled, in the Arctic, both to reject the noble savage idealisation of native peoples and also to refrain from judging by appearances when someone was drunk, stoned, depressed or all three. It was extraordinary to realise that even at the beginning of the twentieth century outsiders could imbue the inhabitants of the Arctic Circle with prelapsarian innocence (or was that pre-Lappsarian?). Munthe's Lapps were the Hyperboreans of Greek myth: a race who inhabited a fertile land of perpetual sunshine in the northernmost region of the earth. According to the ancients, they lived to be 1,000 yet never grew old, and they did not know the meaning of sickness, work, or war. Hyperboreans were happy all the time ('*Never the muse is absent from their ways,*' Pindar wrote), and they enjoyed continuous festivals of song and dance ('*And everywhere maiden choruses whirling*'). As for Munthe, he was a figure of uncompromising idealism and had already clashed, in his youthful writings, with the prevailing ideology and aesthetics. He lived his whole life in a no-man's-land between fact and fiction, a fabricator par excellence, though his portrait of the Lapps rings true, whether or not he ever forded a stream with Ristin. His contemporary Norman Douglas, the improper hedonist who redefined the travel book for a new era, called him a portentous fake; it didn't quite take one to know one, but similarity helped. Munthe grew more irritable with age – who doesn't? – and vainer, especially when, well into his seventies, *The Story of San Michele* (written in English) emerged as an international bestseller, and there was talk of the Nobel Prize. He knew the true value of social success – nothing – but still wanted it; it makes him almost likeable. *San Michele* reflects both the romantic revival and the world weariness of the twenties. The author, like his contemporary Nansen and the other architects of the League of Nations, pursues a misty vision of a better world. But Scott Fitzgerald got the measure of them all, as he always did. 'So we beat on,' asserts Nick in the last line of *The Great Gatsby*, 'boats against the current, borne back ceaselessly into the past.'

Munthe's idea of a 1920s idyll shattered when Ristin and her generation faced fresh horror: the Second World War. This was a shared past that brought the Sámi close. As a result of the triangulation of history that squashed Finland, Norway and the Soviet Union together in one Lappish corner, for settler and Sámi alike the war years were tumultuous by the standards of any displaced peoples. Many died; hundreds of thousands were evacuated and returned to find they had no home left. Survivors did not even have the (admittedly slim) moral comfort of participating in the great battle of good against evil, as at one point the embattled Finns changed sides. Sámi fought Sámi, and then were told to stop, and to start attacking other Sámi, previously allies. Before that turnabout, more than 25,000 Finns had perished in the Russo–Finnish Winter War of 1939–40. Stalin sent the Red Army in over the whole frontier, a 900 km line from the Baltic to the Arctic Ocean. The campaign was a disaster for the freshly purged Soviet army. The newly installed high command was incompetent, junior officers revealed a fatal lack of spirit and the country with the longest Arctic coast in the world despatched men to winter war in their usual brown uniform and without skis or adequate tents. Soldiers regularly froze to death in the frosted silence of the forest. The highly adapted Finns, on the other hand, wore white ski apparel and lived in specialised bell tents which they pitched round a portable wood stove, using the flue as the central pole. Their flying columns that worked through the maze of lakes and waterways were so effective that Russians called them *belaya smert*, the white death. Finnish troops even enjoyed shallow sauna dugouts near the front. In the negotiated peace that ended the Winter War the Russo–Finnish border moved east as Stalin had wanted, but the debacle was a pyrrhic victory after 250,000 Red Army men perished.

The following year, German and Austrian armies and their Finnish allies invaded north-west Russia. Their primary aim was to block the Allied supply route through Murmansk and Arkhangel; they also wanted to gain control of the nickel mine at Nikel, formerly Kolosjoki, 20 kilometres south of Kirkenes. The troops had to cross Lapland. At that time a single decent road connected north Finland with its south: it went, like an arrow's trajectory, from Kemi at the head of the Gulf of Bothnia through Rovaniemi and Ivalo to Pechenga and Kirkenes, for the most part across a wilderness of forest and fells. The only other roads were the narrow coastal S-bends that leave the shores of the fjords to traverse mountain passes. The Germans, who could not get any tanks in, needed ten horses to transport one artillery gun. In desperation they built a field railway, but it subsided when the ground thawed. Their maps were so inadequate that a staff officer corrected top-secret information provided by High Command by referring to his 1912 Baedeker. A soldier holed up in an artillery battery defending the coast around Varangerfjord noted in his diary that in the whole of 1943, he had seen the sun seven times. In addition, the retreating Soviets (who did have tanks) set the forests on fire. The pines burned for weeks. As chief of staff Herman Hölter later wrote in his memoirs, 'Arctic warfare is altogether different from that learned in military academies.' Wehrmacht divisions took control of the Nikel nickel mine; by 1944 it was the German armaments industry's only remaining source of the mineral, and almost every time a supply convoy evaded enemy fire both to get in to Kirkenes and get out again, its ships returned to Germany engorged with nickel. The port was among the most crucial polar stations. The Germans posted 100,000 men in frigid barracks close to the Arctic Ocean, and the Soviets raided so relentlessly that hapless Kirkenes became, after Malta, the second most bombed place in the whole war.

Generaloberst Lothar Rendulic assumed control of German forces in Lapland in June 1944, the month the Allies landed in Normandy. On 2 September the Helsinki government announced that diplomatic relations with Germany would cease the next day; President Mannerheim had signed an armistice with the Soviet Union, agreeing, by the terms of the surrender, that Finland would help the Red Army drive its former allies from Scandinavian soil. Rendulic had to get everyone out. The entire civilian population of Finnish Lapland had to get out too — 170,500 of them. And soon the first snow fell.

Retreating German troops destroyed 90 per cent of the buildings in Rovaniemi, 88 per cent of those in Inari and 95 per cent in Savukoski. They burned down 125 Finnish schools. They blew up the nickel mine. One source states that at the end of the war, twenty-four out of 752 bridges in north Finland remained intact. Evacuees who returned throughout the summer and autumn of 1945 found that the ruins of their villages had been systematically mined. A tuberculosis epidemic was probably the result of insanitary domestic conditions during the period of reconstruction. At the beginning, some people lived in holes in the ground. Norwegian Lapland endured the same treatment. While battling snow, exposed rivers and enemy attack to get his demoralised divisions out of Finland, Rendulic received a personal order from Hitler to destroy everything in north Norway too and evacuate the civil population – about 75,000 people – to Tromsø. Despite airdropped propaganda threatening 'death in the Arctic winter without house or food', as many as 25,000 men and women in eastern Finnmark went into hiding rather than evacuate. 'It must be made clear to the troops carrying out [the command]', Hitler's order stipulated, 'that in a few months time the Norwegians will be thankful for having been saved from Bolshevism.' Norwegians had not been praying to keep Reds out; they hated the German occupiers too much. The stories of what the Resistance achieved in Norway rank among the most Homeric of the war. The name that persistently returned as I kicked up the deep peacetime snows of Finnmark was Jan Baalsrud. Antarctic adventurers like to say that if they had to choose a man to get them out of a polar fix, it would be Shackleton. I would nominate Baalsrud as my man in the north.

A member of a Norwegian Resistance commando unit based in the Shetlands, Baalsrud sailed back to his Nazi-occupied country in 1943 in a disguised fishing vessel armed with seven mounted machine-guns. German forces installed on the thinly populated north Norwegian coast had been attacking Allied convoys to devastating effect. Baalsrud's twelve-strong party planned to land on one of the small islands screening the Norwegian mainland and sabotage the crucial German airbase at Bardufoss, south of Tromsø, thereby facilitating safer passage for the convoys. Ice and snow cover the land there, foul weather batters it and unsurveyed mountains cut it off from civilisation. Even before the group made landfall, a frightened shopkeeper on the remote shore of Toftefjord on one of the outermost islands betrayed them. (Perhaps he wanted the case of brandy with which the Germans rewarded him.) Enemy soldiers shot one of the Resistance men and tortured ten others to death. Four Norwegian civilians suspected of complicity died later in concentration camps. So the brandy had cost fifteen lives.

Baalsrud alone escaped. He was a twenty-six-year-old apprentice instrument maker from Oslo. Now he was on the run. Furuflaten to Lyngseidet to Mandal, fjord after fjord, plateau after plateau, for ten weeks, at one stage buried under snow for either four or five days straight, until the final spurt, lashed to a Sámi sledge, into neutral Sweden, which he first saw through four hundred galloping reindeer legs. The Germans had installed a tyranny of fear, even up in the remotest villages. Baalsrud's flight owed everything to the courage of Norwegians who spirited him to safety, handing him on like the baton in a relay. One rowed him across a sound at night even as German searchlights scissored the water. Of the men who hauled him on a sledge up a Lyngenfjord alp after his feet had turned gangrenous, Baalsrud said, 'All four of them had the unending dogged patience which is typical of Arctic people.' In addition to their native qualities, people loathed Germans with a ferocity that inhabitants of unoccupied lands cannot share. Those men and women were tested almost to the limit in the last months of 1944. Baalsrud, meanwhile, although the recipient of generous assistance, was alone almost all the time, often near starvation, outside in falling snow, frostbitten and snow-blind. Obliged to chop off his toes with a penknife, he laid the digits on a high ledge so he didn't have to look at them. His mother had died when he was sixteen, and as he lay mummified in drift and close to death, he said later that he thought of the younger sister he had himself mothered, left now to grow up without him. He had been active since the start of the war, and had not seen her for three years. But he made it to safety, and served his country again. When I first heard this story, I understood why it was a Norwegian who had beaten Scott to the South Pole.

At the end of the conflict, Finland was obliged to cede its mineral-rich territory in the north-east to the USSR, a disaster for the economy of Finnish Lapland as it meant the loss of its only ocean coast. The Sámi there were resettled in Finland around Sevettijärvi and Nellim. From the Lake Inari basin their new land rises gradually north to the tundra plateau, then drops to the sea coast at Varangerfjord and an embayment of the Barents Sea. Those people were Skolt Sámi, the only group in the world named after a skin disease (the condition, to which these particular Sámi were susceptible, has been eradicated). It was Skolt misfortune to live on one of the most geopolitically precipitous borders in the world – the one dividing east and west, Finland and Russia. Sometimes called Petsamo Skolt after the river which flows through their land, they were first evacuated during the Winter War of 1939, and when they subsequently returned it was only to be evacuated again five years later. Resettlement brought them into an undignified relationship of dependency with the Finnish government. Initially, most people ignored them. But in the 'enlightened' cultural climate of the 1970s, charitable organisations and Helsinki well-wishers took an interest in their northern confrères, deluging the bemused Skolt with second-hand clothes and malfunctioning sewing machines. But subsistence yielded to cash and the journey from autonomy to dependency took its course. Two decades after the Skolt resettlement, petrol-powered washing machines appeared on the shores of Lake Inari. Skills have been lost, some for ever, and the complexity of herding has been vastly simplified with the reduction of herding families and the introduction of technology. Technological innovation is a mighty thing but it renders herding economically unworkable: to raise the capital required to service and upgrade a snowmobile, one would be obliged to slaughter an illegal quantity of reindeer. The same applies to outboard motors and fish. No wonder most Sámi have fled to the industrial heartlands of the south. As in Russia, Canada, Alaska and Greenland, polar conditions were not conducive to interventionism in Scandinavia. In that fragile region, transhumance was more productive and sustainable than home-steading, yet the latter triumphed, along with the industrialisation of the mines. Of a pan-Sámi population of about 70,000, none remain nomadic; many no longer live on their ancestral land; few depend economically on herding. Trans-national agreements allow herders to cross borders unmolested, but the lack of 'nationhood' in the modern, political sense has always worked against the Sámi people. As a Lapp recently told the writer Roger Took, 'Sámi don't think about national borders as most people do ... from the middle ages we Sámi had to submit to Danes, Swedes, Norwegians and Russians. We paid tribute and taxes to whoever claimed to have been granted authority over us ... but we're still one nation, although we speak different dialects, and I like to think we can all still look to one another in rough times.'*

In 2007, to celebrate the centenary of the Turi–Munthe journey, Axel's grandson Adam Munthe made a 1,500-kilometre dog-sledge journey through Finnmark from the Barents Sea to the Atlantic. While the team found much to celebrate, they also learned how government intervention and regulation had ratcheted up the economic challenges of herding, as had in-fighting among Sámi themselves, and the warming climate. 'Their ancestors had to adapt to climatic variations,' Munthe told me, 'and Sámi have to meet today's challenges, somehow.' He agreed that the dismissive attitude expressed by Lars Anders in 1907 had barely improved with the passage of time. 'Sámi are not trusted still, like gypsies,' he said sadly. It was in the DNA: hatred of the other.

* Kirsti Paltto, one of the best known Sámi authors, wrote a short story about what it was like being both Finnish and Sámi. In it, the protagonist grows two heads. 'The Two Headed Woman', according to the author, is 'A story about a woman's life between two cultures.' Who said the subtle image was the best?

The year after my visit to the herders, I attended a meeting with Finnish scientists at the National Meteorological Institute in Helsinki. My hosts told me plainly there were too many reindeer in north Finland, that overgrazing was wrecking the land, and that unlike in Sweden, many of those practising reindeer husbandry were not Sámi, thereby implying

that economic privileges granted to the remaining herders on account of their minority status were unfair. Adam Munthe spoke of 'deep distrust'. The meteorologists told me that Finns drink more as the latitude rises. 'Up there,' they said, pointing to the ceiling, 'they run on ethanol.' Discounting the Sámi, the meteorologists were the first sober Finns I had ever met. In the evening they generously took me out to dinner at a famous Sámi restaurant in Helsinki, a theme-park approximation of how Finns would like their Lapps to be.

In November 2002 I was standing on the tundra trying to lasso a reindeer. 'No good!' cried the man holding the walkie-talkie. 'Reindeer laughs!' Three thousand deer were on the loose, and in an hour I hadn't caught one, not even a calf. I picked up the rope at my feet and walked off, towing little Reg in his sledge. My guide in Sápmi was thirty-one-year-old Lennart Pittja, whose family have herded reindeer on their Unna Cerus community land for many generations. Pittja grew up in Sörkaitum near Gällivare in the heart of Norrbotten, Sweden's most remote province. His mother was not Sámi, which explained his height (five feet eleven) and his sandy hair; he looked like an archetypal Viking. 'Officially', he explained as we sat in a stockade slurping reindeer broth, 'I am half Sámi, but I believe you are either Sámi or not.' He had bridled when I asked how many reindeer his family owned. 'Some,' he replied, explaining later that the question is like asking how much a person earns. (He had a good ear for a snappy phrase. 'Our bank', he added to this last exchange, 'is on four legs and has antlers.') Pittja had many qualities and the chief among them was remorseless enthusiasm. When he saw me battling to breastfeed at -10 he launched into a story about a friend who suckled her baby outside in winter by inserting tin foil in her bra to reflect heat back onto her bosom. As he was plainly about to hurry off in search of foil, I steered him back onto the subject of reindeer economics. Inserting kitchen equipment down my shirt was a step too far.*

Pittja had a profound sense of connection with his community land, and a missionary zeal to preserve the traditions of his people. His great-grandparents were among the last *flyt* Sámi (nomads); they had settled in Sörkaitum in the forties. His father and brother were still herding. After bringing the deer down from the mountain pastures at the onset of winter, they must check every animal each day, no joke at -38. As for the animals: the mortality rate among calves is above 50 per cent in an average winter. In a bad one, they can all die. At that

---

* Though improvisation was the key. On the road in small-town America some years earlier with my elder son, then a baby, I went down to reception at our motel to ask if they by chance had a crib (cot). They did not, but kindly set about trying to find something that might do. Half an hour went by, and the receptionist knocked on my door. When I opened it, she wheeled in a shopping trolley.

time, twelve autumns in a row had been unseasonably warm, a disaster for reindeer, as if snow melts in autumn and freezes in winter an ice bark prevents them from sniffing out lichen. Elsewhere the new and previously unknown phenomenon of winter rain had dangerously thinned ice on migration pathways. The rapidity of climate change had already led to a decline in the reindeer population. 'You wonder', said Pittja, 'if we can hold on.'

Pittja talked of modest tax breaks for indigenous businesses, but they failed to add up to much, while health and safety laws stymied the small-scale herder. A Sámi man no longer castrated his deer by biting off the balls, like his grandfather did; but he can still do the job himself with a pair of special pincers. The government, on the other hand, insists on the engagement of an expensive specialist veterinary surgeon. Industry, meanwhile, has taken up the slack. The economy around Gällivare, my point of entry into Lapland, is based on the Malmberget iron-ore and open-cast copper mines. One of the largest iron ore deposits in the world lies in Kiruna fifty miles to the north. Swedish Lapland is also a significant source of hydroelectric power. The Suorva Dam on the Lule an hour upriver from Gällivare has created the biggest water reservoir in Europe. When the dam was built, Pittja's grandfather had to move house four times as the water level rose (it went up 30 metres in total). Each time, his house had to be burned down. Grandpa watched the land on which he had grown up disappear underwater as the five lakes between Suorva and Ritsem turned into one. Valleys where reindeer calved were flooded, forcing cows to give birth at a colder elevation. As my own Arctic journey unfolded, what had appeared to be a series of individual histories had merged into a universal saga. Before my 2002 visit, the Soviet compulsion to extract minerals struck me as an example of that nation's generally brutish behaviour, like Chernobyl. When I went to the Arctic I saw that we were all at it.

Unlike its Norwegian counterpart, Stockholm will not recognise Sámi as indigenous people by ratifying UN International Labour

Organisation Convention 169. Operations that compete with reindeer herding for land are legally obliged to give consideration to the interests of reindeer husbandry, but provisions work poorly in practice. Pittja reeled off case after case in which a herder had effectively been forced to move. 'Look,' he explained, the enthusiastic voice for once exposing a weary undertow. 'We don't consider that we own the land. We just look after it for future generations. But we have to claim ownership now in order to participate in the system. The trouble is – one of the many troubles – other people show papers to prove ownership, but we don't have documents. Ours is an oral culture – our books are flesh and blood.' Nobody minds too much what Sámi do in the mountains, because Swedes don't use that land. The pressure is on winter grazing in developed areas. When Sámi in Härjedalen lost a court case in which they were claiming rights to their traditional winter grazing, other landowners took the opportunity to get Sámi reindeer off their land 'once and for all'. A Sámi parliament of sorts does exist in Sweden, based in Kiruna, the most northerly town, but it has no constitutional status and, according to Pittja, is little more than an advisory service. Down in far-off Stockholm, the government has always shrunk from anything approaching a concession to indigenous land rights. Norway, with a larger Sámi population, has a better record; its own all-wood parliament building is in Karasjok on the *Finnmarksvidda*.* Meanwhile efforts to establish pan-Sámi cultural institutions have found expression in a flag and a football team. When it came to native peoples, even the most humane and advanced welfare

---

* Sometimes things go backwards. In an article in northern Norway's largest-circulation newspaper, *Nordlys*, Sámi language professor and former president of the Norwegian *Sameting* (Sámi parliament) Ole Henrik Magga wrote that he was more optimistic about the possibilities of working Sámi interests into administrative and other bodies twelve years ago than he is today. Magga cited doubts about 'whether the power structure in place is willing to prepare a permanent spot in the country's political and administrative system for Sámi culture'.

states couldn't get it right. All round the Arctic, I had seen every dominant culture grappling with a legacy of miscarried cultural assimilation and racial marginalisation.

Behind his home, the industrious Pittja had made a sturdy tent-house from skins and peat. If you overlooked the aluminium poles, it was a perfect model of the traditional *lávvu*. When Reggie and I arrived for the evening, a pair of draft reindeer were scooping snow outside with their front hooves, burying their noses into the mushy ground beneath and whistling softly as they exhaled. Constellations of white-faced stars hung low, the abutting spruce grove a cavern of moonlight and shadows. Inside, we lounged on pelts as Pittja's herding assistant, Anders, rolled out flatbread and the fire hissed to life, catching first on resin in the birch bark then crackling over pine and juniper. A small hole in the apex of the *lávvu* drew off aromatic smoke. We lay snug in our poled fortress. Pittja had cooked up a *máles*, the Sámi meal prepared at slaughter time, and it bubbled with ominously pungent eructations in a cauldron lashed to a lateral rod between tent poles. A *máles* consists of almost every part of a reindeer boiled in the same pot: liver, tongue, bone and steak with its hump of canary-yellow fat. 'Even the hooves are boiled!' Pittja announced, handing me a green birch skewer with which to poke marrow from bone. I could see the flickering ion-stream of the Northern Lights through the roof opening. Anders offered a chunk of cooked reindeer fat on a plate. 'For the baby,' he said. 'He's not weaned yet,' I said. 'I know,' he said. 'That's what we wean them with.'

We ate the dish with lingonberry relish, black pudding and a patty made with blood and oatmeal. Breastfeeding makes one hungry enough for anything, except perhaps boiled hoof, though fortunately one was not called to put that to the test. Reggie didn't care much for the smoke, however, and I didn't either, as I couldn't see what I was eating, though this had its advantages. Pittja, ladling vigorously, dealt with the problem by sporting a Davy lamp on his forehead. After the meal we drank coffee brewed on the fire in a tin pot. I watched an approaching milk jug with trepidation – reindeer milk is so high in fat that it practically curdles into cheese in your mouth – but it was cow's milk, bought from a shop. It was hard not to feel relieved. But then the other two lobbed cubes of cheese into their coffee.

The day after the herding, we started up Route 45, 'the Route 66 of Sweden', in Pittja's four-wheel-drive Nissan. Through a break in the rim of a mountain bowl the Lule River heads west into the heartlands of Laponia, 9,400 km² of wilderness north of the Arctic Circle from Jokkmokk to the Norwegian border and beyond. The road was built for the hydroelectric plant; before that, Sámi travelled on the Lule. The sky was full of lenticular stratocumulus, and the sun cast the shadows of slender birch trees over the lakes.

Two hours in, I hoisted Reggie into his sling and with Pittja in the lead we hiked eastwards, following lynx tracks across wetlands where whooper swans nested in the grass of the eskers. When Pittja stopped

to examine snow with foot and hand, like the herder he was, I heard again the crisp Arctic silence – the heaped-up orchestra of high latitudes. In the forest a flock of bramblings rustled up from the cotton grass. They were preparing to migrate, fat as the reindeer. It was -15 and the tips of our noses had turned cerise.* Reg slumbered deep within the folds of my multitudinous layers. (I only wished I hadn't been up half the night feeding him; but what a wickedly ungrateful thought that was.) Suddenly, we heard the click-click of walking reindeer. A special bone on the hind feet clicks so they can hear one another in darkness and mist. Today 50,000 reindeer live in the park and twenty of them were looking for angelica not far from where we stood. Pittja got out his binoculars to see if he could identify animals from his own herd. Each deer is labelled with notches cut into the ears. The markings on the left ear record the family, those on the right ear the individual within the family (babies receive a quota of reindeer at their baptism). A directory records the marks, like a telephone book. But a herder like Pittja knows hundreds of different markings on sight.

Emerging from the conifers, we entered a belt of mountain birch, the last cover before the alpine slopes. 'Look,' said Pittja, poking the forest floor with a stick. 'See these blackened stones? They were the hearth of a *goahte*, a herders' camp. People returned to the same sites year after year. Somewhere round here there will be a hunting pit where they snared moose.' Seasonal migration routes have crossed Laponia since the land rose up from the ice, and traces of human habitation date back 8,000 years. We stopped to picnic on the western shore of Lake Satis, among pink bulbils of netted willow that peeped

---

* Cold noses notwithstanding, the deceptions of latitude are most apparent in the Scandinavian north. The topmost points of Finland (Nuorgam at 70°) and Norway (Nordkapp at 71°) are further north than much of Arctic Canada and almost all of Arctic Alaska, yet enjoy a more temperate climate and lighter ice cover as a result of moderating southerly air currents associated with the Gulf Stream. The coasts have a long ice-free period and snow melts everywhere in summer except on high mountains. Inland, on the Norwegian *Finnmarksvidda* and in Swedish and Finnish Lapland, the climate is continental, with warmer summers than along the coast, but considerably colder winters.

cautiously from the lime-rich soil. Along the shore, ice manacled the lower spruce branches. Pittja produced a hunk of smoked reindeer and began stripping off pieces with a pocket knife. As he and I drank coffee from our wooden bowls, I felt ice crystals softening in my nostrils. Baby breath pearled my undershirt. It was a good place to rest. When we finally brushed ourselves down, the sun had already vanished and the slopes of the blue mountain glittered with patches of snow. Pittja carried a GPS unit, but I never saw him use it. 'We know our land,' he said as we hiked back to the Nissan. He lived and worked with a beguiling combination of technology and tradition. As we walked, he fished out a mobile phone and began punching out a number. 'I am ringing the car,' he said. A diesel-burning heater with controls on the dash could be operated remotely by telephone. Pittja had been yakking all day. 'No need for talking here,' he said quietly as we reached the Nissan and looked over at the ice on the birch branches, the spangled glint of the lake and the miles of rounded mountains beyond. 'It speaks for itself.'

And it did.

VIII

Ship of Fools

The Arctic Ocean and its Passages

Their life is death for us
Randall Jarrell, 'The Iceberg'

The fucking world is running out of gas
John Updike, *Rabbit is Rich*

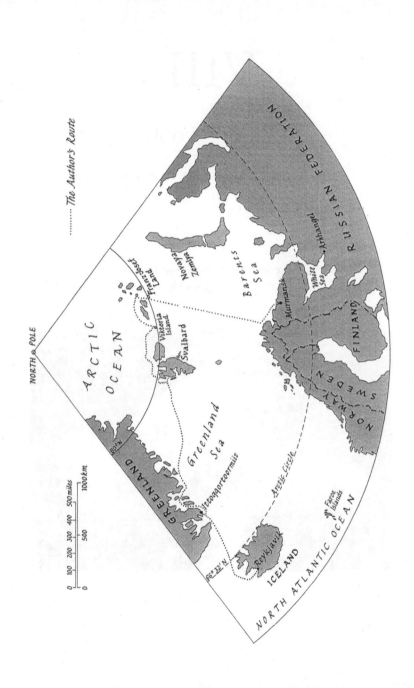

.... The Author's Route

NORTH POLE

ARCTIC OCEAN

GREENLAND

80°N

66°33'N

Greenland Sea

Ittoqqortoormiit

Reykjavik

ICELAND

NORTH ATLANTIC OCEAN

Faroe Islands

Arctic Circle

Svalbard

Viktoria Island

Franz Josef Land

Novaya Zemlya

Barents Sea

Murmansk

White Sea

Arkhangel

NORWAY

SWEDEN

FINLAND

RUSSIAN FEDERATION

0   100 200 300 400 500 miles
0   500   1000 km

As the Arctic took centre stage in the warming climate drama, a cruise industry sprang up to ferry tourists to the polar bears before they all drowned. It was another example of the world moving towards the Arctic. In July 2008 the 15,000-tonne ice-breaker *Kapitan Khlebnikov* sailed from Murmansk on a sixteen-day, 3,256-nautical mile (6,000-kilometre) journey across the Arctic Ocean. I took my wildlife-loving, ten-year-old son on it, Reg's big brother Wilf. It was his future at stake in the Big Melt.

The sun was shining when our charter flight landed at Murmansk, and the pilot announced 69°. Inside the terminal there were no computers at the immigration counters, no trolleys at the baggage carousel and no paper in the lavatory. On the bus into town, Wilf and I gazed out at the wooded slopes of the Kola Peninsula, the quietly glimmering lakes, the timeless melancholy of the far north. A Norwegian conservationist recently called this region of few roads and many bogs 'the largest area of uninterrupted natural landscape in Europe'.

But after half an hour, Murmansk sprang out from behind the beech trees. The city had been built up a hill in tiers of concrete *devyati-etazhki*, the nine-storey blocks that put down root across the Russian permafrost in the Communist period along with the stubbier *khrushchevka.* Beyond the butter-coloured civic buildings on Five Corners Square, and the squashed green cupola of the railway station, seventy-five years of centrally planned vandalism had done their work. The settlement was a study in urban decay, a nasty blur of stained concrete, cracked facades and dribbling rubbish. The sun had gone in. It was hard to imagine the sun ever shining on Murmansk.

The wheezing concertina buses on Prospekt Lenina, once yellow, now kippered with soot, competed with spent trams to climb the hill to St Nikolas' Cathedral, a plain grey, single-domed monument to Russian tenacity, as it was built in 1985 (the Kremlin despatched miners to blow it up, but, in an early indication of the Soviet melt, protesters prevailed – and lived). Few Murmanchaners were on the streets; those who had ventured out appeared hunched and drawn. One-litre plastic beer bottles rolled on the cracked pavements, slewing, drunk themselves, between iron lampposts. Outside the cathedral, a wedding party alighted from a fleet of Ladas, the pasty bride battling to subdue both veil and skirts as a gale swept in from the Kola Gulf, bringing a whiff of salt, and the chief bridesmaid engaged in a private struggle of her own to light and smoke a cigarette in the time it took to walk between the Ladas and the cathedral doors.

Situated in the Sámi heartlands halfway between Moscow and the North Pole, Murmansk was founded in 1916 on the sheltered and deepwater east bank of the Kola Gulf. When Nazi troops arrived in June 1942 having bombed half the port to smithereens, a resistance fighter found a ticket for a banquet to celebrate the city's surrender in the pocket of a dead German's uniform. But there was no surrender. What Murmanchaners withstood, in terms of siege conditions and destruction, was second only to Stalingrad.

We had flown in from Helsinki along with the rest of the ice-breaker's passengers and some replacement crew. Before depositing us at our vessel, the transfer bus stopped at the highest point of the city, a platform dominated by a 42-metre concrete statue of a Russian infantryman facing west across the Kola Gulf towards the River Litsa, where Soviets held the German invasion of 1941. Murmanchaners baptised the statue Alyosha, the Russian John Doe, the boy-man who perished in millions in both wars. On the cargo docks below, steve-dores beetled along the gantries. Next to Alyosha's eternal flame, someone had scrawled *Vechnaya pamyat* on the concrete – eternal memory. Even the graffiti was tragic in Murmansk. Russians were at that time studiously rehabilitating Stalin, and had recently voted him the third greatest Russian of all time. There was to be no sober reflec-tion; 'memory' had barely outlived the century.

The cutaway prow meant we could pick out our ship long before the transfer bus had inched its way through the crowded port lanes. In the days of a command economy the Soviets commissioned the best ice-breakers, and in the struggling market economy that followed the disintegration of the USSR, entrepreneurial tour companies converted several into cruise liners. It was a tourist ice-breaker that brought news in 2000 that there was no ice to break at the North Pole that summer as it had all melted. The *Khlebnikov* was a typical shallow-draft escort vessel designed to enter Siberian deltas in ambient temperatures as low as -50, hopefully not something we were going to put to the test. Foul weather and unexpected sea ice constitute the chief hazards of Arctic travel, but in our case another menace queued up for attention: Russian bureaucracy. Having boarded along with ninety-odd other passengers, and found our cabin on deck 7, we waited thirty hours for 'customs clearance', the international maritime term for a wad of large ones. All we could do was cool our heels, marooned among ziggurats of coal and the low elephant grief of other ships' horns.

The delay gave us a chance to meet fellow passengers as they loafed around the decks taking photographs of the birds, the port, and each other. They were predominantly American, though France, Germany, Switzerland and South Africa were well represented. Many were repeat customers. 'It gets in your blood,' said a Swedish university lecturer. Wilf, the only child on board, reduced the average age by several decades. The eldest cruiser, an eighty-nine-year-old Italian *contessa* travelling alone, was the same size as Wilf. He took to seaboard life immediately. On the second day, one of the logistics team asked if he could help coil some zodiac ropes. A friendship was born. Igor Konyenko was strong and thick-set with cornflake-coloured hair, an excess of energy and a natural disrespect for authority – the perfect companion for a pre-teen.

Murmansk harbour is a major transhipment port for north-west Russia as well as a base for the Barents Sea oil industry and a hub for the fishing trade around its shallow southern banks, a business controlled by gang bosses of the ubiquitous *mafiya*.* From our lookout on the top deck, we watched hundreds of cranes opening bucket jaws over pyramids of coal and slate, piles of anthracite and neat towers of aluminium ingots. Seagulls carved tunnels in vapour from the refinery stacks, and walls of Norilsk Nickel shipping containers that had sailed down the Dudinka dwarfed the cornflower blue customs house, the rusty pontoons and the spaghetti of dented pipes that twirled through the docks. Alongside the *Khlebnikov*, a collier was taking on its freight. The fuel, falling in thunderous booms and discharging acrid black gases, was heading for Siberian coastal villages ahead of the big freeze. Beyond the tarry smells and clattering railyards, tier after tier of identical grey tower blocks reached up the hill, the weak Arctic sun glinting off glassed-in balconies. A mist had closed in on the city and cars crawled through the streets, headlights diffuse in the vapour. On the ridge on the other side of the inlet, the authorities had stuck a model of a fighter plane.

A thousand dollars changed hands in the end. After a decade of turf warfare, racketeering and extortion had regularised themselves in Murmansk; the daytime assassinations of the late nineties had all but

---

* The flat and frugally populated seascape of the Tersky coast in the south and east of the Kola Peninsula, always a smugglers' coast, has turned into a Klondike for a cornucopia of traffickers, the proceeds drunk away or funnelled out through the administrative centre of Umba.

ended and everyone more or less knew their place. We certainly did. The tannoy crackled out an order, and we presented ourselves in the ship's lecture theatre for a passport and face check in front of a row of saurians coiffed in stiff-peaked headwear so huge that one wondered how they remained upright. The tugs finally cast us off at midnight. It was not quite twilight, or even owl light, but it was not daylight either. The brilliance of arc-welding lamps dazzled from the derricks, and, over the low green hill behind one of the loading piers, the eternal flame of Alyosha flickered. For several hours we laboured up the Kola inlet. At Severomorsk, home base of the Northern Fleet, a steel jungle clogged the calm waters of what remained a heavily restricted *zona*, while at the shadowy Nerpa shipyard cranes sheltered the floating dock on which the carcass of *Kursk* bled its nuclear fuel. When the Oscar II-class K-141 sank to the bottom of the Barents Sea after an explosion during a training exercise, the whole world listened to the ghoulish knocking of the trapped submariners. All 118 perished.

At the mouth of the inlet, one last tug whisked off the harbour master. He had to go back to Murmansk, poor thing.

The Arctic Ocean covers in excess of 14 million square kilometres (almost five and a half million square miles), which is one and a half times the area of the United States and sixty United Kingdoms. Ice covers almost all of it in winter, and about half in summer; the ice cap grows and shrinks with the seasons. But in 2007, when satellites revealed record summer shrinkage, news outlets throughout the world led with alarm on this fresh indication of imminent catastrophe. The role of the Arctic Ocean in climate change is complex and occluded in uncertainty. At a macro level, alterations in temperature, salinity and reflective properties affect currents and heat transportation in ways that fundamentally impact on our climate. At a micro level, a warming ocean has begun recalibrating the planet's carbon exchange by heating billions of life forms in the microbial soup at the bottom of the food web. These processes are improperly understood, and outcomes can be good as well as bad. A shifting phytoplankton population might result in an abundance of fish, solving, at a stroke, the planetary protein deficit.

My first close-up experience of the ocean unfolded in the cyclone zone of the Barents Sea, and it was hard to think about anything except not being sick. The ship listed violently to port, and then to starboard, and waves crashed onto the decks with such force that one was denied even the solace of fresh air. Dining saloons stood empty. Like everyone else, I clung to the stair-rails as we plunged in and out of the rollers, reflecting miserably that this was not quite the same as trekking over the flat and solid Greenland ice sheet, or climbing gentle Finnish fells.

The cruise was to trace two sides of a triangle, heading up to the remote Russian archipelago of Franz-Josef Land before turning south-west, skimming the top of the Svalbard group, crossing hemispheres, sailing down the east coast of Greenland and ending up in Iceland's Reykjavik. On this first leg *Khlebnikov* followed the west coast of Novaya Zemlya, an elongated archipelago extending out of the Urals between the Barents and Kara Seas. A pod of humpbacks led the way, cetacean plumes flagging the route. But the history of Novaya Zemlya has little in common with the friendly image of a whale. The islands are uninhabited and far from monitoring stations, and between 1955 and 1990, military personnel detonated 132 nuclear warheads on their rocky tundra. On days when the wind blew east, the fallout landed on Siberian reindeer pastures. Lichens take nutrients from air rather than soil and so absorb many times more radioactive isotopes than green plants. In winter, reindeer eat lichen, and herders eat reindeer. The bio-accumulative effects of radiation must have been worse than even Chernobyl. (Winds were blowing towards the monitoring stations in Sweden on the day Chernobyl went off. So we knew all about that straight away.) After the explosions, workers dumped radioactive waste and spent nuclear reactors in the deep fjords that dissect the northern island of Novaya Zemlya. The development of Soviet nuclear power focussed on the north, and between 1950 and 1970 the Northern Fleet matured from the smallest of the national armadas to one that was larger and more significant than its not diminutive siblings on the Pacific and the Black Sea. Yet the Soviets only had one centre for reprocessing used nuclear fuel, at the Mayak complex in the upper Ob river basin in western Siberia, now the most radioactive place on earth, so the Arctic Ocean became a nuclear rubbish dump. Submarine reactor cores with high radiation levels ended up in the oil and gas-rich Kara Sea.* Wilf's new friend Igor had worked as a bosun for a state hydrological research company. On one job, they measured contamination from the fissionable, enriched uranium control rods of the nuclear ice-breaker *Lenin*. The rods went to the bottom of Tsivolka Bay near Novaya Zemlya following an accident in 1965 involving a loss of coolant. 'After we had finished the landings on Novaya Zemlya,' Igor told me in the bar one night, 'we took bunches of birch twigs back on board for the sauna, like we always do. One day someone was fooling around with a Geiger counter. It went totally crazy near the sauna, and we finally worked out that it was the twigs. They were alive with radiation.'

Meanwhile six new naval bases were operating along the Murman coast from Zapadnaya Litsa in the west to Gremikha in the east. (Soviet bureaucrats had a mania for renaming, and these bases appear on old maps under a variety of disguises: Zapadnaya Litsa was also known as Murmansk-150, Zaozerny, Severomorsk-7 and Andreyeva Bay.) By 1989, Russian Lapland held over one fifth of the world's total nuclear reactor capacity. Obsessive Soviet secrecy once kept this high-specification military matériel hidden from international view. But now the visitor may inspect both stockpiles and infrastructure as it rots on the beaches of the north-west. In 2000, the writer Roger Took counted forty

---

* The Soviet Navy dumped the following three special vessels in the Kara near Novaya Zemlya after the ships had provided technical maintenance to merchant and military nuclear-powered operations; all were heavily contaminated and carried solid radioactive waste. 1) The *Nikolai Bauman*, dumped in 1964 in Tsivolka Bay. 2) The *Olga Bay*, a tugboat, dumped in 1968. 3) A special-purpose technical maintenance vessel, designation PSSN-28, dumped in 1976, which also carried liquid radioactive waste.

decaying nuclear reactors and 900 uranium fuel assemblies in ageing canisters at Gremikha, where Sámi and Pomors processed whale blubber and cod liver for so many generations. As for accidents: environmental groups have uncovered many, and the authorities have owned up to others in order to appeal for clean-up money (which they often get), so imagine the number that must have taken place – the ones never revealed. A series of incidents at Zapadnaya Litsa in the eighties involving spent fuel storage started when the concrete and steel lining of a storage pool cracked due to poor construction and frost effects. Radioactive waste water started to leak at a rate of 30 litres a day, soon reaching ten tonnes an hour. Yes, ten tonnes an hour.* Large quantities of the Northern Fleet's spent nuclear fuel and waste remains in insecure and volatile conditions across Lapland, and a number of fuelled submarines loll like beached killer whales awaiting decommissioning that never comes. In the meantime the industry is working hard on competitive Arctic shelf technologies. A 2008 Bellona report reveals details of the planned construction of nuclear-powered underwater drilling ships to be deployed in the Kara and Barents Seas as well as floating nuclear power plants. That same year, assessors estimated that one field in the Barents Sea contained 3.2 trillion cubic metres of gas in reservoirs 2 kilometres below the seabed.

On the second day, the tumult subsided to oceanic calm. We leant over the rails watching wavelets die under a film of dark grease ice that followed the movement and contours of the swell. When the film thickened, it turned white, like a rind; the Inuit call that *isigoanjazuk*. Green water filled basins under the pressure cracks, and frost smoke wafted from the leads. Later we entered fields of heavy floes that were

---

* According to the science-based environmental organisation Bellona, total radioactivity of spent nuclear fuel and radioactive waste at Zapadnaya Litsa reaches approximately 1,018 Becquerel, or 27 million curies. Overall radioactivity of the release of radioactive substances during the Chernobyl accident was around 50 million curies.

dark blue, like bruises, and twisted at the edges into sinuous galleries of statuary. The Eskimo's multiple words for snow might have an element of the canard, but Inuktituk has a rich fund of expressions for different kinds of sea ice. If, while paddling your *umiak*, you heard a cry of '*Sugainnuq!*', you would look up in alarm and see 'a huge moving mass of ice that threatens the integrity of the lead edge; it might be a large piece of pack ice or an agglomeration of multi-year ice and first-year ice'. *Aluksraq*, on the other hand, would indicate the more benign 'young ice punched by seals forming a blowhole', and *agiuppak* an entirely harmless 'smooth wall of ice along the edge of landfast ice formed by other moving ice'. The wind blew hard, chasing ragged sheets of stratus fractus. When the *Khlebnikov*'s hull broke young ice, rectangles overlapped in quilted patterns of dark and light. On average, ice in the Arctic Ocean is seven years old and ten feet thick. First-year ice is greyish, multi-year ice blueish (another clue: multi-year ice is thicker, so sticks out the water further). Salt gets pushed out when sea ice freezes, as it doesn't fit in the structure of the crystal, and the older the ice, the less salt it contains, which is why, as every expeditioner knew, you can wash with melted first-year ice, cook with second-year ice, and make tea with multi-year ice. Peter Wadhams, professor of ocean physics at Cambridge, has been travelling under the ice cap in Royal Navy submarines since 1976, using an upward-looking echo sounder to measure ice thickness. His published data suggests that for thirty years Arctic sea ice has been thinning everywhere. In March 2007, under the ice in HMS *Tireless*, Wadhams discovered that the thinning rate has accelerated; the ice is now 50 per cent of its 1976 thickness. 'This enormous ice retreat in the last two summers is the culmination of a thinning process that has been going on for decades, and now the ice is just collapsing,' Wadhams said at the end of 2008. 'This is one of the most serious problems the world has ever faced.'

A cold period might allow the ice to recover. But since a blizzard of studies have shown a faster melt than expected (and even a sharp decrease in the extent of winter sea ice), predictions of an ice-free Arctic Ocean are being constantly revised downwards. 'If you look at the papers over the past decade,' says Dr Colin Whiteman, an expert in Quaternary Arctic landscape change, 'the estimated time frame for total melting of summer sea ice shrinks by five years per year.' At the time of writing, most scientists are predicting an Arctic Ocean free of summer ice before the end of the century. When, in 2008, a professor of earth systems at the University of East Anglia invited fifty leading climatologists to nominate their tipping points – likely events involving dramatic outcomes – a massive summer ice melt over ten years appeared at the top of the list. (Second was significant alteration in the Greenland ice sheet within 300 years; third the collapse of the West Antarctic Ice Sheet.) Respondents cited loss of reflective properties as a major factor both in accelerated sea ice melt and in the rapid warming of the Arctic in general. Ice operates as a reflective lid, bouncing the sun's heat back into the atmosphere, whereas open water absorbs about 90 per cent of sunlight that hits it. The albedo of an object – from the Latin for *whiteness* – is the extent to which it diffusely reflects light from the sun; albedo can range from zero per cent (no sunlight reflected – all absorbed – hot earth), to 100 per cent (all sunlight reflected – none absorbed – cold earth). Anything that changes the earth's albedo, such as an increase in sea ice melt, therefore also changes the amount of energy the planet absorbs. As more ice melts, more heat goes in, causing more ice to melt, and so the melt is exponential, which is why a big ice sheet can disappear more rapidly than a small one. A warmed ocean has many thousands of repercussions for marine life. Heating a can of Coca-Cola drives off the fizz, which is carbon dioxide. Heating the oceans does the same thing. As I travelled around the circumpolar lands I met many glaciologists, physicists and other researchers working on the surface heat budget of the ocean. I began this book back in Chukotka with an open mind, but figures recording the loss of sea ice the size of the UK indicate both the potential scale of this particular feedback effect and the extent to which feedback effects in general dominate the earth's complex climate system.

Sidney, a South African passenger travelling with his sister, had returned to the Barents Sea after more than sixty years. He had served as a rating on a convoy. When the German assault on Russia gathered momentum in the second half of 1941, the Allied merchant navy established a supply route through the Barents Sea to the railheads at Arkhangel and Murmansk. The Nazis, recognising the critical importance of the route, sent up dozens of U-boats and surface raiders and hundreds of aircraft; these were the planes Jan Baalsrud's colleagues in the Norwegian Resistance had died to foil. The ocean floor beneath us was a corner of a foreign field tens of thousands of times over. The water seemed to have curdled. 'Nobody can ever know', Sidney told Wilf and me as we lounged on deck, 'what the combination of fear, cold and constant strafing can do. But we were lucky. We were three months ahead of PQ-17.' In the summer of 1942, en route to Murmansk, convoy PQ-17 came under heavy bombardment. The Admiralty radioed orders to switch destination and head for Arkhangel, and, later, to scatter. The convoy lost twenty-five vessels out of thirty-six. Besides killing sailors, the combined action of U-boats and the

Luftwaffe sank 142,500 tons of PQ-17's cargo including 3,350 motor vehicles, 200 bombers and 430 tanks. Horace Carswell served as chief steward on the *Empire Tide*, one of the few ships to survive PQ-17. In the middle of one bombardment he gave a critically wounded rating a fireman's lift down the ladders and, in the absence of a doctor, operated himself using carpentry tools. There was no anaesthetic. 'I summoned the pantryman and a few others of the First Aid party,' Carswell recorded in his diary. '"There's nothing to worry about, son," I assured the patient. "I'll soon fix you up all right . . ." His lurid remarks betokened pain and resentment when I probed the gaping wound in his thigh and the ship lurched to the concussion of a bursting bomb . . . it shook me to find an unexploded shell from an Oerlikon gun embedded in the chap's thigh! . . . Having dug the live shell out, I put sixteen stitches in the wound.' Casualties were so high that the Allies began setting sail in winter, as it was harder to be detected in the dark, but the other enemy, the weather, was almost as bad as the German one, with swells in excess of seventy feet and temperatures so low that the torpedoes froze.

'Land!' yelped Wilf. The rockfaces of Franz-Josef Land glittered beyond the porthole. The sky was streaky, and bergy bits floated in the channel between ship and shore. Taking turns at the porthole, Wilf and I saw the helicopter deck where the crew were reattaching propellers and, on the port side, a crane dropping zodiacs overboard. Igor was in one of the dangling boats, and he saw us at the window as he went past. He waved and beckoned to Wilf, who was by that time worked to such a pitch of excitement that he was unable to manipulate the zips and buckles of his cold-weather safety gear.

Crouched along the rim of the Barents Sea, the 200 uninhabited islands of Franz-Josef Land boast some of the most extraordinary geological formations on the planet, their sequence of crystalline basalt cliffs and sedimentary tableland racked with deep channels. Heavily ice covered and usually tented in fog, the archipelago was not discovered until 1873, when an Austro-Hungarian expedition named it after the emperor. The

crew went exploring, and when the temperature dropped to -55 °C, their eyes froze open and their breath vapour froze, so they tinkled when they walked. But the Arctic Ocean still had secrets, even then. Nobody knew there were 37,000 km² of land between the Kara and Laptex Seas until 1913, when Russians found a fresh archipelago they named Severnaya Zemlya – the last major landmass on the planet to be discovered. As for Franz-Josef: the Soviets kept westerners out.

A zodiac ferried us over to Cape Norway, the western extremity of Jackson Land. Despite a latitude of 81°, purple saxifrage and lemon snow buttercups flourished alongside cushiony moss campion and white poppies, all nourished by the last gasp of the Gulf Stream. Not a single flower grows at that latitude in the southern hemisphere, even in the short burst of summer. Still, Arctic plants engage in a long and laborious energy-storing process in order to produce even a tiny bulb. It can go on for years. On some Arctic islands it takes 10 millennia to form 2 centimetres of topsoil.

In the middle of the vegetation, a few hundred yards from the ocean, a pile of stones lay in a shallow trench covered by a driftwood trunk once used as a roof ridge. It didn't look much. But in 1895 the great Nansen sat out the winter in the hole. The unprepossessing hollow had become one of the most sacred sites of polar history – up there with Scott's hut – just as the drill hole on the Greenland ice sheet represented a hallowed monument to science.

As news trickled in to the Scandinavian nations of the latest round of shoe-eaters frozen into Arctic waters for months and years, Nansen had an idea. If Arctic ice drifted in the direction of the Pole, he argued, why not deliberately allow a ship to freeze in, and drift with it all the way to 90°N? When he tried, the ship failed to reach the top spot, and after two years, refused to come unstuck. In August 1895, Nansen and stoker Hjalmar Johansen set out for help on maple-wood skis and in kayaks, knocking off a Farthest North while they were about it (they got to 86°, just 230 miles short of the Pole. It was the biggest single advance for 400 years). Nansen was a brilliant man but he forgot to wind the clock, so they were unable to chart their longitudinal position. The pair travelled over the ice for 146 days, covering 600 miles, and when they reached what later became Cape Norway they built a hut with stones and walrus hide, copying the dry-stone huts of the Norwegian uplands. This was the trench in which I now made Wilf pose for snaps. It was 10 feet long and 6 feet wide, and it was sunk three feet into the tundra. To celebrate reaching land, Johansen changed his underwear for the first time in four months. 'I like the sound of that,' said Wilf. If only he had been joking.

The pair lived off bear and walrus and spent the winter huddled in the same sleeping bag (Wilf was less attracted to that). Johansen, a short man from Telemark, recorded in his diary that one day Nansen said to him, 'Why don't we start addressing one another in the familiar *du* form now?'* They had no idea where they were. When the ice thawed in May, they paddled for a hundred miles on the wildest of outside chances that they might reach Spitsbergen. Walrus destroyed the kayaks, and food was running out. On 17 June, Nansen heard dogs barking. Leaving Johansen to guard the kayaks, he skied off, and three hours later rounded a hummock on Cape Flora in the south-west of Franz-Josef Land and saw a man in a tweed jacket. It was the English explorer Frederick Jackson, who happened to be on the spot having set off in 1894 on an expedition sponsored by press baron Alfred Harmsworth, later Lord Northcliffe. Nansen skied up to him. The two men shook hands.

'Aren't you Nansen?' asked Jackson, scrutinising the shaggy face of the world's greatest living explorer.

'Yes, I am,' the reply came.

'By Jove,' spluttered the Englishman. 'I'm damned glad to see you.' The whole world thought Nansen had perished. Nansen's first question was about his wife. Then he asked if Norway and Sweden were at war. Jackson noted that he was very fat. Back at Jackson's hut, Nansen ate fried guillemot, rice pudding and jam, had a bath and put on clean clothes while a sledge party went to fetch Johansen. Jackson and Nansen sat up talking till eight the next morning. 'A more remarkable meeting than ours was never heard of,' Jackson wrote in his diary. 'Nansen did not know I was in Franz-Josef Land.' Nansen had not known that he was in Franz-Josef Land himself.

Jackson had applied to join Nansen's expedition, but Nansen had rejected him, as he wanted only Norwegians. Instead, Jackson had persuaded Harmsworth to follow the lead of his American newspaper colleagues and sponsor a polar expedition of his own. It was the equiv-

---

* Shipton said more or less the same thing to Tilman when the pair reached the summit of Nanda Devi, suggesting that they start to use Christian names. But Tilman couldn't do it: surnames or nothing.

alent of owning a football team today. Jackson and his men mapped and explored Franz-Josef Land for three years. In their winter quarters at Cape Flora they washed in a canvas bath once a week, though hot water was banned, as the moisture would have rotted the wood (they made an exception when Nansen appeared). They slept on the floor, rolling up the bags in the day to make more room, and kept a bear cub for company, feeding it tins of condensed milk. They had one two-year-old newspaper, and in the winter learned the contents by heart, even the advertisements.* In his diary, Jackson recorded that when he thought of home, he wondered if they were getting good bags on the moors.

The two Norwegians went home on Jackson's supply ship in July 1886 and reached Christiania at the same time as their own vessel, which in the end had unfrozen. Nansen later named the island where they were rescued after Jackson. To the Norwegian people, Nansen was a hero, but Johansen had no public persona: his is the other face of exploration, that of the failure and misfit. In many ways Nansen's shadow, he was introspective, and seethed with regret and gloom throughout his life, in permanent exile from the rest of humanity. He went to the polar regions to escape himself. Once he reached the open

---

* Like the trapper we met in Svalbard who posted last year's newspaper in his mailbox on the way out to his traps each morning, the tautological antiquity of 'news' means nothing to the polar explorer starved of contact with the outside world. The celebrated French adventurer Jean Charcot put a two-year-old edition of *Le Matin* and *Le Figaro* on the wardroom table of his ship the *Pourquoi Pas?* each morning. He said both news and scandals were as interesting as when he first read of them, and that he was always impatient for the next day's instalment. On the Greely expedition in the High Canadian Arctic, men peeled scraps of soggy newspaper wrapping from their anti-scorbutic lemons and sat around in the evening reading them aloud. When even old news is scarce, any sample of the printed word becomes gripping. A modern day Frozen Beard once recited to me the cooking instructions for porridge oats in Swahili, as they were printed on the packet, which was all the reading material we had in the tent during a week-long blizzard. We had already eaten the porridge.

sea on Jackson's ship, homeward bound at last, he wrote in his diary, 'Now when I think of how wonderful I thought it would be to say goodbye to the ice and to all suffering, and compare that feeling with my reality now, I find that reality, after all, is not so wonderful as it appeared to me in the midst of our hard life.' A champion gymnast and accomplished skier, Johansen went on to explore Antarctica with Amundsen, but the leader left him out of the party that conquered the South Pole. He separated from the woman for whom he had pined in the long winter nights on Franz-Josef Land, and took refuge in alcohol. In 1913 he holed up in a boarding house in Christiania, destitute, and it was there that he shot himself. Nansen paid for his funeral. The refuge at Cape Norway remains, a troglodytic memorial to what men can endure. 'Polar exploration', wrote one of the pioneers, 'is at once the cleanest and most isolated way of having a bad time which has been devised.'

It was one of those perfect Arctic days on which ocean and sky compete to achieve the most vulgar blue. Thickened grease ice lay on the ocean like a rubber blanket, its saltwater pockets flexing with the waves. Back in the zodiac, I trailed a hand in the water and felt the sticky surface of frazil needles. The driver cut the engine, and we listened to mush ice clinking along the edge of the pans. When we floated around a headland, a female polar bear was standing on the fast ice. Her huge front paws were splayed over the ice edge and her raisin eyes focussed on a cub shaking its fur in a starburst of droplets. Sunshine reflected off the newly moulted sheen of her yellow guard hairs. When it sensed that it was too far away, the cub smacked its lips. Mother nosed into soupy ice. Then she went down on her forelegs, and slid silently into the ocean.

The sailor who power-hosed our boots when we returned from landings was a gnome-like figure with a tea-cosy hat and a mouthful of gold teeth. He smiled broadly all the time, and it was pleasant to see a man enjoying his work. After we returned from one outing and he had sluiced us down, he pointed out a bear that was gorging on the entrails of a seal on a floe piled with sugar snow. For an hour we were all hanging over the stern rail taking photographs. That is to say we were absorbed in the wonders of the natural world having burned up hydrocarbons by the tonne to reach them. Knitting at the guillotine? Or fiddling while Rome burned? Either way, this particular ship of fools illustrated the environmental conundrum of our time. When we went down to lunch after watching the bear I talked with the captain, Pavel Ankudonov, an inscrutable chain-smoking Vladivostokan and a veteran of both polar regions. 'On this voyage', he said, 'we burn 439 metric tonnes of IFO, heavy fuel. Average is 35 tonnes per day, though on last trip, through North East Passage from Anadyr, was more ice so we burn 60 tonnes a day.' The presence of my wildlife-loving son attenuated the irony: would all this be here for his children's children? Or would nuclear-powered ice-breakers solve at least this particular problem? I asked Ankudonov if his job would be easier on a nuclear vessel. First he snorted. Then he said, 'Nuclear captains just sit at wheel and go like through butter. We have to steer course. Monkey can pilot nuclear ice-breaker.' It was exactly what jet pilots said about astronauts. Puffing his Troika cigarettes, Ankudonov manfully maintained the ship's Russian flavour despite her international clientele. It was difficult to reconcile the happy images of a pleasure cruise – the grinning boot-hoser, the oldies on holiday, the genial captain and the natural beauty – with the threat of global inundation as the ice melted. Somewhere in the distance, one heard the strains of a band playing on. Hope was one thing. Refusal to listen was another.

When we weren't galumphing over the tundra or cruising the pack, Wilf and I looked out for wildlife, either from the flying bridge, or from Steel Beach on Deck 7 (it was next to the engine vents). There were always birds in the sky. Every day we saw northern fulmar, black-legged kittiwakes and Brünnich's guillemot (called the thick-billed murre in North America), and most days red-throated divers (loons in the

US), creatures so highly adapted to ice that they can barely walk on land. On Viktoria Island, Wilf spotted nesting ivory gulls. Two hundred and forty nautical miles from the other parts of Franz-Josef Land, the lonely Viktoria snow dome marks the westernmost point of Russian territory. The *Khlebnikov* dropped anchor among so much ice that we had to chopper ashore, landing on a shingle spit marked on a military map as Cape Knipovich. On one side of the spit, hundreds of terns had taken refuge in the rusted fuel tanks outside a pair of abandoned stations. One functioned between 1954 and 1993 as a meteorological observatory, the other as a Frontier Guard post. Wiping a circle in a frosted window at the front of the met station, I saw an open book on a desk and an oilskin on a hook with the sleeve turned inside-out. In 1993, having received neither salaries nor supplies for a year, the staff simply walked out of the door when a ship came. There was no money for keeping weather records, or for guarding useless frontiers. Soviet scientists operated 110 Arctic stations before the USSR fell. In 2008 there were three. It was a tragedy for science, as years of good data just stopped. Things would get better, but not yet, and in the meantime, ivory gulls and terns had the island to themselves.

By the time the *KK* approached Greenland four days later the ocean was showing off hundreds of bergs – mast-high fleets of them, towering with spires, funnels and Moorish arabesques. One, the size of a French cathedral, had flipped over, and the ship sailed so close that we were able to inspect whorls of algae on the freshly exposed underside. We had no darkness, but the light changed with the cycling of the day, and late at night long shadows cast the forms of bergs into singular prominence, as shafts of sunlight do in a lamplit room. I started to rise before five, in order not to miss the early morning reds and pinks glowing on the berg pageant. 'There is a glamour about those circumpolar regions,' Arthur Conan Doyle wrote in 1880 after seven months on a whaler. 'You stand on the very brink of the unknown.' We were all facing the unknown now. An undefinable truth of the Arctic was emerging from what I had seen in the beautiful ice.

One thing that was known, however, was that the ship's remorseless three-meals-plus a day regime threatened calorie-induced paralysis. But in the bowels of the vessel, I discovered a gym. Leaving Wilf on bear alert, I joined iron-thighed Russian sailors as they thrusted and flexed to Siberian rap, the crash of waves on the bow directly above adding tympanic rhythm to the piston-pounding from the boom box. The session concluded with a birch-twig thrashing in the sauna. A girl can have a worse time at sea.

From the ship's Mi-2 helicopters we watched the *KK* breaking ice with a bird's eye. As the 45-millimetre steel skirt on the cutaway prow smashed into the pack, it pushed layers up on top of one another until towers of shattered portions tottered sideways, or forced them under the hull, where an ice knife pulverised them into white rubble. The waves formed by the breaking process, as Sylvia Plath wrote about waves somewhere else, went off 'mouthing ice cakes'. As old ice is thicker than young, its dispersal requires increased horsepower, and the *KK* ramped its six diesel engines accordingly, tanking out, at maximum capacity, 24,200 hp. Snug in our cabin, we learned to calibrate the blows. Halfway across the Greenland Sea, at three o'clock in the morning, the ship struck with such ferocity that as he was hurled out of bed Wilfred shouted, 'Yikes!' (or something ruder). 'That must be really old ice!' Alert to the drama, we dressed quickly and hurried to the bridge, where Captain Pavel was smoking inside (a nice touch of *echte Kultur*) and poring over a chart. Sea ice is expressed in tenths on a maritime log, and on that day, at 81° 04' north, the ice master had inscribed '10/10'. Ankudonov had cut thousands of miles of ice at both ends of the earth. 'In satellite images we receive,' he explained as the three of us peered out of the bridge window at the solid white ocean ahead, 'fog obscure the ice cover, so we sail a bit blind. None of this ice at which we look appears on the charts, even though is not first-year ice – probably nobody charted this area last year.' Wilf asked which was harder – north or south. 'Antarctic much easier,' Ankudonov replied, 'as ice down there softer. Has snow on top, so cuts more easily. Up here I see pressure ridges forming and rising before eyes. Also, in Antarctic you only need to break ice close to land. Arctic Ocean has 50 per cent ice cover.'

Managing to smoke, talk and inspect ice all at the same time, the captain revealed that he had joined the *KK* straight out of his naval academy in 1985 and worked his way up, learning on the job the chaotic complexities of sea ice. Years ago he discovered that the key to polar travel is flexibility, and indeed that day, the one on which we reached the unbreakable ice, he changed our course, heading back out to sea and skirting the frozen barrier in order to hit Greenland further south than planned.

There had been a tremendous amount of talk in the bar, where most of the talking went on, about an imminent solar eclipse. Everyone knew something about it, but collective knowledge amounted to nothing at all, so it was a relief when the tannoy summoned us into the lecture theatre for an eclipse briefing. The event (we learned) was one of the Saros 126 1,280-year cycle, and as it turned out, Ankudonov heroically got the *KK* and us into the region of 90 per cent totality. Pinhole viewing boards were distributed, though as there was a bit of gossamer cloud cover we didn't need them, and as we watched the moon steadily blot out the sun, for the first and only time on the expedition, and for two minutes, we experienced something approaching darkness.

When I returned to the bridge later, Ankudonov, still at his post, had a pair of binoculars jammed into his eye sockets. They were pointing south, where there was nothing to see but ocean. When he had lowered the binoculars and put them back into the wooden case attached behind the wheel, he said, I thought almost wistfully, 'Only thousand miles to most important water in world.'

Faroe Bank: heard it on the shipping forecast? The narrow, deep channel south-west of the Faroe Islands has functioned for ten thousand years as a key transit passage for the currents that shift warm and cold water around the planet. But all is not well in the cold and salty deep.

The warm waters of the Gulf Stream flow from the tropics on the surface of the North Atlantic and, in conjunction with associated wind patterns, heat the air around western Europe, creating a climate far warmer than the latitude would otherwise permit. (One limb of the Gulf Stream releases a trillion kilowatts of heat as it powers past Ireland.)* At the same time, cold water flows south from the heart of the Arctic, and the discrete layer of warm water slides over the top of it because the cold, saltier mass is heavier. The warm water gradually releases heat, becoming saltier and heavier, and at pump sites in the Greenland Sea it sinks, piles up and drives the southward flow. (Not many people know that ocean flow is measured in units called Sverdrups, with one Sverdrup equivalent to one million tonnes of water a second.) The exchange of warm water for cold, called the meridional overturning, is a key component of thermohaline circulation, a kind of oceanic conveyor belt driven by salt and temperature (*thermo* heat, *hals* salt). For the exchange to work, extremely large volumes of cold, salty water must sink. But as Greenland glaciers accelerate their melt, they discharge more fresh water into the Arctic Ocean. Without sufficient salinity, the cold water is not dense enough to sink. A series of long-term data-gathering projects have tracked declining salinity in the Faroe Bank gap, while devices attached to narwhal tusks have transmitted valuable information on both reduced salinity and higher temperatures in parts of the ocean inaccessible to research vessels. In one of the many ironies of climate change, were the overturning circulation to stop, Britain would cool even as the planet itself continued to warm. Like most factors that influence a changing climate, overturning circulation is a chaotic and complicated story. Recent studies pioneered by a team from the university of Southampton have

---

* As an American scientist said, the Gulf Stream 'partly explains the accident of European civilisation'.

revealed that Atlantic currents are far more variable than previously understood.

I once asked a group of oceanographers during a coffee break in a polar conference if they considered it likely that the conveyor belt would stop altogether, switching off the overturning circulation. At first, they laughed. 'You can't expect us to agree on that,' one said. 'It won't happen this century – we won't fight about that at least,' said another. 'And certainly not this week, as it did in the movie *The Day After Tomorrow*! The threshold of collapse remains unknown – how much fresh water is needed to shut down thermohaline circulation. There are things we don't understand that play a crucial role. The North Atlantic Oscillation, for example, which is a multi-decadal see-saw of high and low pressure. We do know for sure that the top 1.5 kilometres of water in the seas around the main Greenland pump have freshened rapidly.' Someone said he thought thermohaline circulation might have been responsible for sudden climate shifts in the past, stimulating the switch between ice ages and non-ice ages. The discussion went on for a few minutes, to and fro. 'If the Greenland ice sheet starts to disintegrate – that's the big one in all this,' someone concluded; and we walked back into the conference hall.

The ice has always been uncertain: always the big one. The riches of the Oriental spice trade had lured both European and Russian ships into its traps for many centuries. The prized North-East Passage (following the Russian coast east) and the equally vaunted North-West Passage (threading westwards through the Canadian Arctic) meet at the Bering Strait, the narrow strip of water separating Russia and North America that decants into the priceless Pacific. The pursuit of both passages were epic in scope, involving rescuers who had to be rescued, the mightiest propaganda a country could brew, and many cameo appearances by the Grim Reaper.

Attempts to find a North-East Passage had begun in the sixteenth century, perhaps earlier. (The term refers to the entire Europe-to-

Pacific route along the Russian coast, Murmansk to Vladivostok, dark for half the year and frozen for longer.) The Bering Strait at one end was a notoriously dangerous stretch of water, Vitus Bering himself one of many to have drowned in it. As far as anyone knows, the first man to get through was Baron Adolf Nordenskiöld, a Swede born in Finland who had been contracted to find 'that strait where the Old and the New World seem to shake hands'. Ice stopped his ship, the former whaler *Vega*, 130 miles short of the Strait, and Nordenskiöld and his crew had to spend the winter of 1878-9 in the pincers of a floe off Chukotka before proceeding east into the Pacific.

Meanwhile, in faraway New York, a newsman with an eye for a story decided Nordenskiöld needed rescuing. James Gordon Bennett Jr was the son of the proprietor of the *New York Herald* and at the helm himself for half a century. He had sponsored numerous expeditions and popularised the now standard technique of creating news, the more sensational the better. In a *Herald* story about an earlier Arctic voyage headlined 'Eight Days Between Meals', the reader only learned halfway through the piece that it was the huskies which had gone the eight days. In what turned out to be Bennett's last great attempt at an Arctic scoop, he despatched Navy Captain George Washington DeLong to rescue Nordenskiöld (it didn't matter to Bennett that Nordenskiöld didn't need rescuing) and to find the North Pole by the Pacific route while he was at it.

DeLong, a balding figure with a swanky moustache, steamed out of San Francisco in 1879 in *Jeanette*. As soon as he reached the East Siberian coast, he learned that Nordenskiöld was out of the ice and on his way home, and immediately got stuck himself. In New York, the *Herald* assured the public there was no need to panic, thereby assuring that they did. In June 1881, *Jeanette* sank. The frightened crew set out for the Lena delta on five sledges. The Lena, which drains a million square miles of Siberia, has a coastal outflow 260 miles across, and the men were soon comprehensively lost. Obliged to eat not only their shoes, but also their trousers, they lost body parts to frostbite, and although one party eventually came across a Cossack courier who galloped news to the tsar, twenty out of thirty-three died, including DeLong. It was the biggest American Arctic disaster ever.

The Soviets renamed the North-East Passage *Severnyy Morskoy Put*, or *Sevmorput*, known in English as the Northern Sea Route. Stalin was having a love affair with both industrialisation and polar exploration and when he unleashed the second Five-Year Plan in 1932, he flagged the opening of a Northern Sea Route as top priority. That same year, a former Newfoundland sealer under Soviet command pulled off an Arkhangel-to-Vladivostock transit in one season. Ice off the north coast of Chukotka smashed the ship's propellers, and a trawler towed her the last bit; but still. A year later, Stalin launched the *Chelyuskin* expedition, which was to be the second to sail the length of the Northern Sea Route in a single season. *Chelyuskin* got through the Bering Strait, just, before the pack crushed her. One person died and the other 104 set up camp on the sea ice 80 miles north-east of Vankarem. The story of their survival and rescue hardened into a central Soviet myth. When a plane finally arrived to pick them up, the stranded men allegedly demanded an immediate report on the Seventeenth Party Congress and listened to it without interruption for two and a half hours.

The Arctic, in that lamentable decade, was to play its most sinister role. Stalin deployed his polar aviators and explorers as heroic diversions, trumpeting their achievements across acres of newsprint while hundreds of thousands died and the country moved towards the fully-fledged slaughter of The Great Terror. A couple of hundred miles from the *Chelyuskin* ice camp, a prison ship froze in on its way to Kolyma. The *Dzhurma* was the first vessel to sail a new route from Vladivostok, the 4,000-mile passage to Ambarchik on the Arctic Ocean, at the mouth of the Kolyma River. *Dzhurma* had 12,000 prisoners below decks. When she reached Ambarchik in the spring, they were all dead.

During the thirties Soviet vessels made increasing commercial use of both ends of the Northern Sea Route, and ocean shipping acquired a glamour that the great rivers, economic highways for centuries, entirely lacked. By 1936 the Northern Sea Route Administration, or *Glavsevmorput*, had 40,000 employees on the payroll. In the rush to develop the Arctic coast ships transported whole towns north, prefabricated. Eager *polyarnitsa* and *polyarniki* (polar workers, women and men), in receipt of rations that included twenty-five cigarettes a day, toiled to Stakhanovite targets and built a chain of radio stations to assist navigation and aviation, over fifty polar bases, and a network of towns and cities such as Igarka on the Yenesei, the first port in Arctic Siberia servicing the coal mines. Security agents recruited thousands of Arctic border guards to watch over a frontier as sacred as those to the south facing terrestrial enemies. Propaganda films were made to romanticise these *pogranichniki* (frontier guards). 'Professions are chosen,' went the old KGB slogan, 'but poets and border guards are born.' Otto Yulyevich Shmidt, captain of the *Chelyuskin* and 'Russia's Arctic Hero No. 1', headed *Glavsevmorput*. 'He spoke of the Arctic as Rhodes would have spoken of South Africa or as an eighteenth-century pioneer of America, as a land of promise,' said a *Times* journalist who interviewed Shmidt in Moscow. Under Shmidt's leadership, *Glavsevmorput* even set up an Institute of Arctic Agriculture to coax potatoes out of the permafrost. 'We are really making friends with the polar world,' said the greatest apologist the Arctic has ever known. 'We are bringing it to life, and life to it.'

The next development in Soviet efforts to conquer the ice was the drift station. Stalin had claimed the North-East Passage as one of his countless achievements, but the movements of ice remained enigmatic, and technicians devised camps that floated on moving chunks of solid sea as part of a wider mission to achieve mastery. The first station began its drift in early May 1937, after a 4-engine N-170 landed four men on a 10-foot-thick floe about 12 miles west of the Pole. The leader was Ivan Papanin, a multidisciplinary scientist and zealous first-generation communist born in 1895 in Sevastopol on the Black

Sea. Originally a sailor in the tsarist navy, Papanin was 5 feet 3 and a half with a toothbrush moustache. He and his colleagues lived on the floe in tents which they repegged every day. They ate rations from soldered tin containers; each man had 1,470 grammes of caviare. One had done a short medical course prior to deployment on which he had practised sewing up sutures on hunks of beef. They had a wireless on which they heard the chimes of the Kremlin clock, operatic arias from Paris, and the news that fascists were bombing Barcelona; Eugene Federov also learned that he had become a father. They powered the wireless with a bicycle generator. Two men had to pedal at once in order to transmit just one of the many articles they penned for *Pravda*, *Izvestiya* and other papers; it was a popular job, as pedalling was the only activity during which smoking was permitted (rather a counterproductive regulation, one would imagine). They worked constantly, taking samples and depth soundings and meteorological observations and collecting data on ice dynamics that would unlock the mysteries of the Arctic Ocean. Someone had accidentally left behind the alcohol required for certain experiments, so they distilled some from brandy, possibly the only time the transaction has gone in that direction. They had a rubber boat and a husky called Merry who later had a refrigerated kennel at Moscow zoo; they held Party-Komsomol meetings, and political discussion meetings, and meetings to hear one another talk about the history of the Bolshevik Party. Comrade Stalin, according to Papanin, was 'the greatest man of modern times', and a portrait of him hung in the main tent. 'Stalin has devoted the whole of his life to secure a happy life for the workers,' wrote Papanin. Even Captain Scott, it turned out, would have been all right had he enjoyed the benefits of Soviet society. 'I recall the tragic note written by Captain Scott,' opined Papanin. 'Returning from the South Pole, he was tormented by anxiety as to who would take care of his family if he perished. We have no such anxieties; behind us stands the entire Soviet people, our party and our government; with us is our beloved Joseph . . .'

As they drifted south for a year the floe shrank, the fissures widened and the growling and rumbling grew louder. When the breaking ice was really noisy, they put a record on the gramophone. On 19 February 1938 an ice-breaker picked them up in the southern Greenland Sea, a thousand miles from where they had started. They returned as Heroes of the Soviet Union, and so did the pilots who had flown them in. Aviators were whizzing busily around the Soviet Arctic at the time. 'Our people call it Stalinist aviation,' Papanin wrote, 'because Comrade Stalin himself is so keenly interested in its development.' After one particular pioneering Arctic flight, eight miles of cheering crowds met the three airmen. Again, Papanin and his colleagues were tools – smoke-screen tools. While they were hammering out their reports, the number of arrests based on spurious counter-revolutionary crimes tripled, and the purge extended outwards from the Party and spread to peasants and workers. The show trials had begun, and polar heroes represented progress, youth and triumph to be compared with unenlightened Old Bolsheviks who had to be killed off. While a batch of distinguished military commanders who had pioneered the modernisation of the Red Army were being tried for imaginary crimes in June 1937, a group of polar explorers on Rudolf Island in Franz-Josef Land sent in a message demanding their execution (in fact they had already been shot in secret). According to a leading historian of the Terror, there were at this time – 1938 – about 7 million 'purgees' in the camps.

When heroic deeds went wrong, retribution was swift. Test pilot Valery Chkalov generated the usual vast press coverage when he flew over the North Pole and landed in Washington State in an ANT-25. When he later crashed, Stalin's stooges shot the head of the aircraft industry, the designer of the plane and the director of the plant where it was built. The talented aviation engineer A.N. Tupolev was tortured into a confession of sabotage in October 1937. State security hood-lums murdered weathermen for failing to predict poor weather.

Shortly after the Second World War ended, US air force commander General H.H. Arnold declared, 'If World War 3 should come, its strategic centre will be the North Pole.' His colleagues agreed, and the United States and its allies poured money into the DEW line and the Thule bomber installation which cost a reported $800 million and which rose like an extra-planetary monster among the Greenlandic Inuhuit. At the same time Shmidt and his colleagues pioneered such dramatic advances in nuclear technology and submarine design that an expanded and enhanced Soviet fleet was able to patrol under Arctic ice for months. Some vessels could go four years without refuelling. Throughout the Cold War, both sides knew that the shortest route between them for conventional bombers and intercontinental ballistic missiles was across the Arctic Ocean, as Gino Watkins had recognised. As a result, to complement the work of the submarines, both established dozens of drift stations like the one pioneered by Papanin for reconnaissance purposes. The white and trackless Arctic was perfect war territory. New submarines could dive deeper than their conventional ancestors and so pass under the thickest Arctic ice. In 1958 two US nuclear submarines went all the way to the North Pole. A nuclear capacity had realigned the role of the Arctic, as the general had predicted.

Europeans had been trying to find a way through the fabled North-West Passage since the time of Henry VIII. The channels through what is now the Canadian archipelago were navigable for only two or three months a year, and the pattern and extent of sea ice altered dramatically from one season to the next, as they still do. A glance at the map reveals the names of patrons who had sponsored early expeditions. The fur traders made capital of it. They had little time for unseasoned bunglers. 'In sailing along the Union Coast,' reads an unpublished document found in a trapping station on Hudson Bay, '. . . we also discovered many shoals and islands unnoticed by former Navigators, in particular an extensive sand-bank which at low water forms an Island . . . This Island I have named Brown-Bottom-Island in honour of my Friend and relative Lord Brownbottom.' (Little changes. In 2007 Artur Chilingarov's flag made the North Pole Russian – though at least he didn't try to name it after himself.)

In 1745 a Parliamentary Act in Britain put up a £20,000 reward for the discovery of a route through Hudson Strait north of the bay, the first of many acts and bounties. Captain Cook himself sailed up to have a look, categorically concluding that there was no waterway from the Pacific to the Atlantic. By 1820 any passage that did exist was known to lie too far north to accumulate trade advantage; the quest had become a geographical challenge, and imperial pride was a significant motivator. The hour had its man. He was Mr, later Sir, John Barrow, second secretary at to the Admiralty and once a cabin boy on a whaler. If, Barrow argued, a full traverse of a passage were 'left to be performed by some other power, England by her neglect of it, after having opened the East and West doors, would be laughed at by all the world of having hesitated to cross the threshold'. England was not yet accustomed to being laughed at. Barrow had the tools for the job, as when the Napoleonic Wars ended in 1815, the Admiralty had a glut of idle ships and officers on its hands; and until the Crimean War in 1853, no major conflicts to fight. So Barrow hurled his men again into Arctic waters that made and unmade reputations in a prolonged orgy of shoe-eating and death. William Parry crawled to 82°N. John and James Clark Ross spent four winters locked in the ice, James sledging to the North Magnetic Pole while Uncle John sawed off a stoker's mangled arm. Even as the innovation of the steam engine displaced the rigours of rigging, still the dream lived: the old Arctic dream in which man voyaged over the horizon to find whatever was there. But one figure towers over the rest in the pages of Arctic exploration and its mythology: Sir John Franklin, a household name in his lifetime and, like Captain Scott, more than that beyond it. In 1845 Franklin sailed into the pack with 128 men, determined to nail the Passage once and for all. But it was the other way round. Neither he nor his crew were seen alive again.

What compels in an adventure story? Survival against the odds, as in Maurice Herzog's ascent of Annapurna? Or heroic redemption combining death and deathless prose, as demonstrated by Captain Scott? Or is it perhaps the sheer derring-do of a Livingstone hacking through malarial jungle? Sir John Franklin's story has none of these ingredients, yet he is perceived as a five-star polar hero, commemorated in Westminster Abbey with marble and bad poetry by Tennyson ('*Not here! The white north has thy bones*') and in America with quasi-canonisation. The *New York Times* characterised the Franklin expedition and its aftermath as being 'as noble an epic as that which has immortalised the fall of Troy or the conquest of Jerusalem'. But the story, it turns out, is not about feats of exploration at all, just as the Soviet pursuit of the North-East Passage is not. Both quests reveal the power of myth-making; the manufacturing of national legend; and the manipulation of history.

Franklin was a deeply religious, uneducated Lincolnshire man who joined the Royal Navy at twelve and fought at Trafalgar. By the time he married his ambitious second wife, Jane, he was a veteran of high latitudes and had led two polar expeditions, charting and gathering magnetic data. Jane too was a keen traveller from an early age, racing up mountains on six continents and lugging a customised iron bedstead around the globe. Despite making a cock-up of both his trips to the High Arctic (nearing starvation on one sledging journey, he ate his boots), Franklin, knighted in 1829, had established himself as a celebrity. He was actually a dullard. Jane told him off for writing boring letters. It was his malleability that attracted her, and she controlled his career from the outset, entering the most momentous phase of her own career when she secured her husband another polar command. Weighing in at over twenty stone, fifty-nine-year-old Sir John was hopelessly unsuited to the task. Daguerreotypes taken prior to departure depict a member of the Politburo in an admiral's hat. But in 1845 Franklin sallied blithely north with two ships, HMS *Erebus* and *Terror*, at the head of the last Admiralty expedition to look for a North-West Passage. When neither ship reappeared after two years, Jane began to lobby on her husband's behalf, despatching an armada of rescue ships and even trying to sail north herself. She dragooned Dickens into service. In the pages of his periodical *Household Words* the most famous author in England kept the public rigid with anticipation during the Franklin search, making, at the same time, a significant contribution to the image of the Arctic that was to dominate the public consciousness for decades. 'Think of Christmas in the tremendous wastes of ice and snow', thundered Dickens in 1850 '. . . where crashing mountains of ice, heaped up together, have made a chaos round their ships, which in a moment might have ground them to dust; where hair has frozen up on the face; where blankets have stiffened upon the bodies of men lying asleep . . .' The reading public had been gobbling up stories set in the Arctic since Mary Shelley's *Frankenstein, or, The Modern Prometheus* caused a sensation in 1818 when publication coincided with a revival of British efforts to find a North-West Passage. If subsequent travellers had thought less about artistic embellishments and more about the skills and equipment required to live without actually courting peril in the Arctic, fewer would have died horrible deaths after consuming their footwear.

As for Lady Jane: she handed the captain of each rescue vessel a wax-sealed envelope addressed to her husband. 'I desire nothing', she wrote in one, 'but to cherish you the remainder of your days, however injured and broken your health may be – but in every case I will strive to bow to the Almighty Will, and trust thro' His mercy for a blessed reunion in a better world.' Each time, a gloomy sea dog returned the letter unopened. Manipulative and temperamental, Lady Jane got on people's wicks from Spitsbergen to Sydney (even her loving father eventually disinherited her). Nonetheless, she emerges a far more interesting figure than her useless husband. Many of her rescue ships made important discoveries as well as charting thousands of miles of North American coastline. It was she who created the image of Sir John Franklin that has been handed down to posterity. Newspapers dubbed her 'our English Penelope', and country fairs sold Staffordshire figures of the couple, he peering through a telescope, she anxiously fingering her shawl. Clairvoyants began to see Franklin and his men staggering around on the ice when they stared into their crystal balls. Overheated civic planners named a row of houses near Wormwood Scrubs prison North Pole Road, and an Arctic Street sprang up elsewhere in London. This was the Arctic legacy Gino Watkins inherited.

Lady Jane wrote to President Taylor appealing for an American rescue expedition, but it was a private citizen, New York businessman Henry Grinnell, who came up with real money. Grinnell's second expedition captivated the American public like no other. The equivalent of a ticker-tape parade greeted its leader, Dr Elisha Kent Kane, on his return, and the *New York Times* cleared the front page for a week. Kane published his account of the voyage in 1856, and for a decade the two volumes sold almost as many copies as the Bible. Queen Victoria invited Kane to breakfast when he visited Britain. The furore, once again, was largely based on an illusion: Kane announced that he had found an Open Polar Sea, whereas in fact he had found only a temporarily ice-free stretch of water. In addition, far from being heroic, the expedition could have furnished a script for *Carry On up the Arctic*. Inuit hunters saved Kane and his crew from near starvation, almost everyone had something amputated and rats plagued the ship. Kane tried to fumigate, bivvying the men on deck, but when the cook popped down to the galley to check on the soup, he collapsed from asphyxiation. The ship caught fire, and later sank (the men walked across the ice to Greenland, where they met a rescue ship). Three died. At least Kane didn't go north again, though he wanted to. The effort of writing his book took its toll. 'This book, poor as it is,' he told his publisher when he handed over the type-script, 'has been my coffin.' I know how he felt. Meanwhile Irishman Robert McClure entered the archipelago from the west in HMS *Investigator* to see if Franklin might have broken through to that side. Looping round the east of Banks Island and disembarking, McClure sledged north, and, standing on a peninsula and looking out through a telescope, saw a frozen channel. 'Can it be possible', he wrote in his journal, 'that this water communicates with Barrow's Strait, and shall prove to be the long-sought North-West Passage?' It did, and it was. Trapped for two winters, his crew half-starved and scurvy ridden, McClure then sledged to meet a rescue party coming from the east. So the passage – that part of it now called McClure Strait – had been traversed, though not in a ship. Inevitably, it was an anti-climax.

Of Franklin, however, there was no news until 1854, when Orkneyman and Company surveyor John Rae returned to London. Eskimo hunters, Rae reported, had encountered forty starving members of Franklin's party dragging a boat near the north shore of King William Island (which almost touches the mainland), and later the same season others found thirty-five white corpses near the same island's Great Fish River. The bodies had been partially eaten, and fragments of human flesh floated in the kettles. Nobody wanted to hear that. Dickens sorted it out with magisterial authority by concluding that the chaps were simply too decent to have set about one another with a knife and fork. 'We submit', he declaimed angrily in one of two pieces in *Household Words*, 'that the memory of the lost Arctic voyagers is placed, by reason and experience, high above the taint of this so-easily allowed connection; and that the noble conduct and example of such men, and of their own great leader himself, under similar endurances, belies it, and outweighs by the weight of the whole universe the chatter of a gross handful of uncivilised people, with a domesticity of blood and blubber.' These latter were the Inuit, and Dickens' diatribe constituted propaganda of the Soviet variety. 'We believe every savage to be in his heart covetous, treacherous and cruel,' Dickens insisted. And of course, at bottom he was right about that, because the Inuit are just like us.

Yet more ships now had to sail off to the Great Fish River. In 1857, crewmen found written records stowed in a cairn (only three men died on this, the last of so many Franklin searches). The records revealed that Franklin had expired before most of his crew. In addition, a small party of men, but not Franklin himself, may have found another passage

through to the Pacific, two years before McClure looked out at his. The news only spurred Jane on to higher goals. Through sophistry, tireless hard work and shrewd politicking, she persuaded the Admiralty and the world that the hapless Franklin had discovered the Passage. He had done no such thing. Today it would be called spin.

The public was gasping to transfigure Franklin. Victorians liked transforming earthly journeys into spiritual ones, and they passed the habit down to succeeding generations. People made the most tremendous meal of it in the case of Captain Scott, and after the First World War they were at it again when Mallory vanished on Everest. It was the idealised Arctic that mattered to the armchair explorers, not the protean one on the map; for those reading about it at home the landscape exerted a moral force that conveniently fitted their world view. The explorer, providing he was British, brought order and civilisation and reminded everyone at home that theirs was the greatest nation on earth. Furthermore, explorers were associated with feelings that soared fearlessly above earthbound banalities. Grandeur and violence; cosmic mystery; the primal power of wilderness; the spiritual relationship between man and nature – the Arctic had it all, as Mary Shelley had recognised. Tennyson (poet laureate, as well as Franklin's nephew-in-law) portrayed exploration as a spiritual or intellectual quest. The business of transformation and romanticisation brought out the worst in everyone. Wilkie Collins supplied *The Frozen Deep*, a terrible melodrama loosely based on the Franklin story, the action centring on a group of women waiting for news of their menfolk, these latter having vanished on an Arctic expedition, and on the men themselves, valiantly setting off to relieve stranded colleagues. Collins' friend Dickens helped out with the script, setting to and penning a verse prologue.

> *One savage footprint on the lonely shore,*
> *Where one man listened to the surge's roar;*
> *Not all the winds that stir the mighty sea*
> *Can ever ruffle the memory.*

In his pet role of actor-manager, forty-five-year-old Dickens went on to stage the play with characteristic gusto, and to act the part of the protagonist, Richard Wardour; *The Frozen Deep* was the sensation of the London season, and Dickens so famous that Queen Victoria went to see the play, dragging Princes Leopold of Belgium and Frederick of Prussia. During the course of rehearsals for a short run at the Free Trade Hall in Manchester, Dickens met an eighteen-year-old actress called Nelly Ternan. It was a *coup de foudre*, or perhaps a *coup de glace*, but unlike most strikes, it lasted. For the rest of his life, Dickens maintained a secret home with the blue-eyed Nelly, shuttling between her and his estranged wife Catherine, with whom he had nine children (a tenth had died). It was a set-piece straight out of one of his novels, revealing Dickens as something other than the Pickwickian paterfamilias of legend (another case of the power of myth). Nelly was the one who emerged with her dignity intact, as she never told her story. The theme of double lives occurred often in the Dickensian oeuvre, and the great man cited Wardour as a model for Sydney Carton in *A Tale of Two Cities*. It was encouraging to see the ghost of the Arctic there too.

The glory days of the Northern Sea Route and its passage to Asia are only a memory in the defunct offices of *Glavsevmorput*, Sevmorput and FESCO, the Far Eastern Shipping Company that owns the *Khlebnikov*. FESCO once operated 250 ships on the Northern Sea Route. Now it has fewer than a fifth of that number. To the end (though in truth we have not yet reached the end), polar waterways reflect national concerns. The Russian market economy does not footle with its marine routes: it goes straight for the gasfields. But the 900 miles of deep channels that form the North-West Passage have recently returned to the news pages. Basically they have unfrozen, and once again the commercial potential of the route has set pulses racing. The first vessels to get through did so in two seasons or more, sitting out the winter locked in the ice. In 1944 an ice-strengthened schooner belonging to the Royal Canadian Mounted Police made the first transit in one season. Since then, traverses have been contingent on favourable ice conditions, or on the resources of specialist ships and expeditions. In 2007, however, for the first time, an entirely ice-free passage briefly opened from ocean to ocean. As temperatures rise and ice vanishes, the passage may regularly open to commercial shipping, perhaps even for four or five months a year. This crucially important scenario has ratcheted up a long-running quarrel over ownership of the channels. In April 2007, Canada formally declared that all five routes through its Arctic archipelago constitute inland waterways. Both the USA and the EU, however, insist that these are international waters, which would mean foreign ships could pass through without permission (the USA has sent the odd warship from end to end to prove the point). To reinforce the claim, in February 2008, Washington, via the National Oceanic and Atmospheric Administration and the University of New Hampshire, published a map showing that the continental shelf extending from Alaska includes a portion of the North-West Passage.

Wilf and I continued our adventure. We sailed down the coast of East Greenland among many bergs, and Wilf photographed his first musk ox to add to his first polar bear. The *KK* powered through the Greenland Sea and crossed the Arctic Circle close to Iceland, where we disembarked at Reykjavik. Wilf said he was sad to think he might not be able to repeat the journey with his own son, if the ice really does melt.

IX

The Spirit Lives

The Arctic in European Russia

The glaciers came and went, the granite boulders littered the shores of the lakes; the lakes froze during Solovki winter nights, the sea howled under the wind and was covered with an icy sludge and in places froze; the northern lights blazed across half the sky; and it grew bright once again and warm once again, and the fir trees grew and thickened, and the birds cackled and called, and the young deer trumpeted – and the planet circled through all world history, and kingdoms fell and rose, and here there were still no beasts of prey and no human being.

Alexander Solzhenitsyn, *The Gulag Archipelago*

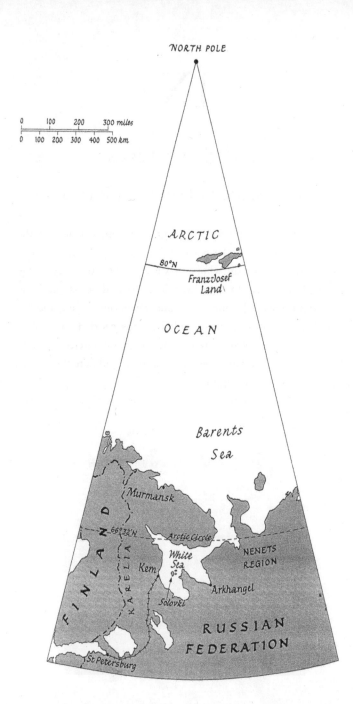

NORTH POLE

0   100   200   300 miles
0   100 200 300 400 500 km

ARCTIC

80°N

Franz Josef
Land

OCEAN

Barents
Sea

Murmansk

FINLAND   66°32'N   Arctic Circle

KARELIA   White   NENETS
           Sea   REGION

Kem

Solovki   Arkhangel

RUSSIAN
FEDERATION

St Petersburg

At the end I returned to Russia, where I had started, lured north-west by the turrets and domes on a 500-rouble note. Set among the fabled White Sea whitecaps, the Solovki monastery, according to generations of true believers, cradles the national soul. Beached in a polar hinterland more than six thousand miles from the Chukchi and their antlered herds, the medieval monastery represents the endurance of hope and faith and the survival of the human spirit against what once seemed like insuperable odds. But the price had been so high. In 1923 Red Guards threw the monks out after 500 years, tore down the icons and set up a prison, shipping in foes by the ten thousand. As the gulag system emerged from the chaos of the twenties, Solovki's model of forced labour multiplied across the USSR. As Solzhenitsyn wrote, from the one cancer cell in that White Sea outpost, a tumour spread all over Russia.* The monks have returned to chant, perhaps for the forgiveness of others. Just as dignified integrity outlasted cultural destruction among the Inuit, a sense of quiet redemption lived on among the bone yards of Stalin's White Sea camp. It was a good place to end.

---

* Other camps existed by 1923, but Solovki is considered the first because of the structured role it acquired as a model for what followed.

To reach Solovki I boarded a Number 22 sleeper train at Petersburg's Ladoga Station for a sixteen-hour rock through the birch forest, though sixteen hours is a hop, in the Russian railway system. Overnight, the birches grew shorter and the air colder. Cars also shrank as the train raced north: rust-bucket Ladas instead of the BMWs of metropolitan mobsters. A sway at the curve before Begeza; gabled snowmobile lock-ups on the shore of Lake Vyg; and, at last, the White Sea port of Kem, half way between the Kandalaksha Gulf and Onega Bay. The landscape had just hung on through winter and was browned out and exhausted. There were no ruined factories here, and no toppled statues of Lenin sneering skyward in Ozymandian reproach. Just the noble rot of the backwoods, and a woman in a housecoat milking a goat. Riding a bus from the railway station to the coast for the three-hour crossing to Solovki, it was difficult not to notice that like the birch trees and the cars, the people too were smaller. These were a short, stubby lot, compared with their stringy Petersburg compatriots. But the paved road was a good one and the bus pressed on, through miles of more snowmobile lock-ups and depleted fences that swayed in the wind. Presently the road collapsed at a jetty. When the bus emptied, the wind dropped suddenly, as if it had been switched off. Four or five fishing boats lay still on the water like sledges on snow. On the churned-up mud of the empty shore, two German shepherds nosed around a motionless Caterpillar truck, its bucket frozen in mid-manoeuvre. And there was my boat: an old trawler.

Ninety devout Karelian pilgrims had already squeezed into the modest cabin. As soon as the captain weighed anchor, a priest and his assistant began intoning a service, both brandishing a large crucifix. The other women passengers whipped headscarves out of their string bags (everyone had a string bag). I like to think of myself as a well-prepared, culturally sensitive traveller, but one had not anticipated an act of worship on a ferry. A polar balaclava wasn't quite the ticket when it came to the Orthodox head-covering rule.

But it was all I had. So I put it on. Outside the porthole, the water sparkled in the morning sunshine. As the mainland shrank to a thin line, the rhythmic rise and fall of the ritual words, mirroring the swell of the sea, invoked the longing for God that played such a living role in old Russia, a country still recognisable up on the fringes of the Federation. The pilgrims intoned, a framed photograph of a saint was passed round to be kissed, and mobile phones trilled again, like the dawn chorus after the stillness of night. Folding her headscarf carefully into her string bag, my neighbour revealed a startling capacity to speak English. A native of the White Sea coast, she had accompanied her husband, a timber specialist, on a two-year professional exchange to Australia. Like everyone on board, she was making a pilgrimage to Solovki. Once she began talking, she could not stop. Having dealt with her extended family tree she moved on to the immanence of the Godhead. After a fraction of a second which was almost a pause, she said, a conspiratorial note entering her tone, 'I have a bad case of *govorukha*.' I said it sounded painful. In fact, *govorukha* describes a mix of garrulousness and taciturnity, an endemic condition in the Russian far north characterised by bursts of direct speech alternating with the silent reserve bred into those who live in geographical isolation.

Paper twists of boiled sweets went from hand to hand. The maritime roll combined with sporadic blasts of hot air from the engine ventilator to induce a drowsy fug. Hard by the Finnish border, the White Sea, *Beloye More*, forms the most southerly gulf of the Barents Sea and Arctic Ocean, a three-pronged embayment sheltered by the motherly arm of the Kola Peninsula. Named after its foamy rollers and known to sailors as 'the bandit sea', its waves gather at the whim of capricious winds that can whisk up five storms a day. The winds in the north have a name – *Moryana, Obyednik, Polunoshrik*. After two hours, perhaps longer, a dark sequence of turrets and domes rose from the distant waves, a low-lying, tightly self-contained silhouette pulling the currents into its own magnetic field. It seemed wondrous: it must have seemed a miracle to a medieval pilgrim. My own pilgrims reached into their string bags for bulky Horizon cameras, and streamed on deck to start snapping.

Between the Karelian coast and what Russians call the summer coast, the islands and islets of the Solovki archipelago lie half a degree south of the Arctic Circle. Although a microclimate sustains cherry trees and cabbages, as well as 600 lakes and swamps, Solovki winters are still long, dark and brutal. On Great Solovki, where we disembarked, a thousand civilians inured to hardship live alongside the holy fathers, servicing the pilgrim trade, harvesting salt and struggling to maintain a power supply. Beyond the coastal sorrel and Siberian cedars, violet mists curled through the larches, the scent of hagberries cut the air, and lakes shone through vertical slits between the forest trunks. The ubiquitous dun-coloured mud of the north spread inland in what Dostoevsky called 'a sort of pea jelly'. My companions from the ferry vanished to a hostel in the forest, so I had lunch alone in my hotel. The waiter, a youth in an embroidered tunic, understood instinctively there was no point fooling around with incomprehensible menus. Without a word he brought a dish of minced perch and salted boletus mushrooms, and watched me as I ate. I had never had a better lunch, and told him so, the phrases translated by my empty dish.

The tour guide Anna was an old-style Russian who spoke wonderful English despite never having set foot outside the motherland. An Arkhangel-born historian and curator, she had worked in the monastic archives for many years, and her worn sheepskin coat, buttoned to the neck, gave her the look of a robust countrywoman. Above all, she radiated enthusiasm. 'Oh it's such a tremendous story,' she said, setting off on the four-hour tour at an Olympic pace. 'Solovki is the place where faith triumphs over death.'

The bulky, reddish-brown boulders at the base of the fortifications seemed to grow organically out of the shingle in a blaze of crystalline light. In a cobbled courtyard on the other side of the arched Holy Gates and the twenty-feet-thick walls, a monk with his soft black *skufia* hat pulled down over his ears was towing a wooden wheelbarrow. His earliest predecessors, St Savvatii and St German, settled on Solovki in 1429. The White Sea islands offered exceptional anchorage, plentiful fresh water, berries and limitless fishing, and the benefits of inaccessibility guaranteed isolation: the crossing from the mainland could only be made between June and August, and then it took two days rowing the stalwart medieval *karbas*. What Mount Athos and the Tibetan plateau offered in height, Solovki had in latitude. But it was more than a quiet place for contemplation. Following the path of St Anthony, Savvatii and German chose one of the harshest places on earth in which to wage spiritual warfare through prayer. Eastern Christian ascetics conceived monasticism as self-martyrdom, voluntarily killing the ego to become a vessel of divine light. On Solovki, the faithful sacrificed their earthly selves to battle the elemental darkness of winter and the bugs and storms of a White Sea summer. As an act of renewal within that context, in the middle of the fifteenth century St Zosima founded a monastery under the titular control of the archbishopric of Novgorod, the powerful mercantile city-state that vied with Moscow. Solovki was to become a mirror of the complex, shifting relationship between church and state.

Muscovite princes were at that time plotting against Novgorod, and once they had beaten its rulers into submission – in most cases literally – and taken over its fur trade (in 1478), they looked to Solovki to protect their empire on the northern borders of Rus. To that end, they lavished the monastery with endowments. The community prospered, accumulating wealth while its holy fathers in theory and often in practice relinquished both money and personal ambition. Savvatii and Zosima supplanted St Nikolas as patron saints of seafarers in the north, where the sea controlled life and death, and the Solovki monks promoted their cult to encourage patronage. In

1539 Ivan IV granted the monastery incomes from the villages along the Vyg River, and, later, from the Tersky coast of the Kola Peninsula and the settlements on two of its largest rivers. On the tour, Anna strode around the courtyard before pausing in front of the chipped white stone wall of a refectory. A group of monks hurried out of its heavy doors and crossed to an arched passageway, coughing into their black sleeves. 'They try', she said, 'to maintain the isolation of their predecessors. When Putin visited in 2001 as president of the Federation, the abbot had to gather his flock in advance and explain who Putin was.' This strained the limits of the credible. But it was an attractive notion of unworldliness. Putin had gone to Solovki to mark the tenth anniversary of the collapse of the Soviet Union. He used the visit to laud the achievements of the state and the contribution of Orthodox Christianity, 'without which Russia could hardly exist'. Then he said that all peoples were equal before God, and that Russia had always guaranteed that equality. Now Solovki really had heard it all.

In 1555 Ivan commanded the abbot to set up a jail for exiled priests, part of an increasingly monomaniacal crusade to establish absolute power. According to one historian, Ivan's *oprichniki*, or secret police, 'felt no shame when killing defenceless people for fun or robbing and raping them ... Ivan wallowed in orgies and debauchery and surrounded himself with reprobates, allowing them everything their licentiousness demanded.' In the words of another scholar, and foreshadowing the future, to Ivan, 'prayer and torture were but two aspects of piety'. Both found a legitimised place in Solovki. Later in the sixteenth century Tsar Fedor Ivanovich commissioned the monastery's most distinctive architectural feature – its fortified walls. He wanted a mighty defensive barricade to ward off 'the Germans and all warring people ... because of how close the Swedish border has become'. The foundation stones were 7 metres long, and according to one source, 'it took at least two or three hundred men to drag the largest'. Designed by a monk and a master builder from Vologda, the walls followed a pentagonal formation, with five corner towers and two side towers equipped with gun rooms and topped by wooden tent roofs and cupolas. The builders did not cut their stones, instead wedging small ones into gaps, thinning the walls as they rose and crowning the lot with bricks from the monastic works. Inside the Cathedral of the Transfiguration, Anna gestured to a portrait of Ivan. 'From his time,' she said, 'Solovki was the focal point of economic, religious, and cultural life along the White Sea coast. Hundreds of craftsmen worked in sheepskin, copper and timber. But the salt trade was the most lucrative.' Without its salt production, Solovki would have remained a minor monastery with little influence on Russian history. Even the name 'Solovki' derives from the Russian word for salt. Annual production peaked at 2 million kilograms, all of it extracted from highly salinated brine deep in the earth, a natural occurrence around the White Sea, which is itself exceptionally salty. Solovki was soon the second richest monastery in Old Russia, behind only Trinity Lavra in Sergiyev Posad.

The good times ended when the monks dug in against the infamous Nikonian reforms that split the Russian Church, an event which Solzhenitsyn claimed influenced the national destiny more than the Bolshevik Revolution. Promulgated by Patriarch Nikon, the 1653–56 reforms aimed to cleanse and improve spiritual practice. But Orthodox traditions were the beating heart of old Russia, and its rituals sacrosanct to those who linked change with western contamination. Conservatives considered the reforms heretical, and became known as Old Believers. They had always crossed themselves with two fingers, and were not minded to change when Nikon introduced the three-fingered cross to bring Russia in line with the Greek Church. Some cut off their index fingers; hundreds walled themselves up in their churches and immolated themselves; thousands settled in Siberia. Waves of dissenters headed north to the White Sea, where peasants and Solovki monks alike were among the most stubborn adherents of the old rituals. The north had a far higher number of tiny wayside chapels (*tchasovnyi*) than other parts of Russia, and no God-fearing man would ever pass without a prayer to the solitary icon that kept a freezing vigil.

Troops mustered to bring Solovki into line and the monks settled down for what turned into a seven-year siege. Anyone caught outside the fortified walls had a bad time of it. 'So they mangled him and burned him', according to the records of one monk apprehended by the military, 'and tore out a rib from his half-burned body, shaved his head and poured cold water on it from a height, and after forty-eight hours of tortures beheaded him on the Saturday after Pentecost, and would not even let him be buried.' When the end came, as it had to, many monks had already died of scurvy and others escaped to take alms in the villages dotting the White Sea coast where Old Believers had found their Arctic utopias. Sensing that the Nikonian reforms signalled imminent apocalypse, and perceiving themselves in flight from the decadence of European Russia, many true believers formed themselves into sects, the crazier the better. The Skoptsy cut off their testicles, reasoning that salvation lay in the association between the Russian words *iskuplenie* (redemption) and *oskoplenie* (castration). Castration sects continued to flourish in Russia in general and in the revived Solovki prisons in particular long after Nikon's reforms (women joined in by chopping off their breasts and vulvas). But the Old Believers were not mad. They were sustained by deep religious consciousness and a refusal to compromise. Their crime was to walk out of step with the Enlightenment insistence on finding the most reasonable path to happiness. Beyond the sects, they consolidated into a broad social movement of religious and political dissent. Nineteenth-century sympathisers included Mussorgsky, who expressed the conviction in his opera *Khovanshchina*, sometimes translated as *The Khovansky Affair*, that Old Believers were the last authentic Russians; and the Cossack painter Vasily Surikov, who did the same thing in the tremendous *Boyarynya Morozova* (The

Boyar's Wife Morozova), a vast canvas, now in the Tretyakov, depicting a fierce-eyed heretic being sledged to her execution with her arm raised in the two-fingered sign. Meanwhile a fresh intake

of monks arrived at Solovki and made overtures to the Tsar. The reformist, 6-foot 8-inch Peter the Great recognised the strategic potential of Solovki: besides wishing to intimidate unwelcome Swedish settlers in the region, he was looking for trade routes out of the White Sea.

Although the old ways never quite died at Solovki, prudence and secrecy prevailed and the monastery flourished once more, the fathers responding to one tsar after another in a fine display of Darwinian adaptation. Anna showed me the water mill, the icon-painting workshop and the kvass brewery, and, outside the kremlin walls, the rope works, the tar distillery and the canning factory, as well as a complex system of canals and reservoirs. In the nineteenth

century, engineers from Arkhangel outfitted Solovki as a shipyard
with northern Russia's only dry dock. Long after their western counterparts had lost the struggle for wealth and influence to secular
rivals, a mystical tradition persisted in the monasteries of the east,
exerting a powerful hold over the elite. As a modern historian puts
it, eastern monks 'ringed a careworn society with the shimmering
hope of paradise regained'. Visitors poured in to Solovki. In summer,
pilgrims disembarked at the pier from a steamship, or from an over-
crowded barge towed behind it. The monastery's own steamship,
captained by a sailor-monk, transported the devout on the seven-
teen-hour voyage from Arkhangel, third-class passage in the hold a
test of the most robust faith. Guest houses sprang up to house the
pilgrims and souvenir stalls to sell them a ten-kopek crucifix fash-
ioned in monastic workshops. The most popular chapel held the
relics of Savvatii and Zosima. 'Countless offerings of candles were
blazing around the tombs of the Solovetski saints,' wrote a rare
English visitor, 'and the floor of the chapel, with its black and white
pavements, was covered with a dense mass of kneeling humanity
all worshipping towards the rich shrines glittering with gold – a
contrast to the two simple old men who lie there.' Others were less
impressed, trotting back to Moscow with tales of boys and drink.

At least two millennia before the first monks cast anchor, about the
time Celtic peoples brought ironwork to Britain and an elite emerged
among the trading peoples of the lower Mississippi delta, the boun-
tiful catch and safe harbours of the White Sea islands attracted
nomadic fishermen and hunter-gatherers. Besides tools and burial
mounds, they left a mysterious sequence of labyrinths, most of them
on Bolshoi Zayatski, a turbulent forty-minute boat journey from
Big Solovki. I had arranged another tour, and was expecting Anna
to meet me at the wharf; but the young woman who approached
me was not Anna. Except she was. She was another Anna, a younger
museum employee. 'Yesterday's Anna', the new version explained in

flawless English, 'is indisposed.' Six Russians pressed indecorously into the cabin while Anna junior and I leant against the bow rail and shouted over the dyspeptic growl of the engine. Cheerful and lively, and formerly a military lawyer, Anna was born in Petrozavodsk and had been brought up speaking Karelian at home. In the 1937–8 campaign against non-Russians, Karelia was among the nations that virtually ceased to exist. 'What made you decide to come here?' I shouted. 'God decided!' she yelled back with a warm smile.

A tint of sage and cadmium overlaid the scene, as if the landscape had been washed. Boulders, juniper bushes, lichen – even the cranberries blushed green and yellow. Entirely different from its forested neighbour, the island was all tundra, the horizon a swathe of merged land and sea; the landscape was apocalyptic in its broad scope. Wanderers in the far north often write of being on the edge of the world, and of life. I could have laid out a cosmic labyrinth myself.

Across the open land, the aspen boards of a church had silvered in the fine rain and brown juices from the swampy earth seeped up the lower rows. Inside, stacked timber rose above my head. It was exceptionally cold that day, and the loons on the lakes had taken refuge in the sedge. A bank of cloud obscured the sun, but towards the end of the afternoon a thin line of orange light appeared along the lower edge of the cloud, like the line that glows after the flame on burning paper. The Bronze Age spirals we had come to see spread over the plain. Their fat mossy whorls – essentially rings of concentric circles – ranged from a metre in diameter to 25 metres; the moss and lichen that formed the rings had grown over carefully positioned stones, and rough pyramids of bare stones lay in random piles. Nobody knows who made the labyrinths, or why. Experts agree only that early nomadic hunter-fishers laid circular patterns to fulfil the requirements of customs, rituals or beliefs. It turns out that the labyrinth is among the oldest human symbols, and that ancient stone spirals exist on every continent except Antarctica. As well as the unidentified marine nomads, Sámi once fished the Solovki archipelago, and some historians believe they laid the Bolshoi Zayatski labyrinths and that the formations represented the one-way journey to the other world, which, according to Sámi belief, is a mirror image of this one. The ground formed the barrier between the here-and-now and the underworld, while the Solovki islands in the middle of the White Sea were, in Sámi mythology, a halfway stop on the journey to the grave. Anna picked out a route back to the tiny wharf. Before reboarding the bobbing boat, we both looked back over the tundra. Vaporous draughts of air blew in from the east and hung over the labyrinths. Anna had finished her history lesson, and stood in silence. The meaning of the patterns lay in a country beyond words. Like poetry, or music, or the aspen wood cross of a Christian ascetic, the sturdy stone rings ratified the transcendental impulse, that dark grope towards truth that lies at the heart of being human.

Arctic European Russia sweeps from the Finnish border to the Urals. It takes in the regions of Murmansk and Arkhangel, the White Sea, and the National Region of Nenets (*Nenetskiy Avtonomnyy Okrug*), which itself stretches along the coast from Kanin Nos at the mouth of the White Sea to the River Kara. The stunted birches of its tundra drown in oceans of mud and lakes like mirrors grown black with age, while to the south, fish-rich rivers curl through the taiga, their glides reflecting hatches of caddisflies and mosquitoes, the biblical locusts of the far north. The region was and remains isolated, culturally as well as geographically, an outpost that during the Revolution remained white in every sense of the word. In September 1918, 5,000 Americans landed in Arkhangel to shore up the Whites and protect the seaboard. The Great War had ceded to the Civil War and in a shifting sea of allegiances, foreign political leaders never quite answered the question frequently asked both on the home front and in the tundra camps, 'Are we at war with the Bolsheviks?' The Americans, mostly Michigan doughboys of the 339th Infantry Regiment, stayed on long after the Armistice in a cold winter during which they went out on snowshoe patrol and befriended local girls as well as fighting Bolsheviks who attacked their dug-in positions. They had been on the defensive from the moment they landed. Michigan-born Captain Robert Boyd expressed the frustrations of many in the 339th when he wrote to his commanding officers asking bluntly, 'Why are we here?' On 14 November, John Cudahy, a young lieutenant, led a counter-attack that routed 1,000 Bolsheviks who had fired on 600 American, Canadian and Royal Scots soldiers holding the village of Toulgas on the Northern Dvina River. But Cudahy later expressed his disillusionment with the campaign in his book *Arkhangel: The American War with Russia*. Still, the boys who made it home to Michigan took sentimental memories back with them from that cold and little known front. 'This is Russia,' wrote Cudahy of the landscape in which he served, 'of the American soldier, a cluster of dirty huts, dominated by the severe white church, and encircling all, fields and fields of spotless snows; Russia, terrible in the grasp of devastating Arctic cold; the squalor and fulsome filth of the villages; the *moujik* [peasant], his mild eyes, his patient bearded face – the grey drudgery and gaping ignorance of his starved life; the little shaggy pony, docile and uncomplaining in winds icy as the breath of the sepulchre; Russia, her dread mystery, and that intangible quality of melodrama that throngs the air, and lingers in the air, persistently haunts the spirit, and is as consciously perceptible as the dirty villages, the white church, and the grief-laden skies.'

The archipelago had functioned as a dumping ground for undesirables for centuries: after Ivan, Peter the Great despatched enemies to cells within the monastic walls. With its island isolation and ready-made infrastructure, Solovki was just the spot to get rid of someone you didn't like, and the leaders of the newly-minted Soviet Union were inevitably to take up the baton. First they had to lock the churches, pack off the monks and crate up the valuables. In the Solovki archives, a suite of rooms off a roofed walkway within the kremlin, the first Anna showed me footage of the requisition teams from Moscow, flickering black-and-white images of men in suits stuffing medieval icons into cardboard boxes. 'It all went off uncatalogued, without notes,' said Anna. It was still agony to a curator. 'The requisition teams were sent by Lenin at the time of the famine, and they said the icons and jewels were going to be sold abroad to buy bread.' And the pigs of the island flew.*

In 1923, revolutionary authorities sent the first 150 Soviet prisoners to Solovki. Under Lenin's portrait in the cathedral, guards hung the inscription, 'We are showing mankind a new road. Labour will be the master of the world.' That year the administration for the entire system of northern camps also moved to Solovki. It was called *Severnye Lagerya Osobogo Naznacheniya*, which means Northern Special Purposes Camps, and its acronym was SLON, the Russian word for elephant. It was the seed which grew into the *Glavnoe Upravlenie Lagerei*, or Main Camp Administration, the acronym of which was GULAG. In the last week of the year, the camp chief, called, believe it or not, Eichmanns, ordered the first massacre. In those early days, funerals were held; the surviving prisoners, according to Solzhenitsyn, 'sang in chorus across the Solovetsky wilderness' and pushed a boulder over the common grave carved with the names of the dead. Meanwhile Lenin had had his third stroke, and in January 1924 he died. Stalin was the Party General Secretary.

In the archives Anna pulled out cardboard boxes and the two of us sat on the flagged floor sifting through tattered black-and-white

---

* The Bolsheviks requisitioned more in their first eighteen months in power than the Nazis sent to Switzerland during the entire Second World War.

photographs labelled with name, profession and date of death. *Galina Maximovna Yudova, teacher, 23.9.23*; *Ivan Sergeyevich Tsekovski, engineer, 14.2.24*; *Mikhail Nikolayevich Bezborodov, priest, 20.3.24.* Many priests and bishops died on Solovki. 'Their silver locks gleamed', according to Solzhenitsyn, 'in every cell and in every prisoner transport en route to the Solovetsky islands,' actual martyrs sustaining the spirit of self-martyrdom pursued by Savvatii and German and the other founding fathers.* By 1925, the prison population on the islands had reached 6,000, a quarter of whom died of typhus that winter. Anxiety that the prison project was not self-supporting put a stop to talk about re-education and punishment. Stalin wanted labour camps at the heart of the economy, and as a result decreed that production was the primary purpose of the new prisons. In other words, Solovki and the other camps were not set up as death factories, though death was often the result.

Anna disappeared into a storeroom, returning with a sheaf of grainy photographs of the cathedral-barracks. Eight hundred and fifty *zeki*, or prisoners, some of them children, slept stacked on top of one another. During the day they worked in the forests and peat bogs, permitted to take the lunch ration only if they completed unrealistic quotas. The logging camps burgeoned after the camp won a contract to sell timber to foreign lands. Few prisoner-loggers recorded their memories. But one who did, a Latvian called E.I. Solovieff, had arrived in 1925. Years later his daughter found his neatly typed story at the bottom of a suitcase. Having arisen at four, wrote Solovieff, 'if one couldn't complete the *urok* [quota of prescribed work] by night, then one had to work through the night and continue back in the woods after check-in and have very little food. In such cases the prisoner frequently collapsed from exhaustion

---

* In 1927 interned bishops issued a statement known thereafter as The Solovki Declaration emphasising the basic inconsistency between communist ideology and Christian faith.

and crawled into bushes to sleep, only to be found asleep for ever. Almost every day some were missing from the groups, having fallen asleep in tents under a spruce and then frozen to death.' Frozen limbs were ignored, and many died of untreated gangrene. One particular guard, Vanka Potapov, enjoyed lighting a fire at night and shooting any prisoner who crept within the ambit of its heat. Many asked guards to beat them to death. Others mutilated themselves by chopping off their hands or feet in order to obtain a hospital transfer, but when this turned into an epidemic, all *samorubi* ('self-inflictionists') were left in the forest to die. Prisoners had to jump off bridges into rivers when a particular guard shouted, 'Dolphin!' And every morning, wrote prisoner Y. Danzas, 'people armed with long sea hooks, through slightly opened gates, hook the dead bodies in order to take out the corpses. At the same time live prisoners attempt to hold on to the dead bodies, to serve them instead of mattresses.' Camp administrators kept groups of women in separate accommodation for use as a personal harem. In the thirties, many Ukrainian women arrived, having escaped from the artificially-induced famine in the south during which their relations had eaten one another.

In 1929 the random terror of the early Soviet years yielded to a more systematic persecution of the regime's perceived opponents. Stalin's 'great turning point' signalled the onset of collectivisation, which, according to gulag historian Anne Applebaum, 'destroyed – for ever – rural Russia's sense of continuity with the past'. As a result of the doomed collectivisation policies, kulaks swamped the gulag. Anna recounted the story of an old Ukrainian on one of her monastery tours. 'At the end of the tour, he explained that he came from a family of kulaks, or rich peasants. When he was five, he was in a neighbour's house and saw through the window his parents and four siblings being taken away. He never saw them again. His hands were shaking when he told me all this. He was going round the camps, trying to find a trace in the records, so he would know.'

Solovki records cover a small percentage of inmates. Nonetheless, Anna said she would ask the colleague responsible to look through the lists in the morning. 'When I got to my office the next day, the Ukrainian was waiting,' Anna continued. 'My colleague arrived. They looked at the lists. But the name wasn't there. The man started crying. He said he was so old, he couldn't carry on looking much longer.' By 1930, the prison population at Solovki had swollen to 28,000, and 44 per cent of them had typhus. (From 1929 to 1934, the overall Soviet prison population multiplied by twenty-three.) As waves of political terror washed over Russia in the thirties, party members arrived at Solovki as prisoners, transported in rail boxcars in which they lay on shelved slats, unable to sit, stand or protect themselves from the vomit, urine and excrement of those on the slats above. Most prisoners lasted a year, perhaps two. The guards were corrupt and inefficient, and every so often a commission arrived from Moscow and shot half of them.

Something indefinably resilient rose out of the glass cabinets displaying newspapers produced by *zeki* on the monks' lithography press. At Solovki these publications reached a level of sophistication unmatched in any other camp. One could subscribe to the weekly *Novye Solovky* (New Solovki) anywhere in the Soviet Union. In the twenties, Anna said, the island was the intellectual centre of Russia, as half the intellectuals lived there. Copies of *Solovetskie ostrova* (Solovki Islands) faintly typed on an old Underwood, ran to 250 pages, with illustrations, poems and articles.

Bizarrely, at some camps 'Culture and Education Departments' showed films to entertain the *zeki*. When there was a large criminal population, which was often, prisoners took advantage of the darkened rooms to kill one of their colleagues, and during the credits a corpse would be carried out. It was a crazy para-world. The same departments organised singing and dancing ensembles featuring songs such as 'The Ballad of Stalin', 'The Cossack Meditation on Stalin' and 'Let's Smoke'. They appointed in-house camp artists and set up theatre troupes; in 1924 prisoners staged *Uncle Vanya* in the Solovki mess hall. Camp 'educators' also encouraged prisoners to design inventions which would increase productivity. Cunning *zeki* used the scheme to engineer a less horrible life. When a former chauffeur said he could make a car that could run on oxygen, he was given a lab in which to toil in peace. It was not funny, but also, it is funny.

Clandestine religious life persisted. In the twenties a priest-prisoner known as Father Nikodim kept a small cup on a string round his neck with which to celebrate the Eucharist. A prisoner who gave birth in the camp remembered, 'We walked together into the forest, to where there was a small wooden chapel, some benches, and a spring. There the priest, who had a cross and was wearing a cassock, baptised my son.' Could one imagine how much that meant to her? Or what happened to the boy?

The salted herring we ate at lunch seemed miraculous in its ordinariness. When we had finished, the first Anna asked if I would care to accompany her to collect a box of archive material from Sekirka, a hill church eleven kilometres away on the east of the island. We were to travel in the old museum Land Rover, virtually an exhibit itself. The mud road was exceptionally bumpy, and we hit our heads numerous times on the (fortunately canvas) roof of the vehicle. Loons were feeding on the lakes in the softwood forest. We could see the Sekirka belfry above the treetops long before we arrived at the foot of the hill. The church there was the only one in the world with a lighthouse on top. Three monks lived in the cloisters. One of them came out to greet Anna when we walked up. I asked him if the lighthouse still functioned. 'Oh yes!' translated Anna. 'It's used ten months a year – August to May.' The forest there was fragrant with bilberries, and winds had bent the ashes and birches into shapes Anna called 'dancing trees'. As we went into the church, she said, 'Solovki used to be the most revered name in all Russia. Then it became the most feared. But when you actually got to the island, there was a name that was more feared. It was Sekirka. Nobody came back from this place.' A spyhole had been clumsily drilled in the door so guards could observe their prisoners. It would have been an obscene image anywhere; but it was in a church. After a guard spotted him secretly celebrating the Eucharist, Father Nikodim arrived at Sekirka. He slept at the bottom of three layers of other men, piled in the church like firewood, and it was there that he died of asphyxiation. At the same time, naked men were made to sit on a pole for hours high in the unheated nave. When they fell, they were beaten. Prisoners went to desperate lengths to avoid this torture. Solovieff again. 'I saw how people deliberately burned their mouths or sex organs to simulate syphilis . . . people swallowed pieces of glass or nails to get into the hospital . . . the number of deaths was enormous here.' On a small patch of a corner wall, faces on a fresco had been violently scratched out. 'One generation destroys what the previous ones have created,' I said as we walked out into the sunlight of a vegetable garden. 'But they didn't destroy it,' said Anna fiercely. 'The spirit lives.'

Outside the church, the early monks built 365 steps as part of their *podvig*, or ongoing spiritual struggle. But the steps were made for going up. During the gulag, guards tied prisoners to logs and rolled them down, their bodies bouncing on the frosted wooden treads. Anna and I descended in silence and continued along a narrow path cut through the birch forest. 'In the mosquito season,' she said, 'they tied men tightly to trees, naked, and left them there all day.' The mosquitoes, according to Anna, who had seen photographs of one of these events, were 'like a moving carpet'. The crunch of my boots on iced mud released the resinous scent of bog rosemary. But I knew I was walking on bones.

Countrywide, 1937 was the worst year. It was the start of The Great Terror. *That was a time*, wrote Anna Akhmatova in an unforgettable poem, *when only the dead / Could smile, delivered from their struggles*. In Solovki some *zeki* escaped into the forest and took their

chances. According to one source, 'The killing and eating of human beings was not considered something extraordinary above the 65th parallel, as it was a matter of survival and was considered a more or less original way to procure food.' Many of the other prisoners were deliberately worked to death or murdered; at Solovki, in August, the administration announced a death quota: 1,200 prisoners had to be executed. A witness remembered, 'Unexpectedly they forced everyone from the open cells to a general count. At the count they read out an enormous list of names to be taken on transport. They were given two hours to prepare . . . a terrible confusion ensued . . . columns of prisoners marched out with suitcases and knapsacks.' They died near the village of Sandormokh and the killers threw their bodies into a pit. *I should like to call you all by name*, Akhmatova ends the poem, *But they have lost the lists.*

Anna had shown me photographs of a figure in a flat cap standing in front of the cathedral accompanied by a delegation of gormlessly grinning men. The cap-wearer was Maxim Gorky, then, in June 1929, the Soviet Union's most important writer. Initially an urgent socialist (he had assisted in the 'nationalisation' of church artefacts), Gorky had had a difficult relationship with Lenin, and when he visited Solovki he had just returned from self-imposed exile in Sorrento. He toured a Potemkin row of cells, visited an apparently well-stocked hospital and saw contented prisoners reading newspapers in comfortable chairs. But Gorky talked to a fourteen-year-old inmate in private for forty minutes and got the true picture. He wrote approvingly nonetheless of the Solovki set-up once he had left, describing 'healthy lads', flowers on windowsills and 'no resemblance to a prison' – though he said later that the censor had been responsible for much of his essay. Solzhenitsyn accused Gorky of an evil conscience after he failed to speak out. Anne Applebaum, less subjective than Solzhenitsyn, says we do not know what Gorky's motivation was, but we do know that he 'made the institutionalised violence of the Solovki camps seem a logical and natural part of the new order, and helped to reconcile the public to the growing, totalitarian power of the state'. Furthermore, writes Applebaum, 'Gorky's 1929 essay on Solovki was to become an important foundation stone in the forming of both public and official attitudes to the new and far more extensive system of camps which were conceived in that same year.' Guards shot the fourteen-year-old as soon as Gorky boarded his steamship.

On my last day I walked from lake to lake, following whortleberry outcrops and the flight paths of the loons. Close to a dammed reservoir marked on my rudimentary map as St Fillip's Pool, knotweed was making progress over a grid of concrete struts, remnants of an abandoned plan to throw a ring road round the forest. When the economy collapsed, the infrastructure went with it, and Solovki was not immune to the problems experienced across the disintegrating Soviet Union. Public money simply stopped, like the water behind the dam; the hospital was heated just enough to stop the drips freezing, and as in the end it was the only building that was heated at all, the administration moved onto the wards. Polish journalist Mariusz Wilk went to live in Solovki at that time. He wrote that when he arrived in 1990 you could buy sixty loaves for the price of a bottle of vodka. When he left in 1996, it had gone down to three loaves per bottle.

As the afternoon ended I hurried to the public sauna for a final roasting. I had been attending women's sessions at the *banya* behind the monastery, a decrepit brick building with an exterior colonised by milky fungus. In the cold far north, people still regard the ritualised sauna of the public *banya* with particular affection. Having paid the modest entrance fee, I derobed in the small outer *predbannik* and collected a bunch of birch twigs for thrashing purposes, together with a woollen cloche hat to insulate my skull against excessive heat, and a sheet in which to enrobe while cooling off. After a brisk bout of self-flagellation, followed by sweating to the locomotive hiss of liquid on hot stone, and excruciating plunges in a trough of iced water, I swaddled up and took my place among the women in the rest room. At first, nobody spoke. By the end of the week, they wouldn't stop talking. When I could edge in a word, I reflected that with its Bronze Age relics, monastic sanctity and gulag ghosts, Solovki opened a window onto the sweep of Russian history. 'Yes,' said my neighbour, heat radiating from her crêpey skin. 'On Solovki you see Russia in miniature, like the tiniest *matreyoshka* doll.' The island even reflected the shrinking awareness in Russia of the need to condemn the crimes of the gulag ('Say what you like about Stalin, he revived the economy . . .'). Above the quiet chants in the churches and the muttered prayers in the hermitages there was no tone of sober repentance – the Never Again of Dachau or Auschwitz. But the spirit lived in the quiet chants and the muttered prayers; they plucked new life out of death, as they always had. It was easier to believe in when you weren't tied to a tree or starving in an igloo, but it was a kind of humanity that eluded articulation, and I had sensed it everywhere in the muddled and loveable Arctic.

A Solzhenitsyn story came to mind on the trawler back to Kem. In the first volume of *The Gulag Archipelago*, the author describes being transferred under armed guard from one prison camp to another. On the journey, made on public transport, Solzhenitsyn overhears the chattering complaints of free men and women. How can it be of any interest, the fettered prisoner wonders, in the face of the barbarity to which he has been condemned, that a woman squabbles with her daughter-in-law? 'Do not pursue what is illusory', he begs the reader, '– property and position: all that is gained at the expense of your nerves decade after decade, and is confiscated on one fell night. Live with a steady superiority over life – don't be afraid of misfortune, and do not yearn after happiness; it is, after all, all the same: the bitter doesn't last forever, and the sweet never fills the cup to overflowing. It is enough if you don't freeze in the cold and if thirst and hunger don't claw at your insides. If your back isn't broken, if your feet can walk, if both arms can bend, if both eyes see, and if both ears hear, then whom should you envy? And why? Our envy of others devours us most of all. Rub your eyes and purify your heart – and prize above all else in the world those who love you and who wish you well.'

The White Sea wind picked up speed, and out on deck salty spray sent the others hurrying into the cabin. A mist had fallen over the distant domes. What had the first fishermen made of it as they piloted their flimsy craft across this water centuries before Solzhenitsyn? Did they lay out the stones for their labyrinth spirals as a way of reaching towards some unobtainable transcendental truth? Or did the stones mark the edges of a Bronze Age rubbish

dump? The trawler chugged to the coast, over wells of oil specu-
lators had not yet sunk. Either way, the mossy whorls revealed the
human spirit at work, stretching back across oceans of time. They
were manifestations of the human need to make order. It was better
not to know.

Notes

All books published in London, unless otherwise indicated.

Chapter I: Tips about Icebergs

8   **This region accounts for . . . is that of reliably** *Novosti*, 17 September 2008.

8   **It's not about polar** 'Anxiously Watching a Different World', *The Economist*, 26 May 2007, p. 56.

12   **twelve months of winter** Galya Diment & Yuri Slezkine, eds, *Between Heaven and Hell. The Myth of Siberia in Russian Culture*, New York, 1993, p. 73.

15   **to see beneath both** T.S. Eliot, *The Use of Poetry and the Use of Criticism*, 1933, p. 106.

18   **the place of greatest** John Davis, *The Worlde's Hydrographical Description*, 1595, p. 19.

Chapter II: No Cows

29   **One should simply tell** Yuri Slezkine, *Arctic Mirrors. Russia and the Small Peoples of the North*, New York, 1994, p. 278.

32   **the smoky, dreamy mountains** Anton Chekhov, *A Journey to the End of the Russian Empire*, trans. Rosamund Bartlett & Anthony Phillips, 2007, p. 10.

32   **Lithe** *ibid.*, p. 10.

32   **everything hellishly expensive** *ibid.*, p. 13.

32 **no washbasins or objects** *ibid.*, p. 31.

32 **To fish scales** *ibid.*, p. 5.

32 **Our primary concern should** Chekhov, *A Journey to the End of the Russian Empire*, trans. Luba & Michael Terpak, p. 88.

33 **It seems to me** Anton Chekhov, *A Journey to Sakhalin*, trans. B. Reeve, Cambridge, 1993, p. 72.

34 **I would not have** David Magarshack, *Gogol. A Life*, 1957, p. 193.

34 **my separate internal / World** Marina Tsvetaeva, *Selected Poems*, trans. Elaine Feinstein, Oxford, 1993, p. 101.

38 **Oh to go to** Anton Chekhov, *Three Sisters*, 1900, trans. Constance Garnett, Act II.

43 **Moscow came up with . . . wherever the bulldozers crashed** Elena Russell, *The Golden Edge*, 1995, p. 136.

44 **cramped by its banks** Diment & Slezkine, *Between Heaven and Hell*, p. 71.

44 **mission** Leo Tolstoy, *Anna Karenina*, 1873–7, trans. Joel Carmichael, 1960, p. 723 (Penguin Classic edn).

44 **Good . . . Delicious . . . Don't even** Slezkine, *Arctic Mirrors*, p.14.

45 **to give each Ostiak** *ibid.*, pp. 99–100.

45 **It was not heat** Fyodor Dostoevsky, *The House of the Dead*, 1862, trans. Constance Garnett, 1915, p. 100 (Dover Thrift edn).

46 **half-thawed humanity . . . descendants of fish** Diment & Slezkine, *Between Heaven and Hell*, p. 99.

46 **if it were to** Tolstoy, *Anna Karenina*, p. 305.

48 **The village came to** Piers Vitebsky, *Reindeer People*, 2005, p. 238.

49 **inner spiritual life and** *ibid.*, p. 375.

50 **death ships of the** Andrei D. Sakharov, *Progress, Coexistence and Intellectual Freedom*, New York, 1968, p. 53.

50 **There's a herring coming** Anna Reid, *The Shaman's Coat: A Native History of Siberia*, 2002, p. 188.

53 **very, very few healthy** Richard Galpin, Report on Norilsk, BBC Radio 4, 5 April 2007.

53 **For the period up** *ibid.*

53 **the Arctic contains twenty-five** 'The Arctic Ocean basin and coastline: Climate Change, Resources, and Law of the Sea', nd, www.usgs.gov

55 **The world breaks everyone** Ernest Hemingway, *A Farewell to Arms*, 1957, p. 249 (Scribner's edn).

Notes

56 **Way to go** *Moscow Times*, 16 March 2008, p. 20.

57 ***The northern lights are*** Slezkine, *Arctic Mirrors*, p. 287.

58 **You say you can** Reid, *The Shaman's Coat*, p. 7.

58 **the First of May . . . Christmas** Slezkine, *Arctic Mirrors*, p. 242.

59 **a bourgeois alphabet** Diment & Slezkine, *Between Heaven and Hell*, p. 235.

60 **Our biggest task is** *Novosti*, 17 September 2008.

61 **Tomorrow's America** H.P. Smolka, *Forty Thousand Against the Arctic*, 1937, p. 30.

Chapter III: 500 Alaskan Whores

66 **that he could have** Richard Vaughan, *The Arctic. A History*, Stroud, 1994, p. 245.

67 ***There's gold, and it's*** Robert Service, 'The Spell of the Yukon', 1916.

67 **What is the Alaskan** Hudson Stuck, *Ten Thousand Miles with a Dogsled*, 1914, p. 224.

68 **It is unquestionable that** *ibid.*, p. 369.

68 **a native woman in** *ibid.*, p. 24.

68 **my moose-hide breeches froze** *ibid.*, p. 18.

69 **the bounding of the . . . regions of the earth** *ibid.*, pp. 74–5.

70 **a dead letter** *ibid.*, p. 363.

70 **whiskey howl** John Muir, *Travels in Alaska*, 1915, p. 100.

70 **whiskied nearly out of** *ibid.*, p. 180.

73 **The sense of private** John McPhee, *Coming into the Country*, New York, 1977, p. 35.

73 **Eskimos should make laws** *ibid.*, p. 36.

73 **rapid acculturation** John Strohmeyer, *Extreme Conditions: Big Oil and the Transformation of Alaska*, New York, 1993, p. 190.

73 **turn white** McPhee, *Coming into the Country*, p. 422.

85 **If Stefansson could get** Robert Marshall, *Arctic Village*, New York, 1933, p. 235.

86 **the emotional values of** Robert Marshall, *Arctic Wilderness*, Berkeley & Los Angeles, 1956, p. xx.

86 **preserved as hunting grounds** George Eliot, *Middlemarch*, 1871–2, Book 1, p. 107 (Penguin English Library edn).

86 **the glamorous mystery of** Marshall, *Arctic Wilderness*, p. 154.

87   the humility of grandeur *ibid.*, p. 27.
87   Exploration is perhaps the *ibid.*, p. xviii.
87   If we perish what Fridtjof Nansen, *Farthest North*, 1897, p. 156.
88   yearning after light and *ibid.*, p. 1.
90   We as Inupiat have Marla Cone, *Silent Snow*, New York, 2005, p. 220.
92   the unreality of a Marshall, *Arctic Wilderness*, p. 126.
92   humility of grandeur *ibid.*, p. 27.
93   The setting sun fired Muir, *Travels in Alaska*, p. 74.
94   slow as a glacier *ibid.*, p. xviii.
94   one day's exposure to *ibid.*, p. xviii.
94   I was too happy *ibid.*, p. 113.
94   are fond and indulgent *ibid.*, p. 150.
95   Paradise – if you can Miranda Seymour, *Robert Graves. Life on the Edge*, 1995, p. 185.
99   I have been managing Alex Kershaw, *Jack London*, 1997, p. 73.
99   probably the most unpleasant Fergus Fleming, *Ninety Degrees North*, 2001, p. 284.
100   the finish, the cap Robert Peary, *The North Pole*, New York, 1986, p. 316.
100   It was like a Kenn Harper, *Give Me My Father's Body*, Iqaluit, NWT, 1986, p. 27.
100   the loneliest person in *ibid.*, p. 167.

Chapter IV: Rock Talk

110   This time around, however Barry Lopez, *Arctic Dreams*, 1986, p. 11.
111   too much geography William Lyon Mackenzie King, 18 June 1936, speech to the Canadian House of Commons.
113   true and absolute Lordes Vaughan, *The Arctic*, p. 117.
114   First, we war . . . Later Ken McGoogan, *Ancient Mariner*, 2004, p. 151.
114   Witchcraft . . . not peculiar to *ibid.*, p. 290.
115   fabulous land where Indians Robert J. Christopher, *Robert and Frances Flaherty*, Montreal, 2005, p. 20.
118   I went to the Hugh Brody, *The Other Side of Eden*, 2000, p. 177.
119   I remember when I Farley Mowat, *High Latitudes*, 2002, p. 242.
120   the best known Canadian James King, *Farley*, Toronto, 2002, p. xvi.
120   ways of life that Farley Mowat, *People of The Deer*, 1952, p. 9.

120 **a spiritual talisman** *ibid.*, p. 9.

121 **I was very deeply** King, *Farley*, p. 103.

122 **a communization of all** Mowat, *People of The Deer*, p. 147.

122 **disintegration and degradation** *ibid.*, p. 159.

122 **Fuck the facts** King, *Farley*, p. xv.

122 **almost the entire** Mowat, *High Latitudes*, p. 2.

122 **All us young people** *ibid.*, p. 236.

123 **refugees from the Stone** *ibid.*, p. 15.

123 **nothing but lemmings** Gerard Kenney, *Arctic Smoke and Mirrors*, Prescott, Ontario, 1994, p. 78.

123 **You see a small** *ibid.*, p. 90.

127 **In support of the** Mowat, *People of the Deer*, p. 261.

128 ***sukkunartuq*, 'something that destroys** Cone, *Silent Snow*, p. 113.

128 **When it comes to** *ibid.*, p. 111.

130 **The Arctic is Russian** BBC News website, 1 August 2007.

130 **Canada Uses Military Might** *Guardian*, 11 August 2007, p. 14.

130 **Canada's new government understands** *Globe and Mail*, Toronto, 27 August 2008, p. A4.

Chapter V: Beautiful Routes to Knowledge

150 **It's a delicate business** Richard B. Alley, *The Two-Mile Time Machine*, Princeton, 2000, p. 150.

152 **Only disappointed human hopes** Nansen, *Farthest North*, p. 156.

158 **The ice sheet is** *National Geographic*, June 2007, p. 61.

165 **I had started on** Tété-Michel Kpomassie, *An African in Greenland*, trans. James Kirkup, 1981, p. 83.

166 **the crying lack of** *ibid.*, p. 193.

166 **Children are sent to** *ibid.*, p. 112.

167 **I was quite willing** *ibid.*, p. 110.

167 **Greenland morality was beginning** *ibid.*, p. 110.

167 **The house** *ibid.*, p. 270.

167 **These *inue* are not** *ibid.*, p. 285.

168 **In the eyes of** *ibid.*, p. 284.

168 **daily bread . . . daily seal** Lawrence Millman, *Last Places*, 1990, p. 157.

169 **The Arctic in 1950** Jean Malaurie, *The Last Kings of Thule*, trans. Adrienne Foulke, 1982, p. xvi.

170 **I pulled a leg** *ibid.*, p. 93.

170 **Every man calls barbarous** *ibid.*, p. 191.

170 **In that pure state** *ibid.*, p. xix.

170 **The more I think** *ibid.*, p. xvi.

170 **It obliged me to** *ibid.*, p. xix.

171 **had decided** *ibid.*, p. 392.

171 **the decline of this** *ibid.*, p. 417.

171 **the warlike glamour** Rockwell Kent, *Salamina*, 1936, p. 90.

171 **the contentment of merely** *ibid.*, p. 119.

171 **people don't need gadgets** *ibid.*, p. 7.

172 **What do men need?** *ibid.*, p. 160.

172 **In Greenland one discovers** *ibid.*, p. 213.

175 **Exploration is the physical** Apsley Cherry-Garrard, *The Worst Journey in the World*, 1922, p. 597.

176 **They talk of decadence** J.M. Scott, *Gino Watkins*, 1935.

176 **a life bright with** *ibid.*, p. 211.

176 **It was more Gino's** *ibid.*, p. 222.

177 **It is queer how** *ibid.*, p. 301.

178 **By the iniquity of** *The Times*, 30 June 1930, p. 15.

181 **If it was worked** F. Spencer Chapman, *Northern Lights*, 1932, p. 128.

181 **Was almost a god** *ibid.*, p. xiv.

181 **never felt as miserable** *ibid.*, p. 105.

181 **From now on the** *ibid.*, p. 58.

182 **the ascetic nakedness** F. Spencer Chapman, *Watkins' Last Expedition*, 1934, p. xiv.

182 **the first great geographical** Roland Huntford, *Nansen*, 1997, p. 114.

182 **the ultra-Norwegian mania for** *ibid.*, p. 128.

183 **There is nothing to** Nicholas Wollaston, *The Man on the Ice Cap*, 1980, p. 134.

184 **And people who are** *ibid.*, p. 162.

184 **But as we got** Chapman, *Northern Lights*, p. 175.

184 **August! August!** *ibid.*, p. 175.

184 **He looked as if** *ibid.*, p. 176.

184 **Fewest possible servants** Wollaston, *The Man on the Ice Cap*, p. 138.

185 **If it were not** *ibid.*, p. 154.

185 **the curious growing feeling** Chapman, *Northern Lights*, p. 186.

186 **To see Mr Watkins** *The Times*, 9 May 1932, p. 12.

Notes

186 **It is quite clear** Chapman, *Northern Lights*, p. 3.
187 **She was wonderful, but . . . Ten months seems a** Scott, *Gino Watkins*, p. 299.
188 **That he should be** Wollaston, *The Man on the Ice Cap*, p. 192.
189 **The environmentally triggered collapse** Jared Diamond, *Collapse*, 2005, p. 179.
190 **Greenland history conveys the** *ibid.*, p. 21.
190 **long-term planning and willingness . . . crucial in tipping** *ibid.*, p. 522.
191 **the blood-soaked selfishness of** John Updike, *In the Beauty of the Lilies*, 1996.

Chapter VI: Watchdogs and Whales

197 **Never before has the** Cone, *Silent Snow*, p. 219.
200 **outliers on the curve** Victor B. Scheffer, cited in Mariana Gosnell, *Ice: The Nature, the History, and the Uses of an Astonishing Substance*, New York, 2005, p. 255.
200 **Only one man died** A.G.E. Jones, 'The Eighteenth Century Whaling Trade of Bristol', in *Polar Portraits*, Whitby, 1992, p. 116.
200 **not unfrequently fall into** William Scoresby Jr, *An Account of the Arctic Regions*, Edinburgh, 1820, Vol. II, p. 302.
202 *cela halucine l'esprit* Léonie d'Aunet, *Voyage d'une femme au Spitzberg*, Paris, 1854, p. 170.
202 **long fleshless fingers like** *ibid.*, p. 175 (author's translation).
202 *une cimetière sans epitaphes ibid.*, pp. 176–7.
211 **I felt instinctively that** Fridtjof Nansen, *The First Crossing of Greenland*, trans. Hubert Majendie Gepp, 1902, pp. 80–1.
212 **a marvel for its** Sir Martin Conway, *No Man's Land: A History of Spitsbergen*, 1906, p. 279.
214 **We think we can** S.A. Andrée, Nils Strindberg and Knut Fraenkel, *The Andrée Diaries*, trans. E. Adams-Ray, 1931, p. 53.
214 **I am sure that** David Hempleman-Adams with Robert Uhlig, *At the Mercy of the Winds*, 2002, p. 196.
215 **BUILD AN AIRSHIP AND** P.J. Capelotti, *By Airship to the North Pole*, New Jersey, 1999, p. 47.
217 **had been like trying** Wally Herbert, *Across the Top of the World*, 1969, p. 174.

218 **strutting dreamer** Roald Amundsen, *My Life as an Explorer*, 1927, p. 208.

218 **itch for ostentation** *ibid.*, p. 202.

218 **illusions of greatness** *ibid.*, p. 206.

218 **Fortunately I have a** *ibid.*, p. 184.

220 **the Norwegians, almost to** *ibid.*, p. 116.

220 **well and truly railroaded** Wilbur Cross, *Ghost Ship of the Pole*, 1960, p. 284.

220 **a new Dreyfus** *ibid.*, p. 284.

224 **This looks like gold** Vaughan, *The Arctic*, p. 249.

224 **When a man comes** Liv Balstad, *North of the Desolate Sea*, trans. Joan Bulman, 1958, p. 54.

224 **the power of adaptability** *ibid.*, p. 94.

225 **Once she has found** *ibid.*, p. 165.

225 **while the so-called Cold** *ibid.*, p. 178.

226 **They were diehards, these** *ibid.*, p. 180.

226 **a blanket more necessary** James Rodger Fleming, *Historical Perspectives on Climate Change*, New York & Oxford, 1998, p. 71.

226 **perfectly colorless and invisible** *ibid.*

229 **precarious equipoise between survival** Gale E. Christianson, *Greenhouse: The 200-Year Story of Global Warming*, 1999, p. 119.

Chapter VII: Four Legs Good

236 **Lapps are so cunning** Roland Huntford, *Two Planks and a Passion*, 2008, p. 23.

236 **They ski down high** *ibid.*, p. 56.

237 **come to twist everything** Johan Turi, *Turi's Book of Lappland*, trans. Emilie Demant Hatt & E. Gee Nash, 1931, p. 19.

237 **the black-clad ones** *ibid.*, p. 24.

238 **To chase a wolf** *ibid.*, p. 111.

238 **Really the Lapps have** *ibid.*, p. 65.

239 **is so wonderful to** *ibid.*, p. 225.

240 **had crept in and** Axel Munthe, *The Story of San Michele*, 1929, p. 98.

240 **I can hear by** *ibid.*, p. 99.

241 **Through the mist of** *ibid.*, p. 107.

242 **While I was still** *ibid.*, p. 108.

Notes

242 **an easy and comfortable** *ibid.*, p. 119.

243 ***Never the muse is*** Pindar, 'Pythian Ode', *The Odes of Pindar*, trans. Richmond A. Lattimore, Chicago, 1947.

243 ***And everywhere maiden choruses*** *ibid.*

243 **So we beat on** F. Scott Fitzgerald, *The Great Gatsby*, 1925, p. 163.

245 **Arctic warfare is altogether** J.D.M. Blyth, 'The War in Arctic Europe', *Polar Record*, vol. 7, Jan. 1955, no. 49, p. 300.

246 **death in the Arctic** *ibid.*, p. 295.

246 **It must be made** *ibid.*, pp. 294-5.

247 **All four of them** David Hawarth, *We Die Alone*, 1955, p. 141.

249 **Sámi don't think about** Roger Took, *Running with Reindeer*, 2003, p. 37.

249 **A story about a** Elina Helander & Kaarina Kailo, eds, *No Beginning, No End: The Sámi Speak Up*, Edmonton & Helsinki, 1998, p. 32.

253 **whether the power structure** Ole Henrik Magga, trans. John Weinstock, *Nordlys*, No. 129, Tromsø, 8 June 2001.

Chapter VIII: Ship of Fools

261 **the largest area of** Took, *Running with Reindeer*, p. 9.

270 **This enormous ice retreat** *Sunday Times*, 26 October 2008, p. 9.

270 **If you look at** Dr Colin Whiteman, 'Hazards of the Polar Environment', conference address, 20 February 2008, at 'The Polar Environment Past, Present and Future', University of Brighton.

272 **I summoned the pantryman** www.naval-history.net/WW2Memoir-PQ17-Carswell.htm

276 **Why don't we start** Huntford, *Nansen*, p. 324.

276 **Aren't you Nansen . . . Yes** Frederick G. Jackson, *A Thousand Days in the Arctic*, 1899, Vol. 2, p. 61.

276 **A more remarkable meeting . . . Nansen did not know** *ibid.*, p. 66.

278 **Now when I think** Huntford, *Nansen*, p. 354.

278 **Polar exploration is at** Cherry-Garrard, *The Worst Journey in the World*, p. vii.

280 **There is a glamour** Arthur Conan Doyle, *Memories and Adventures*, 1924, p. 168.

281 **mouthing ice cakes** Sylvia Plath, 'A Winter Ship', 1960.

283 **partly explains the accident** Jerry McManus, cited in Gosnell, *Ice*, p. 474.

285 **that strait where the** *ibid.*, p. 196.

285 **Eight Days Between Meals** *New York Herald*, 27 September 1880, cited in Beau Riffenburgh, *The Myth of the Explorer*, Oxford, 1994, p. 75.

287 **He spoke of the** Smolka, *Forty Thousand Against the Arctic*, p. 17.

287 **We are really making** *ibid.*, p. 20.

288 **the greatest man of** Ivan Papanin, *Life on an Icefloe*, 1947, trans. Fanny Smitham, 1947, p. 32.

288 **Stalin has devoted the** *ibid.*, p. 151.

288 **I recall the tragic** *ibid.*, p. 219.

289 **Our people call it** *ibid.*, p. 212.

289 **If World War 3** W.M. Leary & L. LeShack, *Project Coldfeet: Secret Mission to a Soviet Ice Station*, Annapolis, 1996, p. 18.

290 **In sailing along the** Janice Cavell, 'The Hidden Crime of Dr Richardson', in *Polar Record*, Vol. 43, Mar. 2007, No. 2, pp. 155–64.

291 **left to be performed** Fergus Fleming, *Barrow's Boys*, 1998, p. 365.

292 *Not here! The white* Alfred, Lord Tennyson, Epitaph to Sir John Franklin, 1859.

292 **as noble an epic** Pierre Berton, *The Arctic Grail*, 1988, p. 334.

293 **Think of Christmas in** R. McCormick & Charles Dickens, 'Christmas in the Frozen Regions', *Household Words* 2, 1850 (39), p. 306.

293 **I desire nothing but** Ann Savours, *The Search for the North West Passage*, New York, 1999, p. 192.

294 **This book, poor as** William Elder, *Biography of Elisha Kent Kane*, Philadelphia, 1858, p. 218.

294 **Can it be possible** Berton, *The Arctic Grail*, p. 219.

295 **We submit that the** Charles Dickens, 'The Lost Arctic Voyagers', *Household Words* 10, 1854 (246), p. 390.

297 *One savage footprint on* Wilkie Collins, *The Frozen Deep*, 1857.

Chapter IX: The Spirit Lives

306 **a sort of pea** Mariusz Wilk, *The Journals of a White Sea Wolf*, trans. Danusia Stok, 2003, p. 19.

308 **without which Russia could** 20 Aug. 2001, http://www.kremlin.ru

308 **felt no shame when** S.F. Platanov, *Ivan the Terrible*, trans. Joseph L. Wieczynski, Florida, 1974, p. 108.

308 **prayer and torture were** Roy R Robson, *Solovki*, 2004, p. 48.

Notes

308 **the Germans and all** *ibid.*, p. 56.

308 **it took at least** Dmitrii Likhachev, cited in Robson, *ibid.*, p. 57.

310 **So they mangled him** Semen Denisov, 'The History of the Fathers and Martyrs of Solovetskii', in W. Palmer, *The Patriarch and the Tsar*, Vol. 2, 1871, pp. 439–40, cited in Robson, *ibid.*, p. 107.

312 **ringed a careworn society** Peter Brown, cited in 'Where Mammon Meets God', *The Economist*, 18 December 2004, p. 75.

312 **Countless offerings of candles** Alexander A. Boddy, *With Russian Pilgrims*, 1892, p. 88.

315 **Why are we here** John Evangelist Walsh, 'The Strange, Sad Death of Sergeant Kenney', in *Wisconsin Magazine of History*, Madison, WI, 85, No. 2 (Winter 2001/2002), p. 8.

315 **This is Russia** A Chronicler (John Cudahy), *Arkhangel: The American War with Russia*, Chicago, 1924, p. 146.

316 **We are showing mankind** Robson, *Solovki*, p. 214.

316 **sang in chorus across** Alexander Solzhenitsyn, *The Gulag Archipelago*, Vol. 1, 1973, trans. Thomas P. Whitney, 1974, Part I, ch. 12, p. 463.

317 **Their silver locks gleamed** *ibid.*, ch. 2, p. 37.

317 **if one couldn't complete** Robson, *Solovki*, p. 223.

318 **people armed with long** http://www.solovki.ca/english/camp.php

318 **destroyed – for ever – rural** Anne Applebaum, *Gulag*, 2003, p. 64.

320 **We walked together into** Veronica Shapovalov, ed., *Remembering the Darkness: Women in Soviet Prisons*, New York, 2001, pp. 270–5.

321 **I saw how people** Robson, *Solovki*, p. 227.

321 **That was a time** Anna Akhmatova, 'Prologue', from *Requiem*, 1935–40, lines 1–2.

322 **The killing and eating** Robson, *Solovki*, p. 247.

322 **Unexpectedly they forced everyone** Applebaum, *Gulag*, p. 115.

323 **'healthy lads' . . . 'no resemblance to' . . . made the institutionalised violence** Applebaum, *Gulag*, pp. 61–2.

325 **Do not pursue what** Solzhenitsyn, *The Gulag Archipelago*, Vol. 1, Part II, ch. 4, pp. 591–2.

Select Bibliography

All books published in London unless otherwise indicated

Albanov, Valerian, *In the Land of White Death*, trans. Alison Anderson, New York, 2000

Alley, Richard, *The Two-Mile Time Machine*, Princeton, 2000

Amundsen, Roald, *My Life as an Explorer*, 1927

Andrée, S.A., Strindberg, Nils, & Fraenkel, Knut, *The Andrée Diaries*, trans. Edward Adams Ray, 1931

Applebaum, Anne, *Gulag: A History*, 2003

d'Aunet, Léonie, *Voyage d'une jeune femme au Spitzberg*, Paris, 1854

Balstad, Liv, *North of the Desolate Sea*, trans. Joan Bulman, 1958

Beardsley, Martyn, *Deadly Winter: The Life of Sir John Franklin*, 2002

Berton, Pierre, *The Arctic Grail*, 1988

Blyth, J.D.M., 'The War in Arctic Europe, 1941–45', in *Polar Record*, vol. 7, Jan. 1955, no. 49, pp. 278–301

Bogoras, Waldemar, *The Chukchee*, New York, 1904–9

Brody, Hugh, *The Other Side of Eden*, Vancouver & Toronto, 2000

Carpenter, Edmund, *Eskimo Realities*, New York, 1973

Chapman, F. Spencer, *Northern Lights: The Official Account of the British Arctic Air-Route Expedition 1930–1*, 1932

—*Watkins' Last Expedition*, 1934

Chekhov, Anton, *A Journey to the End of the Russian Empire*, 2007 (extracts from *A Life in Letters*, trans. Rosamund Bartlett & Anthony Phillips and *The Island: A Journey to Sakhalin*, trans. Luba & Michael Terpak)

Christianson, Gale E., *Greenhouse: The 200-Year Story of Global Warming*, 1999

Christopher, Robert J., *Robert & Frances Flaherty*, Montreal, 2005

Bibliography

Clark, Bruce, *An Empire's New Clothes*, 1995

Cone, Marla, *Silent Snow*, New York, 2005

Conquest, Robert, *The Great Terror: A Reassessment*, 1968; 2008

—*Kolyma: The Arctic Death Camps*, New York, 1978

Conway, Sir Martin, *No Man's Land: A History of Spitsbergen*, Cambridge, 1906

Cook, Frederick, *My Attainment of the Pole*, New York, 1911

Cross, Wilbur, *Ghost Ship of the Pole: The Incredible Story of the Dirigible Italia*, 1960

Diamond, Jared, *Collapse: How Societies Choose to Fail or Survive*, 2005

Diment, Galia, & Slevkine, Yuri, eds, *Between Heaven and Hell: The Myth of Siberia in Russian Culture*, New York, 1993

Ehrlich, Gretel, *This Cold Heaven: Seven Seasons in Greenland*, 2002

Elbo, J.G., 'The War in Svalbard, 1939–45', in *Polar Record*, vol. 6, July 1952, no. 44, pp. 484–495

Fernández-Armesto, Felipe, *Pathfinders: A Global History of Exploration*, 2006

Figes, Orlando, *Natasha's Dance: A Cultural History of Russia*, 2002

Fleming, Fergus, *Ninety Degrees North*, 2001

—*Barrow's Boys*, 1998

Forsyth, James, *A History of the Peoples of Siberia*, Cambridge, 1992

Ginzburg, Eugenia, *Journey into the Whirlwind*, trans. Paul Stevenson & Max Hayward, New York, 1967

Gosnell, Mariana, *Ice*, New York, 2005

Harper, Kenn, *Give Me My Father's Body: The Life of Minik, the New York Eskimo*, Iqaluit, NWT, 1986

Hawarth, David, *We Die Alone*, 1955

Hearne, Samuel *A Journey from Prince of Wales's Fort in Hudson's Bay to the Northern Ocean*, 1795

Herbert, Wally, *Across the Top of the World: The British Trans-Arctic Expedition*, 1969

—*The Noose of Laurels: The Discovery of the North Pole*, 1989

Hosking, Geoffrey, *Russia and the Russians*, 2001

Huntford, Roland, *Scott and Amundsen*, 1979

—*Nansen*, 1997

—*Two Planks and a Passion*, 2008

Ingold, Tim, *The Skolt Lapps Today*, Cambridge, 1976

Jackson, Frederick G., *A Thousand Days in The Arctic*, 2 vols, 1899

Jangfeldt, Bengt, *Axel Munthe: The Road to San Michele*, trans. Harry Watson, 2008

Kennan, George, *Tent Life in Siberia*, 1871

Kenney, Gerard I., *Arctic Smoke and Mirrors*, Prescott, Ontario, 1994

Kent, Rockwell, *Salamina*, 1936

King, James, *Farley*, Toronto, 2002

Kobalenko, Jerry, *The Horizontal Everest: Extreme Journeys on Ellesmere Island*, New York, 2002

Kolbert, Elizabeth, *Field Notes from a Catastrophe: A Frontline Report on Climate Change*, 2006

Kpomassie, Tété-Michel, *An African in Greenland*, 1981

Krakauer, Jon, *Into the Wild*, 1998

Lähteenmäki, Maria, & Pihlaja, Päivi Maria, eds, *The North Calotte: Perspectives on the Histories and Cultures of Northernmost Europe*, Helsinki, 2005

Lambert, Andrew, *Franklin*, 2009

Lamont, James, *Yachting in Arctic Seas*, 1876

Lewis-Jones, Huw W.G., 'Nelson and the Bear: The Making of an Arctic Myth', *in Polar Record* 41: 335–353 (2005)

London, Jack, *The Call of the Wild*, 1903

Loomis, Chauncey, *Weird and Tragic Shores: The Story of Charles Francis Hall, Explorer*, 1971

Lopez, Barry, *Arctic Dreams*, 1986

McCoy, Roger M., *Ending in Ice: The Revolutionary Idea and Tragic Expedition of Alfred Wegener*, Oxford, 2006

McGrath, Melanie, *The Long Exile*, 2006

McNeill, John, *Something New Under the Sun: An Environmental History of the Twentieth Century*, 2000

McPhee, John, *Coming into the Country*, New York, 1977

Malaurie, Jean, *The Last Kings of Thule*, trans. Adrienne Foulke, 1982

Marcus, Alan, *Out In the Cold: The Legacy of Canada's Inuit Relocation Experiment in the High Arctic*, Cambridge, 1990

Marshall, Robert, *Arctic Wilderness*, Berkeley and Los Angeles, 1956

—*Arctic Village*, 1940

Millman, Lawrence, *Last Places*, 1990

Morgan, Lael, *Good Time Girls of the Alaska-Yukon Gold Rush*, Fairbanks & Seattle, 1998

Mowat, Farley, *High Latitudes: An Arctic Journey*, 2002

—People of the Deer, 1952

Muir, John, *Travels in Alaska*, 1915

Munthe, Axel, *The Story of San Michele*, 1929

Bibliography

Nansen, Fridtjof, *The First Crossing of Greenland*, 1890

—*Farthest North*, 1897

Nelson, Richard K., *Hunters of the Northern Ice*, Chicago & London, 1969

Niven, Jennifer, *The Ice Master: The Doomed 1913 Voyage of the Karluk*, New York, 2000

Pala, C., 'Unlikely Heroes: the Story of the First Men who Stood at the North Pole, in *Polar Record* 35 (195): 337–342 (1999)

Papanin, Ivan, *Life on an Icefloe*, trans. Fanny Smitham, 1947

Peary, Robert E., *Northward over the Great Ice*, 2 vols, New York, 1898

—*The North Pole*, 1910

Pielou, E.C., *A Naturalist's Guide to the Arctic*, Chicago, 1994

Pryde, Duncan, *Nunaga: Ten Years among the Eskimos*, 1972

Reid, Anna, *The Shaman's Coat: A Native History of Siberia*, 2002

Ridgway, John, *Gino Watkins*, 1974

Riffenburgh, Beau, *The Myth of the Explorer*, Oxford, 1994

Roberts, David, *Shipwrecked on the Top of the World*, New York, 2003

Robson, Roy R., *Solovki*, New Haven & London, 2004

Russell, Elena, *The Golden Edge: Growing up in Russian Alaska*, 1995

Savours, Ann, *The Search for the North West Passage*, New York, 1999

Schofield, Ernest, & Conyers Nesbit, Roy, *Arctic Airmen: The RAF in Spitsbergen & North Russia in 1942*, 1987

Scoresby, William Jr, *An Account of the Arctic Regions with a Description of the Northern Whale-Fishery*, 2 vols, Edinburgh, 1820

Scott, J.M., *Gino Watkins*, 1935

Scott, Jeremy, *Dancing on Ice*, 2008

Slevkine, Yuri, *Arctic Mirrors: Russia and the Small Peoples of the North*, Ithaca, New York, 1994

Smolka, H.P., *40 Thousand Against The Arctic*, 1937

Solzhenitsyn, Alexander, *The Gulag Archipelago, 1918–1956*, trans. Thomas Whitney, 1974

Stefansson, Vilhjalmur, *The Friendly Arctic*, New York, 1922

Strohmeyer, John, *Extreme Conditions: Big Oil and the Transformation of Alaska*, New York, 1993

Stuck, Hudson, *Ten Thousand Miles with a Dogsled*, 1914

Taplin, Mark, *Open Lands: Travels through Russia's Once Forbidden Places*, 1997

Tenderini, Mirella, & Shandwick, Michael, *The Duke of the Abruzzi*, 1997

Thomas, D.M., *Alexander Solzhenitsyn*, 1998

Thubron, Colin, *In Siberia*, 1999

Took, Roger, *Running with Reindeer*, 2003

Turi, Johan, *Turi's Book of Lappland*, trans. Emilie Demant Hatt & E. Gee Nash, 1931

Vaughan, Richard, *The Arctic: A History*, Stroud, 1994

Vitebsky, Piers, *Reindeer People*, 2005

Vorren, Ørnulv, & Manker, Ernst, *Lapp Life and Customs: A Survey*, trans. Kathleen McFarlane, 1962

Walk, Ansgar, *Kenojuak: The Life Story of an Inuit Artist*, Manotick, Ontario, 1999

Wilk, Mariusz, *The Journals of a White Sea Wolf*, trans. Danusia Stok, 2003

Williams, Glyn, *Voyages of Delusion: the Search for the Northwest Passage in the Age of Reason*, 2002

Williams, Peter J., *Pipelines and Permafrost: Science in a Cold Climate*, 1986

Wollaston, Nicholas, *The Man on the Ice Cap: The Life of August Courtauld*, 1980

Wood, Alan, & French, R.A., eds, *The Development of Siberia*, 1989

Acknowledgements

I wish to acknowledge numerous debts, with sincere gratitude. Simon N. Stephenson at the Office of Polar Programs in the US grasped the point of *The Magnetic North* from the outset and granted access to American Arctic research camps. Chris Rapley, then of the British Antarctic Survey, which also covers the Arctic, did the same in the UK. In the field, Nick Cox went beyond the call of duty to get me to Ny-Ålesund, facilitate travel while I was there, and unlock a rich store of anecdotes. Glenn Sheehan fought through the interminable bureaucracy of Chukotka, as did Gena Zelinsky; the latter also did a great deal while I was in the Russian Far East. On the Greenland ice cap Cathy Young welcomed me to her camp at Summit; Bella Bergeron, whom I met over a cold borehole in Greenland, later made me feel right at home in the bars of Fairbanks. Mike Abels arranged logistics up the Haul Road in Alaska, and at Toolik, across the Arctic Divide. Lennart Pittja did all he could to show me and Reg Sámi life and land in Sweden: we loved living among his reindeer. Joyia Chakungal invited me to her jointly-run geology project on Southampton Island in the Canadian Arctic, gave me a home in Iqaluit and did much more besides: I learned a lot from her.

For science advice and tuition I must thank in particular Jack Dibb, who instructed me with patience on halogens; Matthew Hart and Kim Marshall-Brown, who guided me through overturning circulation; Maarten Loonen for the truth about barnacle geese; Geir Wing

Gabrielsen for explaining ocean-going polar contaminants; and Nia Mererid Whiteley for illuminating the tenebrous world of the amphipod. All mistakes are my own. Grateful acknowledgement to Shirley Sawtell at the Scott Polar Research Institute in Cambridge for research assistance, and to the staff of the London Library and the British Library.

Several editors assisted the growth of *The Magnetic North* by commissioning pieces, among them Cath Urquhart and Jane Knight at *The Times*, Victoria Mather at *Vanity Fair*, Jessamy Calkin at the *Daily Telegraph* and Sarah Spankie and Sarah Miller at *Condé Nast Traveller*. Thanks also to Hurtigruten, to Quark, and to Gloria Ward at the Ultimate Travel Company.

The many others who helped include Allan Ashworth, Nicholas Blincoe, Nell Butler, Tom Carrell, Bruce Clark, Richard Cohen, Faye Ethridge, Bob Headland, Tobias Holzlehner, Ceri Hutton, Clive James, Don James, Michael Kendall, Phil Kolvin QC, Nick Laing, Jeremy Lewis, Adam Munthe, David Newman, Chris Phipps, Nadia Solovieva, Charles Swithinbank, Taneil Uttal, Jess Vaughan and Nigel Winser. Lucinda Riches toiled through many gruelling drafts, as usual; this time she also submitted to the hospitality of vodka-proffering strangers on Russian sleeper trains. Ellah Allfrey at Jonathan Cape piloted us through the last months with wisdom and courtesy, ably assisted by Tom Avery and Katherine Murphy. I also want to acknowledge Neil Bradford in the production department.

As always, and more warmly than ever, millions and millions of thanks to my publisher Dan Franklin and my agent Gillon Aitken.

Finally I must thank my editor of first resort, Peter Graham, who did more than everyone else put together and is a brilliantly insightful reader. Now put your socks away.

Index

Index

Index

Index